FREEDOM OF INFORMATION ACT 2000 (UK)

Updated as of March 26, 2018

THE LAW LIBRARY

TABLE OF CONTENTS

Introductory Text

Freedom of Information Act 2000

2000 CHAPTER 36

An Act to make provision for the disclosure of information held by public authorities or by persons providing services for them and to amend the Data Protection Act 1998 and the Public Records Act 1958; and for connected purposes.

[30th November 2000]

Be it enacted by the Queen's most Excellent Majesty, by and with the advice and consent of the Lords Spiritual and Temporal, and Commons, in this present Parliament assembled, and by the authority of the same, as follows:—

Modifications etc. (not altering text)

C1. Act: functions of Secretary of State transferred to the Lord Chancellor (26.11.2001) by S.I. 2001/3500, arts. 3, 4, Sch. 1 para. 12

Act (except ss. 15, 23, 24, 36, 46, 65, 66 and s. 53 for certain purposes): functions of the Lord Chancellor transferred to the Secretary of State, and all property, rights and liabilities to which the Lord Chancellor is entitled or subject in connection with any such function transferred to the Secretary of State for Constitutional Affairs (19.8.2003) by The Secretary of State for Constitutional Affairs Order 2003 (S.I. 2003/1887), art. 4, Sch. 1 (with art. 6)

C2. Act: enforcement and appeals provisions applied (with modifications) (1.1.2005) by The Environmental Information Regulations 2004 (S.I. 2004/3391), reg. 18 (with reg. 3)

C3. Act applied (with modifications) (22.11.2012) by The Police and Crime Panels (Application of Local Authority Enactments) Regulations 2012 (S.I. 2012/2734), regs. 1. (1), 3-6, Sch. Pt. 3

C4. Act applied (with modifications) (22.11.2012) by The Police and Crime Panels (Application of Local Authority Enactments) Regulations 2012 (S.I. 2012/2734), regs. 1. (1), 3-6, Sch. Pt. 2

C5. Act applied (with modifications) (E.W.) (22.11.2012) by The Police and Crime Panels (Application of Local Authority Enactments) Regulations 2012 (S.I. 2012/2734), regs. 1. (1), 3-6, Sch. Pt. 1

C6. Act: transfer of functions (9.11.2016) by The Transfer of Functions (Elections, Referendums, Third Sector and Information) Order 2016 (S.I. 2016/997), art. 7. (a) (with arts. 8, 12)

C7. Act: transfer of functions (9.11.2016) by The Transfer of Functions (Elections, Referendums, Third Sector and Information) Order 2016 (S.I. 2016/997), arts. 1. (2), 3. (1), Sch. 1. (i) (with arts. 3. (2), 6, 12)

Part I Access to information held by public authorities

Part I Access to information held by public authorities

1 General right of access to information held by public authorities.

(1) Any person making a request for information to a public authority is entitled—
    (a) to be informed in writing by the public authority whether it holds information of the description specified in the request, and
    (b) if that is the case, to have that information communicated to him.
(2) Subsection (1) has effect subject to the following provisions of this section and to the provisions of sections 2, 9, 12 and 14.
(3) Where a public authority—
    (a) reasonably requires further information in order to identify and locate the information requested, and
    (b) has informed the applicant of that requirement,
the authority is not obliged to comply with subsection (1) unless it is supplied with that further information.
(4) The information—
    (a) in respect of which the applicant is to be informed under subsection (1)(a), or
    (b) which is to be communicated under subsection (1)(b),
is the information in question held at the time when the request is received, except that account may be taken of any amendment or deletion made between that time and the time when the information is to be communicated under subsection (1)(b), being an amendment or deletion that would have been made regardless of the receipt of the request.
(5) A public authority is to be taken to have complied with subsection (1)(a) in relation to any information if it has communicated the information to the applicant in accordance with subsection (1)(b).
(6) In this Act, the duty of a public authority to comply with subsection (1)(a) is referred to as "the duty to confirm or deny".

2 Effect of the exemptions in Part II.

(1) Where any provision of Part II states that the duty to confirm or deny does not arise in relation to any information, the effect of the provision is that where either—
    (a) the provision confers absolute exemption, or
    (b) in all the circumstances of the case, the public interest in maintaining the exclusion of the duty to confirm or deny outweighs the public interest in disclosing whether the public authority holds the information,
section 1. (1)(a) does not apply.
(2) In respect of any information which is exempt information by virtue of any provision of Part II, section 1. (1)(b) does not apply if or to the extent that—
    (a) the information is exempt information by virtue of a provision conferring absolute exemption, or
    (b) in all the circumstances of the case, the public interest in maintaining the exemption outweighs the public interest in disclosing the information.
(3) For the purposes of this section, the following provisions of Part II (and no others) are to be regarded as conferring absolute exemption—
    (a) section 21,
    (b) section 23,
    (c) section 32,
    (d) section 34,
    (e) section 36 so far as relating to information held by the House of Commons or the House of Lords,

[F1. (ea)in section 37, paragraphs (a) to (ab) of subsection (1), and subsection (2) so far as relating to those paragraphs,]

(f) in section 40—

(i) subsection (1), and

(ii) subsection (2) so far as relating to cases where the first condition referred to in that subsection is satisfied by virtue of subsection (3)(a)(i) or (b) of that section,

(g) section 41, and

(h) section 44.

Amendments (Textual)

F1. S. 2. (3)(ea) inserted (19.1.2011) by Constitutional Reform and Governance Act 2010 (c. 25), ss. 46. (1), 52. (2), Sch. 7 para. 2; S.I. 2011/46, art. 3. (b)(i) (with art. 4)

3 Public authorities.

(1) In this Act "public authority" means—

(a) subject to section 4. (4), any body which, any other person who, or the holder of any office which—

(i) is listed in Schedule 1, or

(ii) is designated by order under section 5, or

(b) a publicly-owned company as defined by section 6.

(2) For the purposes of this Act, information is held by a public authority if—

(a) it is held by the authority, otherwise than on behalf of another person, or

(b) it is held by another person on behalf of the authority.

Modifications etc. (not altering text)

C1. S. 3 modified (29.9.2008 at 8.00 a.m.) by The Bradford & Bingley plc Transfer of Securities and Property etc. Order 2008 (S.I. 2008/2546), art. 41

C2. S. 3 modified (7.10.2008 at 9.30 a.m.) by The Heritable Bank plc Transfer of Certain Rights and Liabilities Order 2008 (S.I. 2008/2644), art. 29

C3. S. 3. (1)(b) modified (30.3.2009 at 8.00 a.m.) by The Amendments to Law (Resolution of Dunfermline Building Society) Order (S.I. 2009/814), {art. 8. (1)(a)(2)}

C4. S. 3. (1)(b) modified (22.2.2008) by The Northern Rock plc Transfer Order 2008 (S.I. 2008/432), art. 18. (2)(a)

C5. S. 3. (1)(b) excluded (1.3.2016) by The NRAM plc (formerly Northern Rock plc) Consequential and Supplementary Provisions Order 2016 (S.I. 2016/114), arts. 1. (1), 8. (2)(a)

C6. S. 3. (2) modified (1.4.2012) by Budget Responsibility and National Audit Act 2011 (c. 4), s. 29, Sch. 3 para. 13. (2); S.I. 2011/2576, art. 5

C7. S. 3. (2)(b) modified (30.3.2009 at 8.00 a.m.) by The Amendments to Law (Resolution of Dunfermline Building Society) Order (S.I. 2009/814), {art. 8. (1)(b)(2)}

C8. S. 3. (2)(b) modified (8.10.2008 at 12.15 p.m.) by The Kaupthing Singer & Friedlander Limited Transfer of Certain Rights and Liabilities Order 2008 (S.I. 2008/2674), art. 31

C9. S. 3. (2)(b) modified (22.2.2008) by The Northern Rock plc Transfer Order 2008 (S.I. 2008/432), art. 18. (2)(b)

C10. S. 3. (2)(b) excluded (1.3.2016) by The NRAM plc (formerly Northern Rock plc) Consequential and Supplementary Provisions Order 2016 (S.I. 2016/114), arts. 1. (1), 8. (2)(b)

4 Amendment of Schedule 1.

(1) The [F2. Secretary of State] [F3or the [F4. Minister for the Cabinet Office]] may by order amend Schedule 1 by adding to that Schedule a reference to any body or the holder of any office which (in either case) is not for the time being listed in that Schedule but as respects which both the first and the second conditions below are satisfied.

(2) The first condition is that the body or office—

(a) is established by virtue of Her Majesty's prerogative or by an enactment or by subordinate legislation, or

(b) is established in any other way by a Minister of the Crown in his capacity as Minister, by a government department or by [F5the Welsh Ministers, the First Minister for Wales or the Counsel General to the Welsh Assembly Government].

(3) The second condition is—

(a) in the case of a body, that the body is wholly or partly constituted by appointment made by the Crown, by a Minister of the Crown, by a government department or by [F6the Welsh Ministers, the First Minister for Wales or the Counsel General to the Welsh Assembly Government], or

(b) in the case of an office, that appointments to the office are made by the Crown, by a Minister of the Crown, by a government department or by [F6the Welsh Ministers, the First Minister for Wales or the Counsel General to the Welsh Assembly Government].

(4) If either the first or the second condition above ceases to be satisfied as respects any body or office which is listed in Part VI or VII of Schedule 1, that body or the holder of that office shall cease to be a public authority by virtue of the entry in question.

(5) The [F2. Secretary of State] [F7or the [F8. Minister for the Cabinet Office]] may by order amend Schedule 1 by removing from Part VI or VII of that Schedule an entry relating to any body or office—

(a) which has ceased to exist, or

(b) as respects which either the first or the second condition above has ceased to be satisfied.

(6) An order under subsection (1) may relate to a specified person or office or to persons or offices falling within a specified description.

(7) Before making an order under subsection (1), the [F2. Secretary of State] [F9or the [F10. Minister for the Cabinet Office]] shall—

(a) if the order adds to Part II, III, IV or VI of Schedule 1 a reference to—

(i) a body whose functions are exercisable only or mainly in or as regards Wales, or

(ii) the holder of an office whose functions are exercisable only or mainly in or as regards Wales, consult [F11the Welsh Ministers], and

(b) if the order relates to a body which, or the holder of any office who, if the order were made, would be a Northern Ireland public authority, consult the First Minister and deputy First Minister in Northern Ireland.

(8) This section has effect subject to section 80.

(9) In this section "Minister of the Crown" includes a Northern Ireland Minister.

Amendments (Textual)

F2. Words in s. 4 substituted (19.8.2003) by The Secretary of State for Constitutional Affairs Order 2003 (S.I. 2003/1887), art. 9, Sch. 2 para. 12. (1)(a)

F3. Words in s. 4. (1) inserted (9.12.2015) by The Transfer of Functions (Information and Public Records) Order 2015 (S.I. 2015/1897), art. 1. (2), Sch. para. 2. (2)(a)

F4. Words in s. 4. (1) substituted (9.11.2016) by The Transfer of Functions (Elections, Referendums, Third Sector and Information) Order 2016 (S.I. 2016/997), art. 1. (2), Sch. 2 para. 14. (2)(a) (with art. 12)

F5. Words in s. 4. (2)(b) substituted by The Government of Wales Act 2006 (Consequential Modifications and Transitional Provisions) Order 2007 (S.I. 2007/1388), art. 3, Sch. 1 para. 78. (2) (the amendment coming into force immediately after the end of "the initial period" (which ended with the day of the first appointment of a First Minister on 25.5.2007) in accordance with art. 1. (2)(3) of the amending S.I. and see ss. 46, 161. (5) of Government of Wales Act 2006 (c. 32))

F6. Words in s. 4. (3)(a)(b) substituted by The Government of Wales Act 2006 (Consequential Modifications and Transitional Provisions) Order 2007 (S.I. 2007/1388), art. 3, Sch. 1 para. 78. (3) (the amendment coming into force immediately after the end of "the initial period" (which ended with the day of the first appointment of a First Minister on 25.5.2007) in accordance with art. 1. (2)(3) of the amending S.I. and see ss. 46, 161. (5) of Government of Wales Act 2006 (c. 32))

F7. Words in s. 4. (5) inserted (9.12.2015) by The Transfer of Functions (Information and Public

Records) Order 2015 (S.I. 2015/1897), art. 1. (2), Sch. para. 2. (2)(a)

F8. Words in s. 4. (5) substituted (9.11.2016) by The Transfer of Functions (Elections, Referendums, Third Sector and Information) Order 2016 (S.I. 2016/997), art. 1. (2), Sch. 2 para. 14. (2)(a) (with art. 12)

F9. Words in s. 4. (7) inserted (9.12.2015) by The Transfer of Functions (Information and Public Records) Order 2015 (S.I. 2015/1897), art. 1. (2), Sch. para. 2. (2)(a)

F10. Words in s. 4. (7) substituted (9.11.2016) by The Transfer of Functions (Elections, Referendums, Third Sector and Information) Order 2016 (S.I. 2016/997), art. 1. (2), Sch. 2 para. 14. (2)(a) (with art. 12)

F11. Words in s. 4. (7)(a)(ii) substituted by The Government of Wales Act 2006 (Consequential Modifications and Transitional Provisions) Order 2007 (S.I. 2007/1388), art. 3, Sch. 1 para. 78. (4) (the amendment coming into force immediately after the end of "the initial period" (which ended with the day of the first appointment of a First Minister on 25.5.2007) in accordance with art. 1. (2)(3) of the amending S.I. and see ss. 46, 161. (5) of Government of Wales Act 2006 (c. 32))

Modifications etc. (not altering text)

C11. S. 4. (1) functions made exercisable concurrently (9.12.2015) by The Transfer of Functions (Information and Public Records) Order 2015 (S.I. 2015/1897), arts. 1. (2), 3. (1), (2)(a) (with art. 5)

C12. S. 4. (5)(7) functions made exercisable concurrently (9.12.2015) by The Transfer of Functions (Information and Public Records) Order 2015 (S.I. 2015/1897), arts. 1. (2), 3. (1), (2)(a) (with art. 5)

5 Further power to designate public authorities.

(1) The [F12. Secretary of State] [F13or the [F14. Minister for the Cabinet Office]] may by order designate as a public authority for the purposes of this Act any person who is neither listed in Schedule 1 nor capable of being added to that Schedule by an order under section 4. (1), but who—

(a) appears to the Secretary of State[F13or the [F14. Minister for the Cabinet Office]] to exercise functions of a public nature, or

(b) is providing under a contract made with a public authority any service whose provision is a function of that authority.

(2) An order under this section may designate a specified person or office or persons or offices falling within a specified description.

(3) Before making an order under this section, the [F12. Secretary of State] [F15or the [F16. Minister for the Cabinet Office]] shall consult every person to whom the order relates, or persons appearing to him to represent such persons.

(4) This section has effect subject to section 80.

Amendments (Textual)

F12. Words in s. 5 substituted (19.8.2003) by The Secretary of State for Constitutional Affairs Order 2003 (S.I. 2003/1887), art. 9, Sch. 2 para. 12. (1)(a)

F13. Words in s. 5. (1) inserted (9.12.2015) by The Transfer of Functions (Information and Public Records) Order 2015 (S.I. 2015/1897), art. 1. (2), Sch. para. 2. (2)(b)

F14. Words in s. 5. (1) substituted (9.11.2016) by The Transfer of Functions (Elections, Referendums, Third Sector and Information) Order 2016 (S.I. 2016/997), art. 1. (2), Sch. 2 para. 14. (2)(b) (with art. 12)

F15. Words in s. 5. (3) inserted (9.12.2015) by The Transfer of Functions (Information and Public Records) Order 2015 (S.I. 2015/1897), art. 1. (2), Sch. para. 2. (2)(b)

F16. Words in s. 5. (3) substituted (9.11.2016) by The Transfer of Functions (Elections, Referendums, Third Sector and Information) Order 2016 (S.I. 2016/997), art. 1. (2), Sch. 2 para. 14. (2)(b) (with art. 12)

Modifications etc. (not altering text)

C13. S. 5. (1)(3) functions made exercisable concurrently (9.12.2015) by The Transfer of Functions (Information and Public Records) Order 2015 (S.I. 2015/1897), arts. 1. (2), 3. (1), (2)(b) (with art. 5)

6 Publicly-owned companies.

(1) A company is a "publicly-owned company" for the purposes of section 3. (1)(b) if—
   (a) it is wholly owned by the Crown, F17...
   (b) it is wholly owned by [F18the wider public sector] [F19, or
   (c) it is wholly owned by the Crown and the wider public sector.]
[F20. (2)For the purposes of this section—
   (a) a company is wholly owned by the Crown if, and only if, every member is a person falling within sub-paragraph (i) or (ii)—
(i) a Minister of the Crown, government department or company wholly owned by the Crown, or
(ii) a person acting on behalf of a Minister of the Crown, government department or company wholly owned by the Crown,
   (b) a company is wholly owned by the wider public sector if, and only if, every member is a person falling within sub-paragraph (i) or (ii)—
(i) a relevant public authority or a company wholly owned by the wider public sector, or
(ii) a person acting on behalf of a relevant public authority or of a company wholly owned by the wider public sector, and
   (c) a company is wholly owned by the Crown and the wider public sector if, and only if, condition A, B or C is met.
(2. A)In subsection (2)(c)—
   (a) condition A is met if—
(i) at least one member is a person falling within subsection (2)(a)(i) or (ii),
(ii) at least one member is a person falling within subsection (2)(b)(i) or (ii), and
(iii) every member is a person falling within subsection (2)(a)(i) or (ii) or (b)(i) or (ii),
   (b) condition B is met if—
(i) at least one member is a person falling within subsection (2)(a)(i) or (ii) or (b)(i) or (ii),
(ii) at least one member is a company wholly owned by the Crown and the wider public sector, and
(iii) every member is a person falling within subsection (2)(a)(i) or (ii) or (b)(i) or (ii) or a company wholly owned by the Crown and the wider public sector, and
   (c) condition C is met if every member is a company wholly owned by the Crown and the wider public sector.]
(3) In this section—
"company" includes any body corporate;
"Minister of the Crown" includes a Northern Ireland Minister.
[F21 " relevant public authority " means any public authority listed in Schedule 1 other than—
a government department, or
any authority which is listed only in relation to particular information]
Amendments (Textual)
F17. Word in s. 6. (1)(a) repealed (1.9.2013) by Protection of Freedoms Act 2012 (c. 9), ss. 103. (2)(a), 120, Sch. 10 Pt. 7 (with s. 97); S.I. 2013/1906, art. 3. (b)
F18. Words in s. 6. (1)(b) substituted (1.9.2013) by Protection of Freedoms Act 2012 (c. 9), ss. 103. (2)(b), 120 (with s. 97); S.I. 2013/1906, art. 3. (b)
F19. S. 6. (1)(c) and word inserted (1.9.2013) by Protection of Freedoms Act 2012 (c. 9), ss. 103. (2)(c), 120 (with s. 97); S.I. 2013/1906, art. 3. (b)
F20. S. 6. (2)(2. A) substituted for s. 6. (2) (1.9.2013) by Protection of Freedoms Act 2012 (c. 9), ss. 103. (3), 120 (with s. 97); S.I. 2013/1906, art. 3. (b)
F21. Words in s. 6. (3) inserted (1.9.2013) by Protection of Freedoms Act 2012 (c. 9), ss. 103. (4),

7 Public authorities to which Act has limited application.

(1) Where a public authority is listed in Schedule 1 only in relation to information of a specified description, nothing in Parts I to V of this Act applies to any other information held by the authority.

(2) An order under section 4. (1) may, in adding an entry to Schedule 1, list the public authority only in relation to information of a specified description.

(3) The [F22. Secretary of State] [F23or the [F24. Minister for the Cabinet Office]] may by order amend Schedule 1—

(a) by limiting to information of a specified description the entry relating to any public authority, or

(b) by removing or amending any limitation to information of a specified description which is for the time being contained in any entry.

(4) Before making an order under subsection (3), the [F22. Secretary of State] [F25or the [F26. Minister for the Cabinet Office]] shall—

[F27. (a)if the order relates to the National Assembly for Wales or a Welsh public authority referred to in section 83. (1)(b)(ii) (subsidiary of the Assembly Commission), consult the Presiding Officer of the National Assembly for Wales,

(aa) if the order relates to the Welsh Assembly Government or a Welsh public authority other than one referred to in section 83. (1)(b)(ii), consult the First Minister for Wales,]

(b) if the order relates to the Northern Ireland Assembly, consult the Presiding Officer of that Assembly, and

(c) if the order relates to a Northern Ireland department or a Northern Ireland public authority, consult the First Minister and deputy First Minister in Northern Ireland.

(5) An order under section 5. (1)(a) must specify the functions of the public authority designated by the order with respect to which the designation is to have effect; and nothing in Parts I to V of this Act applies to information which is held by the authority but does not relate to the exercise of those functions.

(6) An order under section 5. (1)(b) must specify the services provided under contract with respect to which the designation is to have effect; and nothing in Parts I to V of this Act applies to information which is held by the public authority designated by the order but does not relate to the provision of those services.

(7) Nothing in Parts I to V of this Act applies in relation to any information held by a publicly-owned company which is excluded information in relation to that company.

(8) In subsection (7) "excluded information", in relation to a publicly-owned company, means information which is of a description specified in relation to that company in an order made by the [F22. Secretary of State] [F28or the [F29. Minister for the Cabinet Office]] for the purposes of this subsection.

(9) In this section "publicly-owned company" has the meaning given by section 6.

Amendments (Textual)

F22. Words in s. 7 substituted (19.8.2003) by The Secretary of State for Constitutional Affairs Order 2003 (S.I. 2003/1887), art. 9, Sch. 2 para. 12. (1)(a)

F23. Words in s. 7. (3) inserted (9.12.2015) by The Transfer of Functions (Information and Public Records) Order 2015 (S.I. 2015/1897), art. 1. (2), Sch. para. 2. (2)(c)

F24. Words in s. 7. (3) substituted (9.11.2016) by The Transfer of Functions (Elections, Referendums, Third Sector and Information) Order 2016 (S.I. 2016/997), art. 1. (2), Sch. 2 para. 14. (2)(c) (with art. 12)

F25. Words in s. 7. (4) inserted (9.12.2015) by The Transfer of Functions (Information and Public Records) Order 2015 (S.I. 2015/1897), art. 1. (2), Sch. para. 2. (2)(c)

F26. Words in s. 7. (4) substituted (9.11.2016) by The Transfer of Functions (Elections,

8 Request for information.

(1) In this Act any reference to a "request for information" is a reference to such a request which—
  (a) is in writing,
  (b) states the name of the applicant and an address for correspondence, and
  (c) describes the information requested.
(2) For the purposes of subsection (1)(a), a request is to be treated as made in writing where the text of the request—
  (a) is transmitted by electronic means,
  (b) is received in legible form, and
  (c) is capable of being used for subsequent reference.

9 Fees.

(1) A public authority to whom a request for information is made may, within the period for complying with section 1. (1), give the applicant a notice in writing (in this Act referred to as a "fees notice") stating that a fee of an amount specified in the notice is to be charged by the authority for complying with section 1. (1).
(2) Where a fees notice has been given to the applicant, the public authority is not obliged to comply with section 1. (1) unless the fee is paid within the period of three months beginning with the day on which the fees notice is given to the applicant.
(3) Subject to subsection (5), any fee under this section must be determined by the public authority in accordance with regulations made by the [F30. Minister for the Cabinet Office].
(4) Regulations under subsection (3) may, in particular, provide—
  (a) that no fee is to be payable in prescribed cases,
  (b) that any fee is not to exceed such maximum as may be specified in, or determined in accordance with, the regulations, and
  (c) that any fee is to be calculated in such manner as may be prescribed by the regulations.
(5) Subsection (3) does not apply where provision is made by or under any enactment as to the fee that may be charged by the public authority for the disclosure of the information.

Amendments (Textual)
F30. Words in s. 9. (3) substituted (9.11.2016) by The Transfer of Functions (Elections, Referendums, Third Sector and Information) Order 2016 (S.I. 2016/997), art. 1. (2), Sch. 2 para. 14. (2)(d) (with art. 12)
Modifications etc. (not altering text)
C16. S. 9. (3) functions transferred (9.12.2015) by The Transfer of Functions (Information and Public Records) Order 2015 (S.I. 2015/1897), arts. 1. (2), 4. (1), (2)(a) (with art. 5)
Commencement Information
I1. S. 9 wholly in force at 1.1.2005; s. 9 in force at Royal Assent to the extent that it confers power to make regulations, see s. 87. (1)(m)(3); s. 9 otherwise in force at 1.1.2005 by S.I. 2004/3122, art. 2

10 Time for compliance with request.

(1) Subject to subsections (2) and (3), a public authority must comply with section 1. (1) promptly and in any event not later than the twentieth working day following the date of receipt.

(2) Where the authority has given a fees notice to the applicant and the fee is paid in accordance with section 9. (2), the working days in the period beginning with the day on which the fees notice is given to the applicant and ending with the day on which the fee is received by the authority are to be disregarded in calculating for the purposes of subsection (1) the twentieth working day following the date of receipt.

(3) If, and to the extent that—

(a) section 1. (1)(a) would not apply if the condition in section 2. (1)(b) were satisfied, or

(b) section 1. (1)(b) would not apply if the condition in section 2. (2)(b) were satisfied,

the public authority need not comply with section 1. (1)(a) or (b) until such time as is reasonable in the circumstances; but this subsection does not affect the time by which any notice under section 17. (1) must be given.

(4) The [F31. Minister for the Cabinet Office] may by regulations provide that subsections (1) and (2) are to have effect as if any reference to the twentieth working day following the date of receipt were a reference to such other day, not later than the sixtieth working day following the date of receipt, as may be specified in, or determined in accordance with, the regulations.

(5) Regulations under subsection (4) may—

(a) prescribe different days in relation to different cases, and

(b) confer a discretion on the Commissioner.

(6) In this section—

"the date of receipt" means—

- the day on which the public authority receives the request for information, or

- if later, the day on which it receives the information referred to in section 1. (3);

"working day" means any day other than a Saturday, a Sunday, Christmas Day, Good Friday or a day which is a bank holiday under the M1. Banking and Financial Dealings Act 1971 in any part of the United Kingdom.

Amendments (Textual)
F31. Words in s. 10. (4) substituted (9.11.2016) by The Transfer of Functions (Elections, Referendums, Third Sector and Information) Order 2016 (S.I. 2016/997), art. 1. (2), Sch. 2 para. 14. (2)(e) (with art. 12)
Modifications etc. (not altering text)
C17. S. 10. (1)(2) modified (1.1.2005) by The Freedom of Information (Time for Compliance with Request) Regulations 2004 (S.I. 2004/3364), regs. 3. (2), 4. (2), 5. (2), 6. (2)
C18. S. 10. (1)(2) modified (26.6.2009) by The Freedom of Information (Time for Compliance with Request) Regulations 2009 (S.I. 2009/1369), reg. 2. (2)
C19. S. 10. (1)(2) modified (18.11.2010) by The Freedom of Information (Time for Compliance with Request) Regulations 2010 (S.I. 2010/2768), regs. 1. (2), 2

C20. S. 10. (4) functions transferred (9.12.2015) by The Transfer of Functions (Information and Public Records) Order 2015 (S.I. 2015/1897), arts. 1. (2), 4. (1), (2)(b) (with art. 5)
Commencement Information
I2. S. 10 wholly in force at 1.1.2005; s. 10 in force at Royal Assent to the extent that it confers power to make regulations, see s. 87. (1)(m)(3); s. 10 otherwise in force at 1.1.2005 by S.I. 2004/3122, art. 2
Marginal Citations
M11971 c. 80.

11 Means by which communication to be made.

(1) Where, on making his request for information, the applicant expresses a preference for communication by any one or more of the following means, namely—

(a) the provision to the applicant of a copy of the information in permanent form or in another form acceptable to the applicant,

(b) the provision to the applicant of a reasonable opportunity to inspect a record containing the information, and

(c) the provision to the applicant of a digest or summary of the information in permanent form or in another form acceptable to the applicant,
the public authority shall so far as reasonably practicable give effect to that preference.
[F32. (1. A)Where—

(a) an applicant makes a request for information to a public authority in respect of information that is, or forms part of, a dataset held by the public authority, and

(b) on making the request for information, the applicant expresses a preference for communication by means of the provision to the applicant of a copy of the information in electronic form,
the public authority must, so far as reasonably practicable, provide the information to the applicant in an electronic form which is capable of re-use.]
(2) In determining for the purposes of this section whether it is reasonably practicable to communicate information by particular means, the public authority may have regard to all the circumstances, including the cost of doing so.
(3) Where the public authority determines that it is not reasonably practicable to comply with any preference expressed by the applicant in making his request, the authority shall notify the applicant of the reasons for its determination.
(4) Subject to [F33subsections (1) and (1. A)], a public authority may comply with a request by communicating information by any means which are reasonable in the circumstances.
[F34. (5)In this Act "dataset" means information comprising a collection of information held in electronic form where all or most of the information in the collection—

(a) has been obtained or recorded for the purpose of providing a public authority with information in connection with the provision of a service by the authority or the carrying out of any other function of the authority,

(b) is factual information which—
(i) is not the product of analysis or interpretation other than calculation, and
(ii) is not an official statistic (within the meaning given by section 6. (1) of the Statistics and Registration Service Act 2007), and

(c) remains presented in a way that (except for the purpose of forming part of the collection) has not been organised, adapted or otherwise materially altered since it was obtained or recorded.]
Amendments (Textual)
F32. S. 11. (1. A) inserted (1.9.2013) by Protection of Freedoms Act 2012 (c. 9), ss. 102. (2)(a), 120 (with s. 97); S.I. 2013/1906, art. 3. (a)
F33. Words in s. 11. (4) substituted (1.9.2013) by Protection of Freedoms Act 2012 (c. 9), ss. 102. (2)(b), 120 (with s. 97); S.I. 2013/1906, art. 3. (a)

[F3511. ARelease of datasets for re-use

(1) This section applies where—

(a) a person makes a request for information to a public authority in respect of information that is, or forms part of, a dataset held by the authority,

(b) any of the dataset or part of a dataset so requested is a relevant copyright work,

(c) the public authority is the only owner of the relevant copyright work, and

(d) the public authority is communicating the relevant copyright work to the applicant in accordance with this Act.

[F36. (1. A)But if the whole of the relevant copyright work is a document to which the Re-use of Public Sector Information Regulations 2015 apply, this section does not apply to the relevant copyright work.

(1. B)If part of the relevant copyright work is a document to which those Regulations apply—

(a) this section does not apply to that part, but

(b) this section does apply to the part to which the Regulations do not apply (and references in the following provisions of this section to the relevant copyright work are to be read as references to that part).]

(2) When communicating the relevant copyright work to the applicant, the public authority must make the relevant copyright work available for re-use by the applicant in accordance with the terms of the specified licence.

(3) The public authority may exercise any power that it has by virtue of regulations under section 11. B to charge a fee in connection with making the relevant copyright work available for re-use in accordance with subsection (2).

(4) Nothing in this section or section 11. B prevents a public authority which is subject to a duty under subsection (2) from exercising any power that it has by or under an enactment other than this Act to charge a fee in connection with making the relevant copyright work available for re-use.

(5) Where a public authority intends to charge a fee (whether in accordance with regulations under section 11. B or as mentioned in subsection (4)) in connection with making a relevant copyright work available for re-use by an applicant, the authority must give the applicant a notice in writing (in this section referred to as a " re-use fee notice ") stating that a fee of an amount specified in, or determined in accordance with, the notice is to be charged by the authority in connection with complying with subsection (2).

(6) Where a re-use fee notice has been given to the applicant, the public authority is not obliged to comply with subsection (2) while any part of the fee which is required to be paid is unpaid.

(7) Where a public authority intends to charge a fee as mentioned in subsection (4), the re-use fee notice may be combined with any other notice which is to be given under the power which enables the fee to be charged.

(8) In this section—

"copyright owner" has the meaning given by Part 1 of the Copyright, Designs and Patents Act 1988 (see section 173 of that Act);

"copyright work" has the meaning given by Part 1 of the Act of 1988 (see section 1. (2) of that Act);

"database" has the meaning given by section 3. A of the Act of 1988;

"database right" has the same meaning as in Part 3 of the Copyright and Rights in Databases Regulations 1997 (S.I. 1997/3032);

"owner", in relation to a relevant copyright work, means—

- the copyright owner, or

- the owner of the database right in the database;

"relevant copyright work" means—
- a copyright work, or
- a database subject to a database right,
but excludes a relevant Crown work or a relevant Parliamentary work;
"relevant Crown work" means—
- a copyright work in relation to which the Crown is the copyright owner, or
- a database in relation to which the Crown is the owner of the database right;
"relevant Parliamentary work" means—
- a copyright work in relation to which the House of Commons or the House of Lords is the copyright owner, or
- a database in relation to which the House of Commons or the House of Lords is the owner of the database right;
"the specified licence" is the licence specified by the [F37. Minister for the Cabinet Office] in a code of practice issued under section 45, and the [F37. Minister for the Cabinet Office] may specify different licences for different purposes.

Amendments (Textual)

F35. Ss. 11. A, 11. B inserted (31.7.2013 for the insertion of s. 11. B, 1.9.2013 in so far as not already in force) by Protection of Freedoms Act 2012 (c. 9), ss. 102. (3), 120 (with s. 97); S.I. 2013/1906, arts. 2, 3. (a)

F36. S. 11. A(1. A)(1. B) inserted (18.7.2015) by The Re-use of Public Sector Information Regulations 2015 (S.I. 2015/1415), regs. 1, 21. (2) (with regs. 5, 11. (4), 21. (8))

F37. Words in s. 11. A(8) substituted (9.11.2016) by The Transfer of Functions (Elections, Referendums, Third Sector and Information) Order 2016 (S.I. 2016/997), art. 1. (2), Sch. 2 para. 14. (2)(f) (with art. 12)

Modifications etc. (not altering text)

C21. S. 11. A(8) functions transferred (9.12.2015) by The Transfer of Functions (Information and Public Records) Order 2015 (S.I. 2015/1897), arts. 1. (2), 4. (1), (2)(c) (with art. 5)

11. BPower to charge fees in relation to release of datasets for re-use

(1)The [F38. Minister for the Cabinet Office] may, with the consent of the Treasury, make provision by regulations about the charging of fees by public authorities in connection with making relevant copyright works available for re-use under section 11. A(2) or by virtue of section 19. (2. A)(c).

(2) Regulations under this section may, in particular—

(a) prescribe cases in which fees may, or may not, be charged,

(b) prescribe the amount of any fee payable or provide for any such amount to be determined in such manner as may be prescribed,

(c) prescribe, or otherwise provide for, times at which fees, or parts of fees, are payable,

(d) require the provision of information about the manner in which amounts of fees are determined,

(e) make different provision for different purposes.

(3) Regulations under this section may, in prescribing the amount of any fee payable or providing for any such amount to be determined in such manner as may be prescribed, provide for a reasonable return on investment.

(4) In this section " relevant copyright work " has the meaning given by section 11. A(8).]

Amendments (Textual)

F35. Ss. 11. A, 11. B inserted (31.7.2013 for the insertion of s. 11. B, 1.9.2013 in so far as not already in force) by Protection of Freedoms Act 2012 (c. 9), ss. 102. (3), 120 (with s. 97); S.I. 2013/1906, arts. 2, 3. (a)

F38. Words in s. 11. B(1) substituted (9.11.2016) by The Transfer of Functions (Elections,

Referendums, Third Sector and Information) Order 2016 (S.I. 2016/997), art. 1. (2), Sch. 2 para. 14. (2)(g) (with art. 12)

Modifications etc. (not altering text)

C22. S. 11. B(1) functions transferred (9.12.2015) by The Transfer of Functions (Information and Public Records) Order 2015 (S.I. 2015/1897), arts. 1. (2), 4. (1), (2)(d) (with art. 5)

12. Exemption where cost of compliance exceeds appropriate limit.

(1) Section 1. (1) does not oblige a public authority to comply with a request for information if the authority estimates that the cost of complying with the request would exceed the appropriate limit.

(2) Subsection (1) does not exempt the public authority from its obligation to comply with paragraph (a) of section 1. (1) unless the estimated cost of complying with that paragraph alone would exceed the appropriate limit.

(3) In subsections (1) and (2) "the appropriate limit" means such amount as may be prescribed, and different amounts may be prescribed in relation to different cases.

(4) The [F39. Minister for the Cabinet Office] may by regulations provide that, in such circumstances as may be prescribed, where two or more requests for information are made to a public authority—

    (a) by one person, or

    (b) by different persons who appear to the public authority to be acting in concert or in pursuance of a campaign,

the estimated cost of complying with any of the requests is to be taken to be the estimated total cost of complying with all of them.

(5) The [F40. Minister for the Cabinet Office] may by regulations make provision for the purposes of this section as to the costs to be estimated and as to the manner in which they are to be estimated.

Amendments (Textual)

F39. Words in s. 12. (4) substituted (9.11.2016) by The Transfer of Functions (Elections, Referendums, Third Sector and Information) Order 2016 (S.I. 2016/997), art. 1. (2), Sch. 2 para. 14. (2)(h) (with art. 12)

F40. Words in s. 12. (5) substituted (9.11.2016) by The Transfer of Functions (Elections, Referendums, Third Sector and Information) Order 2016 (S.I. 2016/997), art. 1. (2), Sch. 2 para. 14. (2)(h) (with art. 12)

Modifications etc. (not altering text)

C23. S. 12. (3)-(5) functions transferred (9.12.2015) by The Transfer of Functions (Information and Public Records) Order 2015 (S.I. 2015/1897), arts. 1. (2), 4. (1), (2)(e) (with art. 5)

Commencement Information

I3. S. 12 wholly in force at 1.1.2005; s. 12 in force at Royal Assent to the extent that it confers power to make regulations, see s. 87. (1)(m)(3); s. 12 otherwise in force at 1.1.2005 by S.I. 2004/3122, art. 2

13. Fees for disclosure where cost of compliance exceeds appropriate limit.

(1) A public authority may charge for the communication of any information whose communication—

    (a) is not required by section 1. (1) because the cost of complying with the request for information exceeds the amount which is the appropriate limit for the purposes of section 12. (1) and (2), and

    (b) is not otherwise required by law,

16

such fee as may be determined by the public authority in accordance with regulations made by the [F41. Minister for the Cabinet Office].

(2) Regulations under this section may, in particular, provide—

(a) that any fee is not to exceed such maximum as may be specified in, or determined in accordance with, the regulations, and

(b) that any fee is to be calculated in such manner as may be prescribed by the regulations.

(3) Subsection (1) does not apply where provision is made by or under any enactment as to the fee that may be charged by the public authority for the disclosure of the information.

Amendments (Textual)

F41. Words in s. 13. (1) substituted (9.11.2016) by The Transfer of Functions (Elections, Referendums, Third Sector and Information) Order 2016 (S.I. 2016/997), art. 1. (2), Sch. 2 para. 14. (2)(i) (with art. 12)

Modifications etc. (not altering text)

C24. S. 13. (1) functions transferred (9.12.2015) by The Transfer of Functions (Information and Public Records) Order 2015 (S.I. 2015/1897), arts. 1. (2), 4. (1), (2)(f) (with art. 5)

Commencement Information

I4. S. 13 wholly in force at 1.1.2005; s. 13 in force at Royal Assent to the extent that it confers power to make regulations, see s. 87. (1)(m)(3); s. 13 otherwise in force at 1.1.2005 by S.I. 2004/3122, art. 2

14 Vexatious or repeated requests.

(1) Section 1. (1) does not oblige a public authority to comply with a request for information if the request is vexatious.

(2) Where a public authority has previously complied with a request for information which was made by any person, it is not obliged to comply with a subsequent identical or substantially similar request from that person unless a reasonable interval has elapsed between compliance with the previous request and the making of the current request.

15 Special provisions relating to public records transferred to Public Record Office, etc.

(1) Where—

(a) the appropriate records authority receives a request for information which relates to information which is, or if it existed would be, contained in a transferred public record, and

(b) either of the conditions in subsection (2) is satisfied in relation to any of that information, that authority shall, within the period for complying with section 1. (1), send a copy of the request to the responsible authority.

(2) The conditions referred to in subsection (1)(b) are—

(a) that the duty to confirm or deny is expressed to be excluded only by a provision of Part II not specified in subsection (3) of section 2, and

(b) that the information is exempt information only by virtue of a provision of Part II not specified in that subsection.

(3) On receiving the copy, the responsible authority shall, within such time as is reasonable in all the circumstances, inform the appropriate records authority of the determination required by virtue of subsection (3) or (4) of section 66.

(4) In this Act "transferred public record" means a public record which has been transferred—

(a) to the Public Record Office,

(b) to another place of deposit appointed by the [F42. Secretary of State] under the M2. Public Records Act 1958, or

(c) to the Public Record Office of Northern Ireland.

(5) In this Act—

"appropriate records authority", in relation to a transferred public record, means—

    - in a case falling within subsection (4)(a), the Public Record Office,

    - in a case falling within subsection (4)(b), the [F43. Secretary of State], and

    - in a case falling within subsection (4)(c), the Public Record Office of Northern Ireland;

"responsible authority", in relation to a transferred public record, means—

    - in the case of a record transferred as mentioned in subsection (4)(a) or (b) from a government department in the charge of a Minister of the Crown, the Minister of the Crown who appears to the [F43. Secretary of State] to be primarily concerned,

    - in the case of a record transferred as mentioned in subsection (4)(a) or (b) from any other person, the person who appears to the [F43. Secretary of State] to be primarily concerned,

    - in the case of a record transferred to the Public Record Office of Northern Ireland from a government department in the charge of a Minister of the Crown, the Minister of the Crown who appears to the appropriate Northern Ireland Minister to be primarily concerned,

    - in the case of a record transferred to the Public Record Office of Northern Ireland from a Northern Ireland department, the Northern Ireland Minister who appears to the appropriate Northern Ireland Minister to be primarily concerned, or

    - in the case of a record transferred to the Public Record Office of Northern Ireland from any other person, the person who appears to the appropriate Northern Ireland Minister to be primarily concerned.

Amendments (Textual)

F42. Words in s. 15. (4)(b) substituted (9.12.2015) by The Transfer of Functions (Information and Public Records) Order 2015 (S.I. 2015/1897), art. 1. (2), Sch. para. 2. (5)(a)

F43. Words in s. 15. (5) substituted (9.12.2015) by The Transfer of Functions (Information and Public Records) Order 2015 (S.I. 2015/1897), art. 1. (2), Sch. para. 2. (5)(a)

Commencement Information

I5. S. 15 wholly in force at 1.1.2005; s. 15 not in force at Royal Assent, see s. 87. (3); s. 15. (4)(5) in force for certain purposes at 1.1.2005 by S.I. 2004/1909, art. 2; s. 15 otherwise in force at 1.1.2005 by S.I. 2004/3122, art. 2

Marginal Citations

M21958 c. 51.

16 Duty to provide advice and assistance.

(1) It shall be the duty of a public authority to provide advice and assistance, so far as it would be reasonable to expect the authority to do so, to persons who propose to make, or have made, requests for information to it.

(2) Any public authority which, in relation to the provision of advice or assistance in any case, conforms with the code of practice under section 45 is to be taken to comply with the duty imposed by subsection (1) in relation to that case.

Refusal of request

17 Refusal of request.

(1) A public authority which, in relation to any request for information, is to any extent relying on a claim that any provision of Part II relating to the duty to confirm or deny is relevant to the request or on a claim that information is exempt information must, within the time for complying with section 1. (1), give the applicant a notice which—

    (a) states that fact,

(b) specifies the exemption in question, and

(c) states (if that would not otherwise be apparent) why the exemption applies.

(2) Where—

(a) in relation to any request for information, a public authority is, as respects any information, relying on a claim—

(i) that any provision of Part II which relates to the duty to confirm or deny and is not specified in section 2. (3) is relevant to the request, or

(ii) that the information is exempt information only by virtue of a provision not specified in section 2. (3), and

(b) at the time when the notice under subsection (1) is given to the applicant, the public authority (or, in a case falling within section 66. (3) or (4), the responsible authority) has not yet reached a decision as to the application of subsection (1)(b) or (2)(b) of section 2,

the notice under subsection (1) must indicate that no decision as to the application of that provision has yet been reached and must contain an estimate of the date by which the authority expects that such a decision will have been reached.

(3) A public authority which, in relation to any request for information, is to any extent relying on a claim that subsection (1)(b) or (2)(b) of section 2 applies must, either in the notice under subsection (1) or in a separate notice given within such time as is reasonable in the circumstances, state the reasons for claiming—

(a) that, in all the circumstances of the case, the public interest in maintaining the exclusion of the duty to confirm or deny outweighs the public interest in disclosing whether the authority holds the information, or

(b) that, in all the circumstances of the case, the public interest in maintaining the exemption outweighs the public interest in disclosing the information.

(4) A public authority is not obliged to make a statement under subsection (1)(c) or (3) if, or to the extent that, the statement would involve the disclosure of information which would itself be exempt information.

(5) A public authority which, in relation to any request for information, is relying on a claim that section 12 or 14 applies must, within the time for complying with section 1. (1), give the applicant a notice stating that fact.

(6) Subsection (5) does not apply where—

(a) the public authority is relying on a claim that section 14 applies,

(b) the authority has given the applicant a notice, in relation to a previous request for information, stating that it is relying on such a claim, and

(c) it would in all the circumstances be unreasonable to expect the authority to serve a further notice under subsection (5) in relation to the current request.

(7) A notice under subsection (1), (3) or (5) must—

(a) contain particulars of any procedure provided by the public authority for dealing with complaints about the handling of requests for information or state that the authority does not provide such a procedure, and

(b) contain particulars of the right conferred by section 50.

F44 The Information Commissioner . . .

Amendments (Textual)
F44. Words in cross-heading preceding s. 18 omitted (18.1.2010) by virtue of The Transfer of Tribunal Functions Order 2010 (S.I. 2010/22), arts. 1. (1), 5. (1), Sch. 2 para. 67

18. The Information Commissioner F45. . .

(1) The Data Protection Commissioner shall be known instead as the Information Commissioner.
F46. (2). . . . .

(3) In this Act—

(a) the Information Commissioner is referred to as "the Commissioner", F47...

F47. (b). . . . .

(4) Schedule 2 (which makes provision consequential on subsections (1) and (2) and amendments of the M3. Data Protection Act 1998 relating to the extension by this Act of the functions of the Commissioner and the Tribunal) has effect.

F48. (5). . . . .

F48. (6). . . . .

F48. (7). . . . .

Amendments (Textual)

F45. Words in s. 18 heading omitted (18.1.2010) by virtue of The Transfer of Tribunal Functions Order 2010 (S.I. 2010/22), arts. 1. (1), 5. (1), Sch. 2 para. 68. (a)

F46. S. 18. (2) omitted (18.1.2010) by virtue of The Transfer of Tribunal Functions Order 2010 (S.I. 2010/22), arts. 1. (1), 5. (1), Sch. 2 para. 68. (b)

F47. S. 18. (3)(b) and preceding word omitted (18.1.2010) by virtue of The Transfer of Tribunal Functions Order 2010 (S.I. 2010/22), arts. 1. (1), 5. (1), Sch. 2 para. 68. (c)

F48. S. 18. (5)-(7) repealed (16.3.2015) by Protection of Freedoms Act 2012 (c. 9), ss. 105. (5), 120, Sch. 10 Pt. 8 (with s. 97); S.I. 2015/587, art. 2. (a)(c)

Commencement Information

I6. S. 18 wholly in force at 1.1.2005; s. 18. (4) in force for certain purposes at Royal Assent, see s. 87. (1)(i); s. 18. (1) wholly in force and s. 18. (4) in force for certain further purposes at 30.1.2001, see s. 87. (2)(a)(c); s. 18. (2)(3)(5)-(7) in force and s. 18. (4) in force for certain further purposes at 14.5.2001 by S.I. 2001/1637, art. 2. (a)(b); s. 18 otherwise in force at 1.1.2005 by S.I. 2004/3122, art. 2

Marginal Citations

M31998 c. 29.

Publication schemes

19 Publication schemes.

(1) It shall be the duty of every public authority—

(a) to adopt and maintain a scheme which relates to the publication of information by the authority and is approved by the Commissioner (in this Act referred to as a "publication scheme"),

(b) to publish information in accordance with its publication scheme, and

(c) from time to time to review its publication scheme.

(2) A publication scheme must—

(a) specify classes of information which the public authority publishes or intends to publish,

(b) specify the manner in which information of each class is, or is intended to be, published, and

(c) specify whether the material is, or is intended to be, available to the public free of charge or on payment.

[F49. (2. A)A publication scheme must, in particular, include a requirement for the public authority concerned—

(a) to publish—

(i) any dataset held by the authority in relation to which a person makes a request for information to the authority, and

(ii) any up-dated version held by the authority of such a dataset,

unless the authority is satisfied that it is not appropriate for the dataset to be published,

(b) where reasonably practicable, to publish any dataset the authority publishes by virtue of paragraph (a) in an electronic form which is capable of re-use,

(c) where [F50subject to subsections (2. AA) and (2. AB)] any information in a dataset published by virtue of paragraph (a) is a relevant copyright work in relation to which the authority is the only owner, to make the information available for re-use in accordance with the terms of the specified licence.

[F51. (2. AA)If the whole of the relevant copyright work is a document to which the Re-use of Public Sector Information Regulations 2015 apply, subsections (2. A)(c) and (2. B) to (2. F) do not apply to the relevant copyright work.

(2. AB)If part of the relevant copyright work is a document to which those Regulations apply—

    (a) subsections (2. A)(c) and (2. B) to (2. F) do not apply to that part, but

    (b) those provisions do apply to the part to which the Regulations do not apply (and references in the following provisions of this section to the relevant copyright work are to be read as references to that part).]

(2. B)The public authority may exercise any power that it has by virtue of regulations under section 11. B to charge a fee in connection with making the relevant copyright work available for re-use in accordance with a requirement imposed by virtue of subsection (2. A)(c).

(2. C)Nothing in this section or section 11. B prevents a public authority which is subject to such a requirement from exercising any power that it has by or under an enactment other than this Act to charge a fee in connection with making the relevant copyright work available for re-use.

(2. D) Where a public authority intends to charge a fee (whether in accordance with regulations under section 11. B or as mentioned in subsection (2. C)) in connection with making a relevant copyright work available for re-use by an applicant, the authority must give the applicant a notice in writing (in this section referred to as a " re-use fee notice ") stating that a fee of an amount specified in, or determined in accordance with, the notice is to be charged by the authority in connection with complying with the requirement imposed by virtue of subsection (2. A)(c).

(2. E)Where a re-use fee notice has been given to the applicant, the public authority is not obliged to comply with the requirement imposed by virtue of subsection (2. A)(c) while any part of the fee which is required to be paid is unpaid.

(2. F)Where a public authority intends to charge a fee as mentioned in subsection (2. C), the re-use fee notice may be combined with any other notice which is to be given under the power which enables the fee to be charged.]

(3) In adopting or reviewing a publication scheme, a public authority shall have regard to the public interest—

    (a) in allowing public access to information held by the authority, and

    (b) in the publication of reasons for decisions made by the authority.

(4) A public authority shall publish its publication scheme in such manner as it thinks fit.

(5) The Commissioner may, when approving a scheme, provide that his approval is to expire at the end of a specified period.

(6) Where the Commissioner has approved the publication scheme of any public authority, he may at any time give notice to the public authority revoking his approval of the scheme as from the end of the period of six months beginning with the day on which the notice is given.

(7) Where the Commissioner—

    (a) refuses to approve a proposed publication scheme, or

    (b) revokes his approval of a publication scheme,

he must give the public authority a statement of his reasons for doing so.

[F52. (8)In this section—

" copyright owner " has the meaning given by Part 1 of the Copyright, Designs and Patents Act 1988 (see section 173 of that Act);

" copyright work " has the meaning given by Part 1 of the Act of 1988 (see section 1. (2) of that Act);

" database " has the meaning given by section 3. A of the Act of 1988;

" database right " has the same meaning as in Part 3 of the Copyright and Rights in Databases Regulations 1997 (S.I. 1997/3032);

" owner ", in relation to a relevant copyright work, means—

    - the copyright owner, or

- the owner of the database right in the database;
" relevant copyright work " means—
- a copyright work, or
- a database subject to a database right,
but excludes a relevant Crown work or a relevant Parliamentary work;
" relevant Crown work " means—
- a copyright work in relation to which the Crown is the copyright owner, or
- a database in relation to which the Crown is the owner of the database right;
" relevant Parliamentary work " means—
- a copyright work in relation to which the House of Commons or the House of Lords is the copyright owner, or
- a database in relation to which the House of Commons or the House of Lords is the owner of the database right;
" the specified licence " has the meaning given by section 11. A(8).]

Amendments (Textual)

F49. S. 19. (2. A)-(2. F) inserted (1.9.2013) by Protection of Freedoms Act 2012 (c. 9), ss. 102. (4)(a), 120 (with s. 97); S.I. 2013/1906, art. 3. (a)

F50. Words in s. 19. (2. A)(c) inserted (18.7.2015) by The Re-use of Public Sector Information Regulations 2015 (S.I. 2015/1415), regs. 1, 21. (3)(a) (with regs. 5, 11. (4), 21. (8))

F51. S. 19. (2. AA)(2. AB) inserted (18.7.2015) by The Re-use of Public Sector Information Regulations 2015 (S.I. 2015/1415), regs. 1, 21. (3)(b) (with regs. 5, 11. (4), 21. (8))

F52. S. 19. (8) inserted (1.9.2013) by Protection of Freedoms Act 2012 (c. 9), ss. 102. (4)(b), 120 (with s. 97); S.I. 2013/1906, art. 3. (a)

Commencement Information

I7. S. 19 wholly in force at 1.1.2005; s. 19 in force for certain purposes at Royal Assent, see s. 87. (1)(b)(3); s. 19. (5)-(7) in force at 30.11.2002 and s. 19. (1)-(4) in force for certain purposes at 28.2.2003 and 30.6.2003 by S.I. 2002/2812, arts. 3, 4, 5 (as amended (1.4.2006) by S.I. 2005/3239, art. 9. (2), Sch. 2 para. 8, S.I. 2006/63, art. 3. (2)(b) and S.I. 2006/64, art. 3. (2)(b)); s. 19. (1)-(4) in force for certain further purposes at 31.10.2003, 29.2.2004 and 30.6.2004 by S.I. 2003/2603, arts. 2, 3, 4; s. 19 in force in so far as not already in force at 1.1.2005 by S.I. 2004/3122, art. 2

20 Model publication schemes.

(1) The Commissioner may from time to time approve, in relation to public authorities falling within particular classes, model publication schemes prepared by him or by other persons.
(2) Where a public authority falling within the class to which an approved model scheme relates adopts such a scheme without modification, no further approval of the Commissioner is required so long as the model scheme remains approved; and where such an authority adopts such a scheme with modifications, the approval of the Commissioner is required only in relation to the modifications.
(3) The Commissioner may, when approving a model publication scheme, provide that his approval is to expire at the end of a specified period.
(4) Where the Commissioner has approved a model publication scheme, he may at any time publish, in such manner as he thinks fit, a notice revoking his approval of the scheme as from the end of the period of six months beginning with the day on which the notice is published.
(5) Where the Commissioner refuses to approve a proposed model publication scheme on the application of any person, he must give the person who applied for approval of the scheme a statement of the reasons for his refusal.
(6) Where the Commissioner refuses to approve any modifications under subsection (2), he must give the public authority a statement of the reasons for his refusal.
(7) Where the Commissioner revokes his approval of a model publication scheme, he must include

in the notice under subsection (4) a statement of his reasons for doing so.

Commencement Information

I8. S. 20 wholly in force at 1.1.2005; s. 20 in force for certain purposes at Royal Assent, see s. 87. (1)(c)(3); s. 20 otherwise in force at 1.1.2005 by S.I. 2004/3122, art. 2

Effect of the exemptions in Part II.

2 Effect of the exemptions in Part II.

(1) Where any provision of Part II states that the duty to confirm or deny does not arise in relation to any information, the effect of the provision is that where either—

(a) the provision confers absolute exemption, or

(b) in all the circumstances of the case, the public interest in maintaining the exclusion of the duty to confirm or deny outweighs the public interest in disclosing whether the public authority holds the information,

section 1. (1)(a) does not apply.

(2) In respect of any information which is exempt information by virtue of any provision of Part II, section 1. (1)(b) does not apply if or to the extent that—

(a) the information is exempt information by virtue of a provision conferring absolute exemption, or

(b) in all the circumstances of the case, the public interest in maintaining the exemption outweighs the public interest in disclosing the information.

(3) For the purposes of this section, the following provisions of Part II (and no others) are to be regarded as conferring absolute exemption—

(a) section 21,

(b) section 23,

(c) section 32,

(d) section 34,

(e) section 36 so far as relating to information held by the House of Commons or the House of Lords,

[F1. (ea)in section 37, paragraphs (a) to (ab) of subsection (1), and subsection (2) so far as relating to those paragraphs,]

(f) in section 40—

(i) subsection (1), and

(ii) subsection (2) so far as relating to cases where the first condition referred to in that subsection is satisfied by virtue of subsection (3)(a)(i) or (b) of that section,

(g) section 41, and

(h) section 44.

Amendments (Textual)

F1. S. 2. (3)(ea) inserted (19.1.2011) by Constitutional Reform and Governance Act 2010 (c. 25), ss. 46. (1), 52. (2), Sch. 7 para. 2; S.I. 2011/46, art. 3. (b)(i) (with art. 4)

Part II Exempt information

Part II Exempt information

21 Information accessible to applicant by other means.

(1) Information which is reasonably accessible to the applicant otherwise than under section 1 is exempt information.

(2) For the purposes of subsection (1)—

(a) information may be reasonably accessible to the applicant even though it is accessible only on payment, and

(b) information is to be taken to be reasonably accessible to the applicant if it is information which the public authority or any other person is obliged by or under any enactment to communicate (otherwise than by making the information available for inspection) to members of the public on request, whether free of charge or on payment.

(3) For the purposes of subsection (1), information which is held by a public authority and does not fall within subsection (2)(b) is not to be regarded as reasonably accessible to the applicant merely because the information is available from the public authority itself on request, unless the information is made available in accordance with the authority's publication scheme and any payment required is specified in, or determined in accordance with, the scheme.

22 Information intended for future publication.

(1) Information is exempt information if—

(a) the information is held by the public authority with a view to its publication, by the authority or any other person, at some future date (whether determined or not),

(b) the information was already held with a view to such publication at the time when the request for information was made, and

(c) it is reasonable in all the circumstances that the information should be withheld from disclosure until the date referred to in paragraph (a).

(2) The duty to confirm or deny does not arise if, or to the extent that, compliance with section 1. (1)(a) would involve the disclosure of any information (whether or not already recorded) which falls within subsection (1).

[F122. AResearch

(1) Information obtained in the course of, or derived from, a programme of research is exempt information if—

(a) the programme is continuing with a view to the publication, by a public authority or any other person, of a report of the research (whether or not including a statement of that information), and

(b) disclosure of the information under this Act before the date of publication would, or would be likely to, prejudice—

(i) the programme,

(ii) the interests of any individual participating in the programme,

(iii) the interests of the authority which holds the information, or

(iv) the interests of the authority mentioned in paragraph (a) (if it is a different authority from that which holds the information).

(2) The duty to confirm or deny does not arise in relation to information which is (or if it were held by the public authority would be) exempt information by virtue of subsection (1) if, or to the extent that, compliance with section 1. (1)(a) would, or would be likely to, prejudice any of the matters mentioned in subsection (1)(b).]

Amendments (Textual)

F1. S. 22. A inserted (1.10.2014) by Intellectual Property Act 2014 (c. 18), ss. 20, 24. (1); S.I. 2014/2330, art. 3, Sch.

23 Information supplied by, or relating to, bodies dealing with security matters.

(1) Information held by a public authority is exempt information if it was directly or indirectly supplied to the public authority by, or relates to, any of the bodies specified in subsection (3).

(2) A certificate signed by a Minister of the Crown certifying that the information to which it applies was directly or indirectly supplied by, or relates to, any of the bodies specified in subsection (3) shall, subject to section 60, be conclusive evidence of that fact.

(3) The bodies referred to in subsections (1) and (2) are—

    (a) the Security Service,

    (b) the Secret Intelligence Service,

    (c) the Government Communications Headquarters,

    (d) the special forces,

    (e) the Tribunal established under section 65 of the Regulation of M1. Investigatory Powers Act 2000,

    (f) the Tribunal established under section 7 of the M2. Interception of Communications Act 1985,

    (g) the Tribunal established under section 5 of the M3. Security Service Act 1989,

    (h) the Tribunal established under section 9 of the M4. Intelligence Services Act 1994,

    (i) the Security Vetting Appeals Panel,

    (j) the Security Commission,

    (k) the National Criminal Intelligence Service, F2. . .

    (l) the Service Authority for the National Criminal Intelligence Service.

    [F3. (m)the Serious Organised Crime Agency.]

    [F4. (n)the National Crime Agency.]

    [F5. (o)the Intelligence and Security Committee of Parliament.]

(4) In subsection (3)(c) "the Government Communications Headquarters" includes any unit or part of a unit of the armed forces of the Crown which is for the time being required by the Secretary of State to assist the Government Communications Headquarters in carrying out its functions.

(5) The duty to confirm or deny does not arise if, or to the extent that, compliance with section 1. (1)(a) would involve the disclosure of any information (whether or not already recorded) which was directly or indirectly supplied to the public authority by, or relates to, any of the bodies specified in subsection (3).

Amendments (Textual)

F2. Word in s. 23. (3)(k) repealed (1.4.2006) by Serious Organised Crime and Police Act 2005 (c. 15), ss. 59, 174, 178, Sch. 4 para. 159, Sch. 17; S.I. 2006/378, art. 4. (1), Sch. para. 10 (subject to art. 4. (2)-(7))

F3. S. 23. (3)(m) inserted (1.4.2006) by Serious Organised Crime and Police Act 2005 (c. 15), ss. 59, 178, Sch. 4 para. 159; S.I. 2006/378, art. 4. (1), Sch. para. 10 (subject to art. 4. (2)-(7))

F4. S. 23. (3)(n) inserted (27.5.2013) by Crime and Courts Act 2013 (c. 22), s. 61. (2), Sch. 8 para. 102; S.I. 2013/1042, art. 3. (l)

F5. S. 23. (3)(o) inserted (25.6.2013) by Justice and Security Act 2013 (c. 18), s. 20. (1), Sch. 2 para. 5. (2); S.I. 2013/1482, art. 2 (with arts. 3, 4)

Marginal Citations

M12000 c. 23.

M21985 c. 56.

M31989 c. 5.

M41994 c. 13.

24 National security.

(1) Information which does not fall within section 23. (1) is exempt information if exemption from section 1. (1)(b) is required for the purpose of safeguarding national security.

(2) The duty to confirm or deny does not arise if, or to the extent that, exemption from section 1. (1)(a) is required for the purpose of safeguarding national security.

(3) A certificate signed by a Minister of the Crown certifying that exemption from section 1. (1)(b), or from section 1. (1)(a) and (b), is, or at any time was, required for the purpose of safeguarding national security shall, subject to section 60, be conclusive evidence of that fact.

(4) A certificate under subsection (3) may identify the information to which it applies by means of a general description and may be expressed to have prospective effect.

25 Certificates under ss. 23 and 24: supplementary provisions.

(1) A document purporting to be a certificate under section 23. (2) or 24. (3) shall be received in evidence and deemed to be such a certificate unless the contrary is proved.

(2) A document which purports to be certified by or on behalf of a Minister of the Crown as a true copy of a certificate issued by that Minister under section 23. (2) or 24. (3) shall in any legal proceedings be evidence (or, in Scotland, sufficient evidence) of that certificate.

(3) The power conferred by section 23. (2) or 24. (3) on a Minister of the Crown shall not be exercisable except by a Minister who is a member of the Cabinet or by the Attorney General, the Advocate General for Scotland or the Attorney General for Northern Ireland.

26 Defence.

(1) Information is exempt information if its disclosure under this Act would, or would be likely to, prejudice—

    (a) the defence of the British Islands or of any colony, or

    (b) the capability, effectiveness or security of any relevant forces.

(2) In subsection (1)(b) "relevant forces" means—

    (a) the armed forces of the Crown, and

    (b) any forces co-operating with those forces,

or any part of any of those forces.

(3) The duty to confirm or deny does not arise if, or to the extent that, compliance with section 1. (1)(a) would, or would be likely to, prejudice any of the matters mentioned in subsection (1).

27 International relations.

(1) Information is exempt information if its disclosure under this Act would, or would be likely to, prejudice—

    (a) relations between the United Kingdom and any other State,

    (b) relations between the United Kingdom and any international organisation or international court,

    (c) the interests of the United Kingdom abroad, or

    (d) the promotion or protection by the United Kingdom of its interests abroad.

(2) Information is also exempt information if it is confidential information obtained from a State other than the United Kingdom or from an international organisation or international court.

(3) For the purposes of this section, any information obtained from a State, organisation or court is confidential at any time while the terms on which it was obtained require it to be held in confidence or while the circumstances in which it was obtained make it reasonable for the State, organisation or court to expect that it will be so held.

(4) The duty to confirm or deny does not arise if, or to the extent that, compliance with section 1. (1)(a)—

(a) would, or would be likely to, prejudice any of the matters mentioned in subsection (1), or

(b) would involve the disclosure of any information (whether or not already recorded) which is confidential information obtained from a State other than the United Kingdom or from an international organisation or international court.

(5) In this section—

"international court" means any international court which is not an international organisation and which is established—

- by a resolution of an international organisation of which the United Kingdom is a member, or

- by an international agreement to which the United Kingdom is a party;

"international organisation" means any international organisation whose members include any two or more States, or any organ of such an organisation;

"State" includes the government of any State and any organ of its government, and references to a State other than the United Kingdom include references to any territory outside the United Kingdom.

28 Relations within the United Kingdom.

(1) Information is exempt information if its disclosure under this Act would, or would be likely to, prejudice relations between any administration in the United Kingdom and any other such administration.

(2) In subsection (1) "administration in the United Kingdom" means—

(a) the government of the United Kingdom,

(b) the Scottish Administration,

(c) the Executive Committee of the Northern Ireland Assembly, or

[F6. (d)the Welsh Assembly Government.]

(3) The duty to confirm or deny does not arise if, or to the extent that, compliance with section 1. (1)(a) would, or would be likely to, prejudice any of the matters mentioned in subsection (1).

Amendments (Textual)

F6. S. 28. (2)(d) substituted by The Government of Wales Act 2006 (Consequential Modifications and Transitional Provisions) Order 2007 (S.I. 2007/1388), art. 3, Sch. 1 para. 80 (the amendment coming into force immediately after the end of "the initial period" (which ended with the day of the first appointment of a First Minister on 25.5.2007) in accordance with art. 1. (2)(3) of the amending S.I. and see ss. 46, 161. (5) of Government of Wales Act 2006 (c. 32))

29 The economy.

(1) Information is exempt information if its disclosure under this Act would, or would be likely to, prejudice—

(a) the economic interests of the United Kingdom or of any part of the United Kingdom, or

(b) the financial interests of any administration in the United Kingdom, as defined by section 28. (2).

(2) The duty to confirm or deny does not arise if, or to the extent that, compliance with section 1. (1)(a) would, or would be likely to, prejudice any of the matters mentioned in subsection (1).

30 Investigations and proceedings conducted by public authorities.

(1) Information held by a public authority is exempt information if it has at any time been held by the authority for the purposes of—

(a) any investigation which the public authority has a duty to conduct with a view to it being ascertained—

(i) whether a person should be charged with an offence, or

(ii) whether a person charged with an offence is guilty of it,

(b) any investigation which is conducted by the authority and in the circumstances may lead to a decision by the authority to institute criminal proceedings which the authority has power to conduct, or

(c) any criminal proceedings which the authority has power to conduct.

(2) Information held by a public authority is exempt information if—

(a) it was obtained or recorded by the authority for the purposes of its functions relating to—

(i) investigations falling within subsection (1)(a) or (b),

(ii) criminal proceedings which the authority has power to conduct,

(iii) investigations (other than investigations falling within subsection (1)(a) or (b)) which are conducted by the authority for any of the purposes specified in section 31. (2) and either by virtue of Her Majesty's prerogative or by virtue of powers conferred by or under any enactment, or

(iv) civil proceedings which are brought by or on behalf of the authority and arise out of such investigations, and

(b) it relates to the obtaining of information from confidential sources.

(3) The duty to confirm or deny does not arise in relation to information which is (or if it were held by the public authority would be) exempt information by virtue of subsection (1) or (2).

(4) In relation to the institution or conduct of criminal proceedings or the power to conduct them, references in subsection (1)(b) or (c) and subsection (2)(a) to the public authority include references—

(a) to any officer of the authority,

(b) in the case of a government department other than a Northern Ireland department, to the Minister of the Crown in charge of the department, and

(c) in the case of a Northern Ireland department, to the Northern Ireland Minister in charge of the department.

[F7. (5)In this section—

" criminal proceedings " includes service law proceedings (as defined by section 324. (5) of the Armed Forces Act 2006);

" offence " includes a service offence (as defined by section 50 of that Act).]

(6) In the application of this section to Scotland—

(a) in subsection (1)(b), for the words from "a decision" to the end there is substituted " a decision by the authority to make a report to the procurator fiscal for the purpose of enabling him to determine whether criminal proceedings should be instituted ",

(b) in subsections (1)(c) and (2)(a)(ii) for "which the authority has power to conduct" there is substituted " which have been instituted in consequence of a report made by the authority to the procurator fiscal ", and

(c) for any reference to a person being charged with an offence there is substituted a reference to the person being prosecuted for the offence.

Amendments (Textual)

F7. S. 30. (5) substituted (28.3.2009 for certain purposes and 31.10.2009 otherwise) by Armed Forces Act 2006 (c. 52), ss. 378. (1), 383. (2), Sch. 16 para. 176; S.I. 2009/812, art. 3; S.I. 2009/1167, art. 4

Modifications etc. (not altering text)

C1. S. 30 modified (24.4.2009 for certain purposes and 31.10.2009 otherwise) by The Armed Forces Act 2006 (Transitional Provisions etc) Order 2009 (S.I. 2009/1059), arts. 1. (3), 205, Sch. 1 para. 46. (1)

C2. S. 30. (5) modified (24.4.2009 for certain purposes and 31.10.2009 otherwise) by The Armed Forces Act 2006 (Transitional Provisions etc) Order 2009 (S.I. 2009/1059), arts. 1. (3), 205, Sch. 1 para. 46. (2)

31 Law enforcement.

(1) Information which is not exempt information by virtue of section 30 is exempt information if its disclosure under this Act would, or would be likely to, prejudice—

(a) the prevention or detection of crime,

(b) the apprehension or prosecution of offenders,

(c) the administration of justice,

(d) the assessment or collection of any tax or duty or of any imposition of a similar nature,

(e) the operation of the immigration controls,

(f) the maintenance of security and good order in prisons or in other institutions where persons are lawfully detained,

(g) the exercise by any public authority of its functions for any of the purposes specified in subsection (2),

(h) any civil proceedings which are brought by or on behalf of a public authority and arise out of an investigation conducted, for any of the purposes specified in subsection (2), by or on behalf of the authority by virtue of Her Majesty's prerogative or by virtue of powers conferred by or under an enactment, or

(i) any inquiry held under the [F8. Inquiries into Fatal Accidents and Sudden Deaths etc. (Scotland) Act 2016] to the extent that the inquiry arises out of an investigation conducted, for any of the purposes specified in subsection (2), by or on behalf of the authority by virtue of Her Majesty's prerogative or by virtue of powers conferred by or under an enactment.

(2) The purposes referred to in subsection (1)(g) to (i) are—

(a) the purpose of ascertaining whether any person has failed to comply with the law,

(b) the purpose of ascertaining whether any person is responsible for any conduct which is improper,

(c) the purpose of ascertaining whether circumstances which would justify regulatory action in pursuance of any enactment exist or may arise,

(d) the purpose of ascertaining a person's fitness or competence in relation to the management of bodies corporate or in relation to any profession or other activity which he is, or seeks to become, authorised to carry on,

(e) the purpose of ascertaining the cause of an accident,

(f) the purpose of protecting charities against misconduct or mismanagement (whether by trustees or other persons) in their administration,

(g) the purpose of protecting the property of charities from loss or misapplication,

(h) the purpose of recovering the property of charities,

(i) the purpose of securing the health, safety and welfare of persons at work, and

(j) the purpose of protecting persons other than persons at work against risk to health or safety arising out of or in connection with the actions of persons at work.

(3) The duty to confirm or deny does not arise if, or to the extent that, compliance with section 1. (1)(a) would, or would be likely to, prejudice any of the matters mentioned in subsection (1).

Amendments (Textual)

F8. Words in s. 31. (1)(i) substituted (S.) (15.6.2017) by Inquiries into Fatal Accidents and Sudden Deaths etc. (Scotland) Act 2016 (asp 2), s. 42. (2), sch. 2 para. 8; S.S.I. 2017/155, reg. 2 (with regs. 4. (2) 5) and words in s. 31. (1)(i) substituted (E.W. N.I.) (15.6.2017) by The Inquiries into Fatal Accidents and Sudden Deaths etc. (Scotland) Act 2016 (Consequential Provisions and Modifications) Order 2016 (S.I. 2016/1142), art. 1. (2), Sch. para. 8 (with art. 7. (2)); ; S.S.I. 2017/155, reg. 2

32 Court records, etc.

(1) Information held by a public authority is exempt information if it is held only by virtue of being contained in—

(a) any document filed with, or otherwise placed in the custody of, a court for the purposes of proceedings in a particular cause or matter,

(b) any document served upon, or by, a public authority for the purposes of proceedings in a particular cause or matter, or

(c) any document created by—

(i) a court, or

(ii) a member of the administrative staff of a court,

for the purposes of proceedings in a particular cause or matter.

(2) Information held by a public authority is exempt information if it is held only by virtue of being contained in—

(a) any document placed in the custody of a person conducting an inquiry or arbitration, for the purposes of the inquiry or arbitration, or

(b) any document created by a person conducting an inquiry or arbitration, for the purposes of the inquiry or arbitration.

(3) The duty to confirm or deny does not arise in relation to information which is (or if it were held by the public authority would be) exempt information by virtue of this section.

(4) In this section—

(a) "court" includes any tribunal or body exercising the judicial power of the State,

(b) "proceedings in a particular cause or matter" includes [F9any investigation under Part 1 of the Coroners and Justice Act 2009, any inquest under the Coroners Act (Northern Ireland) 1959 and any] post-mortem examination,

(c) "inquiry" means any inquiry or hearing held under any provision contained in, or made under, an enactment, and

(d) except in relation to Scotland, "arbitration" means any arbitration to which Part I of the M5. Arbitration Act 1996 applies.

Amendments (Textual)

F9. Words in s. 32. (4)(b) substituted (25.7.2013) by Coroners and Justice Act 2009 (c. 25), s. 182. (4)(e), Sch. 21 para. 44 (with s. 180); S.I. 2013/1869, art. 2. (o)(xvi)

Modifications etc. (not altering text)

C3. S. 32. (2) excluded (7.6.2005) by Inquiries Act 2005 (c. 12), ss. 18. (3), 51. (1) (with ss. 44, 50); S.I. 2005/1432, art. 2

Marginal Citations

M51996 c. 23.

33 Audit functions.

(1) This section applies to any public authority which has functions in relation to—

(a) the audit of the accounts of other public authorities, or

(b) the examination of the economy, efficiency and effectiveness with which other public authorities use their resources in discharging their functions.

(2) Information held by a public authority to which this section applies is exempt information if its disclosure would, or would be likely to, prejudice the exercise of any of the authority's functions in relation to any of the matters referred to in subsection (1).

(3) The duty to confirm or deny does not arise in relation to a public authority to which this section applies if, or to the extent that, compliance with section 1. (1)(a) would, or would be likely to, prejudice the exercise of any of the authority's functions in relation to any of the matters referred to in subsection (1).

34 Parliamentary privilege.

(1) Information is exempt information if exemption from section 1. (1)(b) is required for the purpose of avoiding an infringement of the privileges of either House of Parliament.

(2) The duty to confirm or deny does not apply if, or to the extent that, exemption from section 1.

(1)(a) is required for the purpose of avoiding an infringement of the privileges of either House of Parliament.

(3) A certificate signed by the appropriate authority certifying that exemption from section 1. (1)(b), or from section 1. (1)(a) and (b), is, or at any time was, required for the purpose of avoiding an infringement of the privileges of either House of Parliament shall be conclusive evidence of that fact.

(4) In subsection (3) "the appropriate authority" means—

    (a) in relation to the House of Commons, the Speaker of that House, and

    (b) in relation to the House of Lords, the Clerk of the Parliaments.

35 Formulation of government policy, etc.

(1) Information held by a government department or by [F10the Welsh Assembly Government] is exempt information if it relates to—

    (a) the formulation or development of government policy,

    (b) Ministerial communications,

    (c) the provision of advice by any of the Law Officers or any request for the provision of such advice, or

    (d) the operation of any Ministerial private office.

(2) Once a decision as to government policy has been taken, any statistical information used to provide an informed background to the taking of the decision is not to be regarded—

    (a) for the purposes of subsection (1)(a), as relating to the formulation or development of government policy, or

    (b) for the purposes of subsection (1)(b), as relating to Ministerial communications.

(3) The duty to confirm or deny does not arise in relation to information which is (or if it were held by the public authority would be) exempt information by virtue of subsection (1).

(4) In making any determination required by section 2. (1)(b) or (2)(b) in relation to information which is exempt information by virtue of subsection (1)(a), regard shall be had to the particular public interest in the disclosure of factual information which has been used, or is intended to be used, to provide an informed background to decision-taking.

(5) In this section—

"government policy" includes the policy of the Executive Committee of the Northern Ireland Assembly and the policy of [F11the Welsh Assembly Government];

"the Law Officers" means the Attorney General, the Solicitor General, the Advocate General for Scotland, the Lord Advocate, the Solicitor General for Scotland [F12, the Counsel General to the Welsh Assembly Government] and the Attorney General for Northern Ireland;

"Ministerial communications" means any communications—

    - between Ministers of the Crown,

    - between Northern Ireland Ministers, including Northern Ireland junior Ministers, or

    - [F13between members of the Welsh Assembly Government]

and includes, in particular, proceedings of the Cabinet or of any committee of the Cabinet, proceedings of the Executive Committee of the Northern Ireland Assembly, and proceedings of [F14the Cabinet or any committee of the Cabinet of the Welsh Assembly Government];

"Ministerial private office" means any part of a government department which provides personal administrative support to a Minister of the Crown, to a Northern Ireland Minister or a Northern Ireland junior Minister or [F15any part of the administration of the Welsh Assembly Government providing personal administrative support to the members of the Welsh Assembly Government];

"Northern Ireland junior Minister" means a member of the Northern Ireland Assembly appointed as a junior Minister under section 19 of the M6. Northern Ireland Act 1998.

Amendments (Textual)

F10. Words in s. 35. (1) substituted by The Government of Wales Act 2006 (Consequential Modifications and Transitional Provisions) Order 2007 (S.I. 2007/1388), art. 3, Sch. 1 para. 81. (2)

(the amendment coming into force immediately after the end of "the initial period" (which ended with the day of the first appointment of a First Minister on 25.5.2007) in accordance with art. 1. (2)(3) of the amending S.I. and see ss. 46, 161. (5) of Government of Wales Act 2006 (c. 32))

F11. S. 35. (5): words in definition of "government policy" substituted by The Government of Wales Act 2006 (Consequential Modifications and Transitional Provisions) Order 2007 (S.I. 2007/1388), art. 3, Sch. 1 para. 81. (3)(a) (the amendment coming into force immediately after the end of "the initial period" (which ended with the day of the first appointment of a First Minister on 25.5.2007) in accordance with art. 1. (2)(3) of the amending S.I. and see ss. 46, 161. (5) of Government of Wales Act 2006 (c. 32))

F12. S. 35. (5): words in definition of "the Law Officers" substituted by The Government of Wales Act 2006 (Consequential Modifications and Transitional Provisions) Order 2007 (S.I. 2007/1388), art. 3, Sch. 1 para. 81. (3)(b) (the amendment coming into force immediately after the end of "the initial period" (which ended with the day of the first appointment of a First Minister on 25.5.2007) in accordance with art. 1. (2)(3) of the amending S.I. and see ss. 46, 161. (5) of Government of Wales Act 2006 (c. 32))

F13. S. 35. (5): para. (c) in definition of "Ministerial communications" substituted by The Government of Wales Act 2006 (Consequential Modifications and Transitional Provisions) Order 2007 (S.I. 2007/1388), art. 3, Sch. 1 para. 81. (c)(i) (the amendment coming into force immediately after the end of "the initial period" (which ended with the day of the first appointment of a First Minister on 25.5.2007) in accordance with art. 1. (2)(3) of the amending S.I. and see ss. 46, 161. (5) of Government of Wales Act 2006 (c. 32))

F14. S. 35. (5): words in definition of "Ministerial communications" substituted by The Government of Wales Act 2006 (Consequential Modifications and Transitional Provisions) Order 2007 (S.I. 2007/1388), art. 3, Sch. 1 para. 81. (c)(ii) (the amendment coming into force immediately after the end of "the initial period" (which ended with the day of the first appointment of a First Minister on 25.5.2007) in accordance with art. 1. (2)(3) of the amending S.I. and see ss. 46, 161. (5) of Government of Wales Act 2006 (c. 32))

F15. S. 35. (5): words in definition of "Ministerial private office" substituted by The Government of Wales Act 2006 (Consequential Modifications and Transitional Provisions) Order 2007 (S.I. 2007/1388), art. 3, Sch. 1 para. 81. (d) (the amendment coming into force immediately after the end of "the initial period" (which ended with the day of the first appointment of a First Minister on 25.5.2007) in accordance with art. 1. (2)(3) of the amending S.I. and see ss. 46, 161. (5) of Government of Wales Act 2006 (c. 32))

Marginal Citations
M61998 c. 47.

36 Prejudice to effective conduct of public affairs.

(1) This section applies to—
    (a) information which is held by a government department or by [F16the Welsh Assembly Government] and is not exempt information by virtue of section 35, and
    (b) information which is held by any other public authority.
(2) Information to which this section applies is exempt information if, in the reasonable opinion of a qualified person, disclosure of the information under this Act—
    (a) would, or would be likely to, prejudice—
(i) the maintenance of the convention of the collective responsibility of Ministers of the Crown, or
(ii) the work of the Executive Committee of the Northern Ireland Assembly, or
[F17. (iii)the work of the Cabinet of the Welsh Assembly Government.]
    (b) would, or would be likely to, inhibit—
(i) the free and frank provision of advice, or
(ii) the free and frank exchange of views for the purposes of deliberation, or
    (c) would otherwise prejudice, or would be likely otherwise to prejudice, the effective conduct

of public affairs.

(3) The duty to confirm or deny does not arise in relation to information to which this section applies (or would apply if held by the public authority) if, or to the extent that, in the reasonable opinion of a qualified person, compliance with section 1. (1)(a) would, or would be likely to, have any of the effects mentioned in subsection (2).

(4) In relation to statistical information, subsections (2) and (3) shall have effect with the omission of the words "in the reasonable opinion of a qualified person".

(5) In subsections (2) and (3) "qualified person"—

(a) in relation to information held by a government department in the charge of a Minister of the Crown, means any Minister of the Crown,

(b) in relation to information held by a Northern Ireland department, means the Northern Ireland Minister in charge of the department,

(c) in relation to information held by any other government department, means the commissioners or other person in charge of that department,

(d) in relation to information held by the House of Commons, means the Speaker of that House,

(e) in relation to information held by the House of Lords, means the Clerk of the Parliaments,

(f) in relation to information held by the Northern Ireland Assembly, means the Presiding Officer,

[F18. (g)in relation to information held by the Welsh Assembly Government, means the Welsh Ministers or the Counsel General to the Welsh Assembly Government,

(ga) in relation to information held by the National Assembly for Wales, means the Presiding Officer of the National Assembly for Wales,

(gb) in relation to information held by any Welsh public authority (other than one referred to in section 83. (1)(b)(ii) (subsidiary of the Assembly Commission), the Auditor General for Wales [F19, the Wales Audit Office] or the Public Services Ombudsman for Wales), means—
(i) the public authority, or
(ii) any officer or employee of the authority authorised by the Welsh Ministers or the Counsel General to the Welsh Assembly Government",

(gc) in relation to information held by a Welsh public authority referred to in section 83. (1)(b)(ii), means—
(i) the public authority, or
(ii) any officer or employee of the authority authorised by the Presiding Officer of the National Assembly for Wales,]

(i) in relation to information held by the National Audit Office [F20or the Comptroller and Auditor General], means the Comptroller and Auditor General,

(j) in relation to information held by the Northern Ireland Audit Office, means the Comptroller and Auditor General for Northern Ireland,

(k) in relation to information held by the Auditor General for Wales [F21or the Wales Audit Office], means the Auditor General for Wales,

[F22. (ka)in relation to information held by the Public Services Ombudsman for Wales, means the Public Services Ombudsman for Wales,]

(l) in relation to information held by any Northern Ireland public authority other than the Northern Ireland Audit Office, means—
(i) the public authority, or
(ii) any officer or employee of the authority authorised by the First Minister and deputy First Minister in Northern Ireland acting jointly,

(m) in relation to information held by the Greater London Authority, means the Mayor of London,

(n) in relation to information held by a functional body within the meaning of the M7. Greater London Authority Act 1999, means the chairman of that functional body, and

(o) in relation to information held by any public authority not falling within any of paragraphs (a) to (n), means—
(i) a Minister of the Crown,

(ii) the public authority, if authorised for the purposes of this section by a Minister of the Crown, or

(iii) any officer or employee of the public authority who is authorised for the purposes of this section by a Minister of the Crown.

(6) Any authorisation for the purposes of this section—

(a) may relate to a specified person or to persons falling within a specified class,

(b) may be general or limited to particular classes of case, and

(c) may be granted subject to conditions.

(7) A certificate signed by the qualified person referred to in subsection (5)(d) or (e) above certifying that in his reasonable opinion—

(a) disclosure of information held by either House of Parliament, or

(b) compliance with section 1. (1)(a) by either House,

would, or would be likely to, have any of the effects mentioned in subsection (2) shall be conclusive evidence of that fact.

Amendments (Textual)

F16. Words in s. 36. (1)(a) substituted by The Government of Wales Act 2006 (Consequential Modifications and Transitional Provisions) Order 2007 (S.I. 2007/1388), art. 3, Sch. 1 para. 82. (2) (the amendment coming into force immediately after the end of "the initial period" (which ended with the day of the first appointment of a First Minister on 25.5.2007) in accordance with art. 1. (2)(3) of the amending S.I. and see ss. 46, 161. (5) of Government of Wales Act 2006 (c. 32))

F17. S. 36. (2)(a)(iii) substituted by The Government of Wales Act 2006 (Consequential Modifications and Transitional Provisions) Order 2007 (S.I. 2007/1388), art. 3, Sch. 1 para. 82. (3) (the amendment coming into force immediately after the end of "the initial period" (which ended with the day of the first appointment of a First Minister on 25.5.2007) in accordance with art. 1. (2)(3) of the amending S.I. and see ss. 46, 161. (5) of Government of Wales Act 2006 (c. 32))

F18. S. 36. (5)(g)-(gc) substituted for s. 36. (g)(h) by The Government of Wales Act 2006 (Consequential Modifications and Transitional Provisions) Order 2007 (S.I. 2007/1388), art. 3, Sch. 1 para. 82. (4)(a) (the amendment coming into force immediately after the end of "the initial period" (which ended with the day of the first appointment of a First Minister on 25.5.2007) in accordance with art. 1. (2)(3) of the amending S.I. and see ss. 46, 161. (5) of Government of Wales Act 2006 (c. 32))

F19. Words in s. 36. (5)(gb) inserted (E.W.) (1.4.2014) by Public Audit (Wales) Act 2013 (anaw 3), s. 35. (2), Sch. 4 para. 18. (2) (with Sch. 3 para. 3); S.I. 2013/1466, art. 3. (1)

F20. Words in s. 36. (5)(i) inserted (1.4.2012) by Budget Responsibility and National Audit Act 2011 (c. 4), s. 29, Sch. 5 para. 22. (1); S.I. 2011/2576, art. 5

F21. Words in s. 36. (5)(k) inserted (E.W.) (1.4.2014) by Public Audit (Wales) Act 2013 (anaw 3), s. 35. (2), Sch. 4 para. 18. (3) (with Sch. 3 para. 3); S.I. 2013/1466, art. 3. (1)

F22. S. 36. (5)(ka) inserted by The Government of Wales Act 2006 (Consequential Modifications and Transitional Provisions) Order 2007 (S.I. 2007/1388), art. 3, Sch. 1 para. 82. (4)(b) (the amendment coming into force immediately after the end of "the initial period" (which ended with the day of the first appointment of a First Minister on 25.5.2007) in accordance with art. 1. (2)(3) of the amending S.I. and see ss. 46, 161. (5) of Government of Wales Act 2006 (c. 32))

Modifications etc. (not altering text)

C4. S. 36. (5)(i) amended (1.4.2012) by Budget Responsibility and National Audit Act 2011 (c. 4), s. 29, Sch. 5 para. 22. (2); S.I. 2011/2576, art. 5

Marginal Citations

M71999 c. 29.

37 Communications with Her Majesty, etc. and honours.

(1) Information is exempt information if it relates to—

[F23. (a)communications with the Sovereign,

(aa) communications with the heir to, or the person who is for the time being second in line of succession to, the Throne,

(ab) communications with a person who has subsequently acceded to the Throne or become heir to, or second in line to, the Throne,

(ac) communications with other members of the Royal Family (other than communications which fall within any of paragraphs (a) to (ab) because they are made or received on behalf of a person falling within any of those paragraphs), and

(ad) communications with the Royal Household (other than communications which fall within any of paragraphs (a) to (ac) because they are made or received on behalf of a person falling within any of those paragraphs), or]

(b) the conferring by the Crown of any honour or dignity.

(2) The duty to confirm or deny does not arise in relation to information which is (or if it were held by the public authority would be) exempt information by virtue of subsection (1).

Amendments (Textual)

F23. S. 37. (1)(a)-(ad) substituted for s. 37. (1)(a) (19.1.2011) by Constitutional Reform and Governance Act 2010 (c. 25), ss. 46. (1), 52. (2), Sch. 7 para. 3; S.I. 2011/46, art. 3. (b)(i) (with art. 4)

38 Health and safety.

(1) Information is exempt information if its disclosure under this Act would, or would be likely to—

(a) endanger the physical or mental health of any individual, or

(b) endanger the safety of any individual.

(2) The duty to confirm or deny does not arise if, or to the extent that, compliance with section 1. (1)(a) would, or would be likely to, have either of the effects mentioned in subsection (1).

39 Environmental information.

(1) Information is exempt information if the public authority holding it—

(a) is obliged by [F24environmental information regulations] to make the information available to the public in accordance with the regulations, or

(b) would be so obliged but for any exemption contained in the regulations.

[F25. (1. A) In subsection (1) " environmental information regulations " means—

(a) regulations made under section 74, or

(b) regulations made under section 2. (2) of the European Communities Act 1972 for the purpose of implementing any [F26. EU] obligation relating to public access to, and the dissemination of, information on the environment.]

(2) The duty to confirm or deny does not arise in relation to information which is (or if it were held by the public authority would be) exempt information by virtue of subsection (1).

(3) Subsection (1)(a) does not limit the generality of section 21. (1).

Amendments (Textual)

F24. Words in s. 39. (1)(a) substituted (1.1.2005) by The Environmental Information Regulations 2004 (S.I. 2004/3391), reg. 20. (2) (with reg. 3)

F25. S. 39. (1. A) inserted (1.1.2005) by The Environmental Information Regulations 2004 (S.I. 2004/3391), reg. 20. (3) (with reg. 3)

F26. Words in s. 39. (1. A)(b) substituted (22.4.2011) by The Treaty of Lisbon (Changes in Terminology) Order 2011 (S.I. 2011/1043), arts. 3, 6. (1)(e)

40 Personal information.

(1) Any information to which a request for information relates is exempt information if it constitutes personal data of which the applicant is the data subject.

(2) Any information to which a request for information relates is also exempt information if—

　(a) it constitutes personal data which do not fall within subsection (1), and

　(b) either the first or the second condition below is satisfied.

(3) The first condition is—

　(a) in a case where the information falls within any of paragraphs (a) to (d) of the definition of "data" in section 1. (1) of the M8. Data Protection Act 1998, that the disclosure of the information to a member of the public otherwise than under this Act would contravene—

(i) any of the data protection principles, or

(ii) section 10 of that Act (right to prevent processing likely to cause damage or distress), and

　(b) in any other case, that the disclosure of the information to a member of the public otherwise than under this Act would contravene any of the data protection principles if the exemptions in section 33. A(1) of the M9. Data Protection Act 1998 (which relate to manual data held by public authorities) were disregarded.

(4) The second condition is that by virtue of any provision of Part IV of the M10. Data Protection Act 1998 the information is exempt from section 7. (1)(c) of that Act (data subject's right of access to personal data).

(5) The duty to confirm or deny—

　(a) does not arise in relation to information which is (or if it were held by the public authority would be) exempt information by virtue of subsection (1), and

　(b) does not arise in relation to other information if or to the extent that either—

(i) the giving to a member of the public of the confirmation or denial that would have to be given to comply with section 1. (1)(a) would (apart from this Act) contravene any of the data protection principles or section 10 of the M11. Data Protection Act 1998 or would do so if the exemptions in section 33. A(1) of that Act were disregarded, or

(ii) by virtue of any provision of Part IV of the M12. Data Protection Act 1998 the information is exempt from section 7. (1)(a) of that Act (data subject's right to be informed whether personal data being processed).

(6) In determining for the purposes of this section whether anything done before 24th October 2007 would contravene any of the data protection principles, the exemptions in Part III of Schedule 8 to the M13. Data Protection Act 1998 shall be disregarded.

(7) In this section—

"the data protection principles" means the principles set out in Part I of Schedule 1 to the M14. Data Protection Act 1998, as read subject to Part II of that Schedule and section 27. (1) of that Act;

"data subject" has the same meaning as in section 1. (1) of that Act;

"personal data" has the same meaning as in section 1. (1) of that Act.

Marginal Citations

M81998 c. 29.

M91998 c. 29.

M101998 c. 29.

M111998 c. 29.

M121998 c. 29.

M131998 c. 29.

M141998 c. 29.

41 Information provided in confidence.

(1) Information is exempt information if—

　(a) it was obtained by the public authority from any other person (including another public authority), and

(b) the disclosure of the information to the public (otherwise than under this Act) by the public authority holding it would constitute a breach of confidence actionable by that or any other person.
(2) The duty to confirm or deny does not arise if, or to the extent that, the confirmation or denial that would have to be given to comply with section 1. (1)(a) would (apart from this Act) constitute an actionable breach of confidence.
Modifications etc. (not altering text)
C5. S. 41. (1) extended (E.W.) (5.11.2013) by Mobile Homes (Wales) Act 2013 (anaw 6), ss. 61. (8), 64. (1) (with Sch. 5 para. 7)

42 Legal professional privilege.

(1) Information in respect of which a claim to legal professional privilege or, in Scotland, to confidentiality of communications could be maintained in legal proceedings is exempt information.
(2) The duty to confirm or deny does not arise if, or to the extent that, compliance with section 1. (1)(a) would involve the disclosure of any information (whether or not already recorded) in respect of which such a claim could be maintained in legal proceedings.

43 Commercial interests.

(1) Information is exempt information if it constitutes a trade secret.
(2) Information is exempt information if its disclosure under this Act would, or would be likely to, prejudice the commercial interests of any person (including the public authority holding it).
(3) The duty to confirm or deny does not arise if, or to the extent that, compliance with section 1. (1)(a) would, or would be likely to, prejudice the interests mentioned in subsection (2).

44 Prohibitions on disclosure.

(1) Information is exempt information if its disclosure (otherwise than under this Act) by the public authority holding it—
    (a) is prohibited by or under any enactment,
    (b) is incompatible with any [F27. EU] obligation, or
    (c) would constitute or be punishable as a contempt of court.
(2) The duty to confirm or deny does not arise if the confirmation or denial that would have to be given to comply with section 1. (1)(a) would (apart from this Act) fall within any of paragraphs (a) to (c) of subsection (1).
Amendments (Textual)
F27. Words in s. 44. (1)(b) substituted (22.4.2011) by The Treaty of Lisbon (Changes in Terminology) Order 2011 (S.I. 2011/1043), arts. 3, 6. (1)(e)
Modifications etc. (not altering text)
C6. S. 44 excluded (1.12.2007) by Statistics and Registration Service Act 2007 (c. 18), ss. 40. (1)(2), 74; S.I. 2007/3388, art. 2. (f)
C7. S. 44. (1)(a) modified (7.4.2005 at 5:45 p.m.) by Commissioners for Revenue and Customs Act 2005 (c. 11), ss. 23, 53. (1); S.I. 2005/1126, art. 2. (1)

Part III General functions of Minister for the Cabinet Office, Secretary of State and Information Commissioner

Part III General functions of [F1[F2. Minister for the Cabinet Office], Secretary of State] and Information Commissioner

Amendments (Textual)
F1. Words in Pt. III heading substituted (9.12.2015) by virtue of The Transfer of Functions (Information and Public Records) Order 2015 (S.I. 2015/1897), art. 1. (2), Sch. para. 2. (6)
F2. Words in Pt. III heading substituted (9.11.2016) by The Transfer of Functions (Elections, Referendums, Third Sector and Information) Order 2016 (S.I. 2016/997), art. 1. (2), Sch. 2 para. 14. (2)(j) (with art. 12)

45 Issue of code of practice [F3by the Minister for the Cabinet Office].

(1) The [F4. Minister for the Cabinet Office] shall issue, and may from time to time revise, a code of practice providing guidance to public authorities as to the practice which it would, in his opinion, be desirable for them to follow in connection with the discharge of the authorities' functions under Part I.

(2) The code of practice must, in particular, include provision relating to—

    (a) the provision of advice and assistance by public authorities to persons who propose to make, or have made, requests for information to them,

    (b) the transfer of requests by one public authority to another public authority by which the information requested is or may be held,

    (c) consultation with persons to whom the information requested relates or persons whose interests are likely to be affected by the disclosure of information,

    (d) the inclusion in contracts entered into by public authorities of terms relating to the disclosure of information,

    [F5. (da)the disclosure by public authorities of datasets held by them,] and

    (e) the provision by public authorities of procedures for dealing with complaints about the handling by them of requests for information.

[F6. (2. A)Provision of the kind mentioned in subsection (2)(da) may, in particular, include provision relating to—

    (a) the giving of permission for datasets to be re-used,

    (b) the disclosure of datasets in an electronic form which is capable of re-use,

    (c) the making of datasets available for re-use in accordance with the terms of a licence,

    (d) other matters relating to the making of datasets available for re-use,

    (e) standards applicable to public authorities in connection with the disclosure of datasets.]

(3) [F7. Any code under this section] may make different provision for different public authorities.

(4) Before issuing or revising any code under this section, the [F8. Minister for the Cabinet Office] shall consult the Commissioner.

(5) The [F9. Minister for the Cabinet Office] shall lay before each House of Parliament any code or revised code made under this section.

Amendments (Textual)
F3. Words in s. 45 heading substituted (9.11.2016) by The Transfer of Functions (Elections, Referendums, Third Sector and Information) Order 2016 (S.I. 2016/997), art. 1. (2), Sch. 2 para. 14. (4) (with art. 12)
F4. Words in s. 45. (1) substituted (9.11.2016) by The Transfer of Functions (Elections, Referendums, Third Sector and Information) Order 2016 (S.I. 2016/997), art. 1. (2), Sch. 2 para. 14. (2)(k) (with art. 12)
F5. S. 45. (2)(da) inserted (1.9.2013) by Protection of Freedoms Act 2012 (c. 9), ss. 102. (5)(a), 120 (with s. 97); S.I. 2013/1906, art. 3. (a)

46 Issue of code of practice by [F10. Secretary of State].

(1) The [F11. Secretary of State] shall issue, and may from time to time revise, a code of practice providing guidance to relevant authorities as to the practice which it would, in his opinion, be desirable for them to follow in connection with the keeping, management and destruction of their records.

(2) For the purpose of facilitating the performance by the Public Record Office, the Public Record Office of Northern Ireland and other public authorities of their functions under this Act in relation to records which are public records for the purposes of the M1. Public Records Act 1958 or the Public Records Act (Northern Ireland) 1923, the code may also include guidance as to—

(a) the practice to be adopted in relation to the transfer of records under section 3. (4) of the M2. Public Records Act 1958 or section 3 of the M3. Public Records Act (Northern Ireland) 1923, and

(b) the practice of reviewing records before they are transferred under those provisions.

(3) In exercising his functions under this section, the [F12. Secretary of State] shall have regard to the public interest in allowing public access to information held by relevant authorities.

(4) The code may make different provision for different relevant authorities.

(5) Before issuing or revising any code under this section the [F13. Secretary of State] shall consult—

[F14. (a)the [F15. Minister for the Cabinet Office],]

(b) the Commissioner, and

(c) in relation to Northern Ireland, the appropriate Northern Ireland Minister.

(6) The [F16. Secretary of State] shall lay before each House of Parliament any code or revised code made under this section.

(7) In this section "relevant authority" means—

(a) any public authority, and

(b) any office or body which is not a public authority but whose administrative and departmental records are public records for the purposes of the M4. Public Records Act 1958 or the Public Records Act (Northern Ireland) 1923.

Public Records) Order 2015 (S.I. 2015/1897), art. 1. (2), Sch. para. 2. (5)(b)
F12. Words in s. 46. (3) substituted (9.12.2015) by The Transfer of Functions (Information and Public Records) Order 2015 (S.I. 2015/1897), art. 1. (2), Sch. para. 2. (5)(b)
F13. Words in s. 46. (5) substituted (9.12.2015) by The Transfer of Functions (Information and Public Records) Order 2015 (S.I. 2015/1897), art. 1. (2), Sch. para. 2. (5)(b)
F14. S. 46. (5)(a) inserted (19.8.2003) by The Secretary of State for Constitutional Affairs Order 2003 (S.I. 2003/1887), art. 9, Sch. 2 para. 12. (2)
F15. Words in s. 46. (5)(a) substituted (9.11.2016) by The Transfer of Functions (Elections, Referendums, Third Sector and Information) Order 2016 (S.I. 2016/997), art. 1. (2), Sch. 2 para. 14. (2)(l) (with art. 12)
F16. Words in s. 46. (6) substituted (9.12.2015) by The Transfer of Functions (Information and Public Records) Order 2015 (S.I. 2015/1897), art. 1. (2), Sch. para. 2. (5)(b)
Modifications etc. (not altering text)
C3. S. 46. (1) functions transferred (9.12.2015) by The Transfer of Functions (Information and Public Records) Order 2015 (S.I. 2015/1897), arts. 1. (2), 6. (1)(b), (3)(a) (with art. 7)
C4. S. 46. (3) functions transferred (9.12.2015) by The Transfer of Functions (Information and Public Records) Order 2015 (S.I. 2015/1897), arts. 1. (2), 6. (1)(b), (3)(a) (with art. 7)
C5. S. 46. (5)(6) functions transferred (9.12.2015) by The Transfer of Functions (Information and Public Records) Order 2015 (S.I. 2015/1897), arts. 1. (2), 6. (1)(b), (3)(a) (with art. 7)
C6. S. 46. (5)(a) functions transferred (9.12.2015) by The Transfer of Functions (Information and Public Records) Order 2015 (S.I. 2015/1897), arts. 1. (2), 4. (1), (2)(h) (with art. 5)
Commencement Information
I2. S. 46 wholly in force at 30.11.2002; s. 46 in force at Royal Assent to the extent that it confers power to make code of practice, see s. 87. (1)(m)(3); s. 46 otherwise in force at 30.11.2002 by S.I. 2002/2812, art. 2. (b)
Marginal Citations
M11958 c. 51.
M21958 c. 51.
M31923 c. 20 (N.I.)
M41958 c. 51.

47 General functions of Commissioner.

(1) It shall be the duty of the Commissioner to promote the following of good practice by public authorities and, in particular, so to perform his functions under this Act as to promote the observance by public authorities of—

(a) the requirements of this Act, and

(b) the provisions of the codes of practice under sections 45 and 46.

(2) The Commissioner shall arrange for the dissemination in such form and manner as he considers appropriate of such information as it may appear to him expedient to give to the public—

(a) about the operation of this Act,

(b) about good practice, and

(c) about other matters within the scope of his functions under this Act,

and may give advice to any person as to any of those matters.

(3) The Commissioner may, with the consent of any public authority, assess whether that authority is following good practice.

(4) The Commissioner may charge such sums as he may F17... determine for any [F18relevant] services provided by the Commissioner under this section.

[F19. (4. A) In subsection (4) " relevant services " means—

(a) the provision to the same person of more than one copy of any published material where each of the copies of the material is either provided on paper, a portable disk which stores the material electronically or a similar medium,

    (b) the provision of training, or

    (c) the provision of conferences.

(4. B)The [F20. Minister for the Cabinet Office] may by order amend subsection (4. A).

(4. C)An order under subsection (4. B) may include such transitional or saving provision as the [F20. Minister for the Cabinet Office] considers appropriate.

(4. D)The [F20. Minister for the Cabinet Office] must consult the Commissioner before making an order under subsection (4. B).]

(5) The Commissioner shall from time to time as he considers appropriate—

    (a) consult the Keeper of Public Records about the promotion by the Commissioner of the observance by public authorities of the provisions of the code of practice under section 46 in relation to records which are public records for the purposes of the M5. Public Records Act 1958, and

    (b) consult the Deputy Keeper of the Records of Northern Ireland about the promotion by the Commissioner of the observance by public authorities of those provisions in relation to records which are public records for the purposes of the M6. Public Records Act (Northern Ireland) 1923.

(6) In this section "good practice", in relation to a public authority, means such practice in the discharge of its functions under this Act as appears to the Commissioner to be desirable, and includes (but is not limited to) compliance with the requirements of this Act and the provisions of the codes of practice under sections 45 and 46.

Amendments (Textual)

F17. Words in s. 47. (4) repealed (1.9.2013) by Protection of Freedoms Act 2012 (c. 9), ss. 107. (3)(a)(i), 120, Sch. 10 Pt. 8 (with s. 97); S.I. 2013/1906, art. 3. (d)

F18. Word in s. 47. (4) inserted (1.9.2013) by Protection of Freedoms Act 2012 (c. 9), ss. 107. (3)(a)(ii), 120 (with s. 97); S.I. 2013/1906, art. 3. (d)

F19. S. 47. (4. A)-(4. D) inserted (1.9.2013) by Protection of Freedoms Act 2012 (c. 9), ss. 107. (3)(b), 120 (with s. 97); S.I. 2013/1906, art. 3. (d)

F20. Words in s. 47. (4. B)-(4. D) substituted (9.11.2016) by The Transfer of Functions (Elections, Referendums, Third Sector and Information) Order 2016 (S.I. 2016/997), art. 1. (2), Sch. 2 para. 14. (2)(m) (with art. 12)

Modifications etc. (not altering text)

C7. S. 47 applied (with modifications) (1.1.2005) by The Environmental Information Regulations 2004 (S.I. 2004/3391), reg. 16. (5) (with reg. 3)

C8. S. 47. (4. B)-(4. D) functions transferred (9.12.2015) by The Transfer of Functions (Information and Public Records) Order 2015 (S.I. 2015/1897), arts. 1. (2), 4. (1), (2)(i) (with art. 5)

Commencement Information

I3. S. 47 wholly in force at 30.11.2002; s. 47. (2)-(6) in force at Royal Assent, see s. 87. (1)(d); s. 47. (1) in force at 30.11.2002 by S.I. 2002/2812, art. 2. (c)

Marginal Citations

M51958 c. 51.

M61923 c. 20.

48 Recommendations as to good practice.

(1) If it appears to the Commissioner that the practice of a public authority in relation to the exercise of its functions under this Act does not conform with that proposed in the codes of practice under sections 45 and 46, he may give to the authority a recommendation (in this section referred to as a "practice recommendation") specifying the steps which ought in his opinion to be taken for promoting such conformity.

(2) A practice recommendation must be given in writing and must refer to the particular provisions of the code of practice with which, in the Commissioner's opinion, the public authority's practice

does not conform.

(3) Before giving to a public authority other than the Public Record Office a practice recommendation which relates to conformity with the code of practice under section 46 in respect of records which are public records for the purposes of the M7. Public Records Act 1958, the Commissioner shall consult the Keeper of Public Records.

(4) Before giving to a public authority other than the Public Record Office of Northern Ireland a practice recommendation which relates to conformity with the code of practice under section 46 in respect of records which are public records for the purposes of the Public Records Act (Northern Ireland) 1923, the Commissioner shall consult the Deputy Keeper of the Records of Northern Ireland.

Modifications etc. (not altering text)

C9. S. 48 applied (with modifications) (1.1.2005) by The Environmental Information Regulations 2004 (S.I. 2004/3391), reg. 16. (5) (with reg. 3)

Commencement Information

I4. S. 48 wholly in force at 1.1.2005; s. 48 not in force at Royal Assent, see s. 87. (3); s. 48. (1)(2) in force for certain purposes at 30.11.2002 by S.I. 2002/2812, art. 2. (d); s. 48 in force for certain further purposes at 1.1.2005 by S.I. 2004/1909, art. 2; s. 48 otherwise in force at 1.1.2005 by S.I. 2004/3122, art. 2

Marginal Citations

M71958 c. 51.

49 Reports to be laid before Parliament.

(1) The Commissioner shall lay annually before each House of Parliament a general report on the exercise of his functions under this Act.

(2) The Commissioner may from time to time lay before each House of Parliament such other reports with respect to those functions as he thinks fit.

Part IV Enforcement

Part IV Enforcement

50 Application for decision by Commissioner.

(1) Any person (in this section referred to as "the complainant") may apply to the Commissioner for a decision whether, in any specified respect, a request for information made by the complainant to a public authority has been dealt with in accordance with the requirements of Part I.

(2) On receiving an application under this section, the Commissioner shall make a decision unless it appears to him—

    (a) that the complainant has not exhausted any complaints procedure which is provided by the public authority in conformity with the code of practice under section 45,

    (b) that there has been undue delay in making the application,

    (c) that the application is frivolous or vexatious, or

    (d) that the application has been withdrawn or abandoned.

(3) Where the Commissioner has received an application under this section, he shall either—

    (a) notify the complainant that he has not made any decision under this section as a result of the application and of his grounds for not doing so, or

    (b) serve notice of his decision (in this Act referred to as a "decision notice") on the complainant and the public authority.

(4) Where the Commissioner decides that a public authority—

(a) has failed to communicate information, or to provide confirmation or denial, in a case where it is required to do so by section 1. (1), or

(b) has failed to comply with any of the requirements of sections 11 and 17,

the decision notice must specify the steps which must be taken by the authority for complying with that requirement and the period within which they must be taken.

(5) A decision notice must contain particulars of the right of appeal conferred by section 57.

(6) Where a decision notice requires steps to be taken by the public authority within a specified period, the time specified in the notice must not expire before the end of the period within which an appeal can be brought against the notice and, if such an appeal is brought, no step which is affected by the appeal need be taken pending the determination or withdrawal of the appeal.

(7) This section has effect subject to section 53.

Modifications etc. (not altering text)

C1. S. 50 applied (with modifications) (31.12.2009) by The INSPIRE Regulations 2009 (S.I. 2009/3157), {reg. 11. (1)-(3)(4)(9)}

C2. S. 50 applied (with modifications) (18.7.2015) by The Re-use of Public Sector Information Regulations 2015 (S.I. 2015/1415), regs. 1, 18 (with regs. 5, 11. (4))

C3. S. 50 applied (with modifications) (18.7.2015) by The Re-use of Public Sector Information Regulations 2015 (S.I. 2015/1415), regs. 1, 19 (with regs. 5, 11. (4))

Commencement Information

I1. S. 50 wholly in force at 1.1.2005; s. 50 not in force at Royal Assent, see s. 87. (3); s. 50 in force for certain purposes at 1.1.2005 by S.I. 2004/1909, art. 2 and otherwise in force at 1.1.2005 by S.I. 2004/3122, art. 2

51 Information notices.

(1) If the Commissioner—

(a) has received an application under section 50, or

(b) reasonably requires any information—

(i) for the purpose of determining whether a public authority has complied or is complying with any of the requirements of Part I, or

(ii) for the purpose of determining whether the practice of a public authority in relation to the exercise of its functions under this Act conforms with that proposed in the codes of practice under sections 45 and 46,

he may serve the authority with a notice (in this Act referred to as "an information notice") requiring it, within such time as is specified in the notice, to furnish the Commissioner, in such form as may be so specified, with such information relating to the application, to compliance with Part I or to conformity with the code of practice as is so specified.

(2) An information notice must contain—

(a) in a case falling within subsection (1)(a), a statement that the Commissioner has received an application under section 50, or

(b) in a case falling within subsection (1)(b), a statement—

(i) that the Commissioner regards the specified information as relevant for either of the purposes referred to in subsection (1)(b), and

(ii) of his reasons for regarding that information as relevant for that purpose.

(3) An information notice must also contain particulars of the right of appeal conferred by section 57.

(4) The time specified in an information notice must not expire before the end of the period within which an appeal can be brought against the notice and, if such an appeal is brought, the information need not be furnished pending the determination or withdrawal of the appeal.

(5) An authority shall not be required by virtue of this section to furnish the Commissioner with

any information in respect of—

(a) any communication between a professional legal adviser and his client in connection with the giving of legal advice to the client with respect to his obligations, liabilities or rights under this Act, or

(b) any communication between a professional legal adviser and his client, or between such an adviser or his client and any other person, made in connection with or in contemplation of proceedings under or arising out of this Act (including proceedings before the Tribunal) and for the purposes of such proceedings.

(6) In subsection (5) references to the client of a professional legal adviser include references to any person representing such a client.

(7) The Commissioner may cancel an information notice by written notice to the authority on which it was served.

(8) In this section "information" includes unrecorded information.

Modifications etc. (not altering text)

C4. S. 51 applied (with modifications) (31.12.2009) by The INSPIRE Regulations 2009 (S.I. 2009/3157), {reg. 11. (1)-(3)(5)(9)}

C5. S. 51 applied (with modifications) (18.7.2015) by The Re-use of Public Sector Information Regulations 2015 (S.I. 2015/1415), regs. 1, 18 (with regs. 5, 11. (4))

Commencement Information

I2. S. 51 wholly in force at 1.1.2005; s. 51 not in force at Royal Assent, see s. 87. (3); s. 51 in force for certain purposes at 30.11.2002 by S.I. 2002/2812, art. 2. (d)(e); s. 51 in force for certain further purposes at 1.1.2005 by S.I. 2004/1909, art. 2 and otherwise in force at 1.1.2005 by S.I. 2004/3122, art. 2

52 Enforcement notices.

(1) If the Commissioner is satisfied that a public authority has failed to comply with any of the requirements of Part I, the Commissioner may serve the authority with a notice (in this Act referred to as "an enforcement notice") requiring the authority to take, within such time as may be specified in the notice, such steps as may be so specified for complying with those requirements.

(2) An enforcement notice must contain—

(a) a statement of the requirement or requirements of Part I with which the Commissioner is satisfied that the public authority has failed to comply and his reasons for reaching that conclusion, and

(b) particulars of the right of appeal conferred by section 57.

(3) An enforcement notice must not require any of the provisions of the notice to be complied with before the end of the period within which an appeal can be brought against the notice and, if such an appeal is brought, the notice need not be complied with pending the determination or withdrawal of the appeal.

(4) The Commissioner may cancel an enforcement notice by written notice to the authority on which it was served.

(5) This section has effect subject to section 53.

Modifications etc. (not altering text)

C6. S. 52 applied (with modifications) (31.12.2009) by The INSPIRE Regulations 2009 (S.I. 2009/3157), {reg. 11. (1)-(3)(6)(9)}

C7. S. 52 applied (with modifications) (18.7.2015) by The Re-use of Public Sector Information Regulations 2015 (S.I. 2015/1415), regs. 1, 18 (with regs. 5, 11. (4))

C8. S. 52 excluded (18.7.2015) by The Re-use of Public Sector Information Regulations 2015 (S.I. 2015/1415), regs. 1, 22. (7) (with regs. 5, 11. (4))

Commencement Information

I3. S. 52 wholly in force at 1.1.2005; s. 52 not in force at Royal Assent, see s. 87. (3); s. 52 in force for certain purposes at 30.11.2002 by S.I. 2002/2812, art. 2. (e), s. 52 in force for certain further purposes at 1.1.2005 by S.I. 2004/1909, art. 2 and otherwise in force at 1.1.2005 by S.I. 2004/3122, art. 2

53 Exception from duty to comply with decision notice or enforcement notice.

(1) This section applies to a decision notice or enforcement notice which—

(a) is served on—

(i) a government department,

[F1. (ii)the Welsh Assembly Government, or]

(iii) any public authority designated for the purposes of this section by an order made by the [F2. Minister for the Cabinet Office], and

(b) relates to a failure, in respect of one or more requests for information—

(i) to comply with section 1. (1)(a) in respect of information which falls within any provision of Part II stating that the duty to confirm or deny does not arise, or

(ii) to comply with section 1. (1)(b) in respect of exempt information.

(2) A decision notice or enforcement notice to which this section applies shall cease to have effect if, not later than the twentieth working day following the effective date, the accountable person in relation to that authority gives the Commissioner a certificate signed by him stating that he has on reasonable grounds formed the opinion that, in respect of the request or requests concerned, there was no failure falling within subsection (1)(b).

(3) Where the accountable person gives a certificate to the Commissioner under subsection (2) he shall as soon as practicable thereafter lay a copy of the certificate before—

(a) each House of Parliament,

(b) the Northern Ireland Assembly, in any case where the certificate relates to a decision notice or enforcement notice which has been served on a Northern Ireland department or any Northern Ireland public authority, or

[F3. (c)the National Assembly for Wales, in any case where the certificate relates to a decision notice or enforcement notice which has been served on—

(i) the Welsh Assembly Government,

(ii) the National Assembly for Wales, or

(iii) any Welsh public authority.]

(4) In subsection (2) "the effective date", in relation to a decision notice or enforcement notice, means—

(a) the day on which the notice was given to the public authority, or

(b) where an appeal under section 57 is brought, the day on which that appeal (or any further appeal arising out of it) is determined or withdrawn.

(5) Before making an order under subsection (1)(a)(iii), the [F4. Minister for the Cabinet Office] shall—

(a) if the order relates to a Welsh public authority, consult [F5the Welsh Ministers],

[F6. (aa)if the order relates to the National Assembly for Wales, consult the Presiding Officer of that Assembly,]

(b) if the order relates to the Northern Ireland Assembly, consult the Presiding Officer of that Assembly, and

(c) if the order relates to a Northern Ireland public authority, consult the First Minister and deputy First Minister in Northern Ireland.

(6) Where the accountable person gives a certificate to the Commissioner under subsection (2) in relation to a decision notice, the accountable person shall, on doing so or as soon as reasonably practicable after doing so, inform the person who is the complainant for the purposes of section 50 of the reasons for his opinion.

(7) The accountable person is not obliged to provide information under subsection (6) if, or to the extent that, compliance with that subsection would involve the disclosure of exempt information.

(8) In this section "the accountable person"—

(a) in relation to a Northern Ireland department or any Northern Ireland public authority, means the First Minister and deputy First Minister in Northern Ireland acting jointly,

[F7. (b)in relation the Welsh Assembly Government, the National Assembly for Wales or any Welsh public authority, means the First Minister for Wales, and]

(c) in relation to any other public authority, means—

(i) a Minister of the Crown who is a member of the Cabinet, or

(ii) the Attorney General, the Advocate General for Scotland or the Attorney General for Northern Ireland.

(9) In this section "working day" has the same meaning as in section 10.

Amendments (Textual)

F1. S. 53. (1)(a)(ii) substituted by The Government of Wales Act 2006 (Consequential Modifications and Transitional Provisions) Order 2007 (S.I. 2007/1388), art. 3, Sch. 1 para. 83. (2) (the amendment coming into force immediately after the end of "the initial period" (which ended with the day of the first appointment of a First Minister on 25.5.2007) in accordance with art. 1. (2)(3) of the amending S.I. and see ss. 46, 161. (5) of Government of Wales Act 2006 (c. 32))

F2. Words in s. 53. (1)(a)(iii) substituted (9.11.2016) by The Transfer of Functions (Elections, Referendums, Third Sector and Information) Order 2016 (S.I. 2016/997), art. 1. (2), Sch. 2 para. 14. (2)(n) (with art. 12)

F3. S. 53. (3)(c) substituted by The Government of Wales Act 2006 (Consequential Modifications and Transitional Provisions) Order 2007 (S.I. 2007/1388), art. 3, Sch. 1 para. 83. (3) (the amendment coming into force immediately after the end of "the initial period" (which ended with the day of the first appointment of a First Minister on 25.5.2007) in accordance with art. 1. (2)(3) of the amending S.I. and see ss. 46, 161. (5) of Government of Wales Act 2006 (c. 32))

F4. Words in s. 53. (5) substituted (9.11.2016) by The Transfer of Functions (Elections, Referendums, Third Sector and Information) Order 2016 (S.I. 2016/997), art. 1. (2), Sch. 2 para. 14. (2)(n) (with art. 12)

F5. Words in s. 53. (5)(a) substituted by The Government of Wales Act 2006 (Consequential Modifications and Transitional Provisions) Order 2007 (S.I. 2007/1388), art. 3, Sch. 1 para. 83. (4)(a) (the amendment coming into force immediately after the end of "the initial period" (which ended with the day of the first appointment of a First Minister on 25.5.2007) in accordance with art. 1. (2)(3) of the amending S.I. and see ss. 46, 161. (5) of Government of Wales Act 2006 (c. 32))

F6. S. 53. (5)(aa) inserted by The Government of Wales Act 2006 (Consequential Modifications and Transitional Provisions) Order 2007 (S.I. 2007/1388), art. 3, Sch. 1 para. 83. (4)(b) (the amendment coming into force immediately after the end of "the initial period" (which ended with the day of the first appointment of a First Minister on 25.5.2007) in accordance with art. 1. (2)(3) of the amending S.I. and see ss. 46, 161. (5) of Government of Wales Act 2006 (c. 32))

F7. S. 53. (8)(b) substituted by The Government of Wales Act 2006 (Consequential Modifications and Transitional Provisions) Order 2007 (S.I. 2007/1388), art. 3, Sch. 1 para. 83. (5) (the amendment coming into force immediately after the end of "the initial period" (which ended with the day of the first appointment of a First Minister on 25.5.2007) in accordance with art. 1. (2)(3) of the amending S.I. and see ss. 46, 161. (5) of Government of Wales Act 2006 (c. 32))

Modifications etc. (not altering text)

C9. S. 53. (1)(a)(iii) functions transferred (9.12.2015) by The Transfer of Functions (Information and Public Records) Order 2015 (S.I. 2015/1897), arts. 1. (2), 4. (1), (2)(j) (with art. 5)

C10. S. 53. (5) functions transferred (9.12.2015) by The Transfer of Functions (Information and Public Records) Order 2015 (S.I. 2015/1897), arts. 1. (2), 4. (1), (2)(j) (with art. 5)

Commencement Information

I4. S. 53 wholly in force at 1.1.2005; s. 53 in force at Royal Assent to the extent that it confers power to make an order, see s. 87. (1)(m)(3); s. 53 in force for certain further purposes at 1.1.2005 by S.I. 2004/1909, art. 2 and otherwise in force at 1.1.2005 by S.I. 2004/3122, art. 2

54 Failure to comply with notice.

(1) If a public authority has failed to comply with—
  (a) so much of a decision notice as requires steps to be taken,
  (b) an information notice, or
  (c) an enforcement notice,
the Commissioner may certify in writing to the court that the public authority has failed to comply with that notice.
(2) For the purposes of this section, a public authority which, in purported compliance with an information notice—
  (a) makes a statement which it knows to be false in a material respect, or
  (b) recklessly makes a statement which is false in a material respect,
is to be taken to have failed to comply with the notice.
(3) Where a failure to comply is certified under subsection (1), the court may inquire into the matter and, after hearing any witness who may be produced against or on behalf of the public authority, and after hearing any statement that may be offered in defence, deal with the authority as if it had committed a contempt of court.
(4) In this section "the court" means the High Court or, in Scotland, the Court of Session.
Modifications etc. (not altering text)
C11. S. 54 applied (with modifications) (31.12.2009) by The INSPIRE Regulations 2009 (S.I. 2009/3157), {reg. 11. (1)-(3)(9)}
C12. S. 54 excluded (18.7.2015) by The Re-use of Public Sector Information Regulations 2015 (S.I. 2015/1415), regs. 1, 22. (7) (with regs. 5, 11. (4))
C13. S. 54 applied (with modifications) (18.7.2015) by The Re-use of Public Sector Information Regulations 2015 (S.I. 2015/1415), regs. 1, 18 (with regs. 5, 11. (4))
Commencement Information
I5. S. 54 wholly in force at 1.1.2005; s. 54 not in force at Royal assent, see s. 87. (3); s. 54 in force for certain purposes at 30.11.2002 by S.I. 2002/2812, art. 2. (d)(e); s. 54 in force for certain further purposes at 1.1.2005 by S.I. 2004/1909, art. 2 and otherwise in force at 1.1.2005 by S.I. 2004/3122, art. 2

55 Powers of entry and inspection.

Schedule 3 (powers of entry and inspection) has effect.
Modifications etc. (not altering text)
C14. S. 55 applied (with modifications) (31.12.2009) by The INSPIRE Regulations 2009 (S.I. 2009/3157), {reg. 11. (1)-(3)(9)}
Commencement Information
I6. S. 55 wholly in force at 1.1.2005; s. 55 not in force at Royal Assent, see s. 87. (3); s. 55 in force for certain purposes at 30.11.2002 by S.I. 2002/2812, art. 2. (d)(f); s. 55 in force for certain further purposes at 1.1.2005 by S.I. 2004/1909, art. 2 and otherwise in force at 1.1.2005 by S.I. 2004/3122, art. 2

56 No action against public authority.

(1) This Act does not confer any right of action in civil proceedings in respect of any failure to comply with any duty imposed by or under this Act.
(2) Subsection (1) does not affect the powers of the Commissioner under section 54.
Modifications etc. (not altering text)
C15. S. 56 applied (with modifications) (31.12.2009) by The INSPIRE Regulations 2009 (S.I. 2009/3157), {reg. 11. (1)-(3)(7)(9)}

C16. S. 56 applied (with modifications) (18.7.2015) by The Re-use of Public Sector Information Regulations 2015 (S.I. 2015/1415), regs. 1, 19 (with regs. 5, 11. (4))
C17. S. 56 applied (with modifications) (18.7.2015) by The Re-use of Public Sector Information Regulations 2015 (S.I. 2015/1415), regs. 1, 18 (with regs. 5, 11. (4))
C18. S. 56 excluded (18.7.2015) by The Re-use of Public Sector Information Regulations 2015 (S.I. 2015/1415), regs. 1, 22. (7) (with regs. 5, 11. (4))

Part V Appeals

Part V Appeals

57 Appeal against notices served under Part IV.

(1) Where a decision notice has been served, the complainant or the public authority may appeal to the Tribunal against the notice.
(2) A public authority on which an information notice or an enforcement notice has been served by the Commissioner may appeal to the Tribunal against the notice.
(3) In relation to a decision notice or enforcement notice which relates—
    (a) to information to which section 66 applies, and
    (b) to a matter which by virtue of subsection (3) or (4) of that section falls to be determined by the responsible authority instead of the appropriate records authority,
subsections (1) and (2) shall have effect as if the reference to the public authority were a reference to the public authority or the responsible authority.
Modifications etc. (not altering text)
C1. S. 57 applied (with modifications) (31.12.2009) by The INSPIRE Regulations 2009 (S.I. 2009/3157), {reg. 11. (1)-(3)(8)(9)}
C2. S. 57 applied (with modifications) (18.7.2015) by The Re-use of Public Sector Information Regulations 2015 (S.I. 2015/1415), regs. 1, 18 (with regs. 5, 11. (4))
C3. S. 57 excluded (18.7.2015) by The Re-use of Public Sector Information Regulations 2015 (S.I. 2015/1415), regs. 1, 22. (7) (with regs. 5, 11. (4))
C4. S. 57 applied (with modifications) (18.7.2015) by The Re-use of Public Sector Information Regulations 2015 (S.I. 2015/1415), regs. 1, 19 (with regs. 5, 11. (4))
Commencement Information
I1. S. 57 wholly in force at 1.1.2005; s. 57 not in force at Royal Assent, see s. 87. (3); s. 57. (2) in force at 30.11.2002 by S.I. 2002/2812, art. 2. (g); s. 57. (1)(3) in force for certain purposes at 1.1.2005 by S.I. 2004/1909, art. 2; s. 57. (1)(3) otherwise in force at 1.1.2005 by S.I. 2004/3122, art. 2

58 Determination of appeals.

(1) If on an appeal under section 57 the Tribunal considers—
    (a) that the notice against which the appeal is brought is not in accordance with the law, or
    (b) to the extent that the notice involved an exercise of discretion by the Commissioner, that he ought to have exercised his discretion differently,
the Tribunal shall allow the appeal or substitute such other notice as could have been served by the Commissioner; and in any other case the Tribunal shall dismiss the appeal.
(2) On such an appeal, the Tribunal may review any finding of fact on which the notice in question was based.
Modifications etc. (not altering text)

C5. S. 58 applied (with modifications) (31.12.2009) by The INSPIRE Regulations 2009 (S.I. 2009/3157), {reg. 11. (1)-(3)(9)}
C6. S. 58 applied (with modifications) (18.7.2015) by The Re-use of Public Sector Information Regulations 2015 (S.I. 2015/1415), regs. 1, 18 (with regs. 5, 11. (4))
C7. S. 58 applied (with modifications) (18.7.2015) by The Re-use of Public Sector Information Regulations 2015 (S.I. 2015/1415), regs. 1, 19 (with regs. 5, 11. (4))
C8. S. 58 excluded (18.7.2015) by The Re-use of Public Sector Information Regulations 2015 (S.I. 2015/1415), regs. 1, 22. (7) (with regs. 5, 11. (4))

59 Appeals from decision of Tribunal.

F1. . . . .
Amendments (Textual)
F1. S. 59 omitted (18.1.2010) by virtue of The Transfer of Tribunal Functions Order 2010 (S.I. 2010/22), arts. 1. (1), 5. (1), Sch. 2 para. 69

60 Appeals against national security certificate.

(1) Where a certificate under section 23. (2) or 24. (3) has been issued—
    (a) the Commissioner, or
    (b) any applicant whose request for information is affected by the issue of the certificate,
may appeal to the Tribunal against the certificate.
(2) If on an appeal under subsection (1) relating to a certificate under section 23. (2), the Tribunal finds that the information referred to in the certificate was not exempt information by virtue of section 23. (1), the Tribunal may allow the appeal and quash the certificate.
(3) If on an appeal under subsection (1) relating to a certificate under section 24. (3), the Tribunal finds that, applying the principles applied by the court on an application for judicial review, the Minister did not have reasonable grounds for issuing the certificate, the Tribunal may allow the appeal and quash the certificate.
(4) Where in any proceedings under this Act it is claimed by a public authority that a certificate under section 24. (3) which identifies the information to which it applies by means of a general description applies to particular information, any other party to the proceedings may appeal to the Tribunal on the ground that the certificate does not apply to the information in question and, subject to any determination under subsection (5), the certificate shall be conclusively presumed so to apply.
(5) On any appeal under subsection (4), the Tribunal may determine that the certificate does not so apply.
Commencement Information
I2. S. 60 wholly in force at 1.1.2005; s. 60 not in force at Royal Assent, see s. 87. (3); s. 60 in force for certain purposes at 1.1.2005 by S.I. 2002/1909, art. 2 and otherwise in force at 1.1.2005 by S.I. 2004/3122, art. 2

61 Appeal proceedings.

[F2. The provisions of Schedule 6 to the Data Protection Act 1998 have effect (so far as applicable) in relation to appeals under this Part.]
Amendments (Textual)
F2. Words in s. 61 substituted for s. 61. (1)(2) (18.1.2010) by The Transfer of Tribunal Functions Order 2010 (S.I. 2010/22), arts. 1. (1), 5. (1), Sch. 2 para. 70
Modifications etc. (not altering text)
C9. S. 61 applied (with modifications) (31.12.2009) by The INSPIRE Regulations 2009 (S.I.

2009/3157), {reg. 11. (1)-(3. (9))}
Commencement Information
I3. S. 61 wholly in force at 1.1.2005; s. 61 not in force at Royal Assent, see s. 87. (3); s. 61 in force for certain purposes at 14.5.2001 by S.I. 2001/1637, art. 2. (c); s. 61. (1) in force for certain purposes and s. 61. (2) wholly in force at 30.11.2002 by S.I. 2002/2812, art. 2. (g)(i); s. 61. (1) in force for certain further purposes at 1.1.2005 by S.I. 2004/1909, art. 2 and otherwise in force at 1.1.2005 by S.I. 2004/3122, art. 2

Appeal against notices served under Part IV.

57 Appeal against notices served under Part IV.

(1) Where a decision notice has been served, the complainant or the public authority may appeal to the Tribunal against the notice.
(2) A public authority on which an information notice or an enforcement notice has been served by the Commissioner may appeal to the Tribunal against the notice.
(3) In relation to a decision notice or enforcement notice which relates—
    (a) to information to which section 66 applies, and
    (b) to a matter which by virtue of subsection (3) or (4) of that section falls to be determined by the responsible authority instead of the appropriate records authority,
subsections (1) and (2) shall have effect as if the reference to the public authority were a reference to the public authority or the responsible authority.
Modifications etc. (not altering text)
C1. S. 57 applied (with modifications) (31.12.2009) by The INSPIRE Regulations 2009 (S.I. 2009/3157), {reg. 11. (1)-(3)(8)(9)}
C2. S. 57 applied (with modifications) (18.7.2015) by The Re-use of Public Sector Information Regulations 2015 (S.I. 2015/1415), regs. 1, 18 (with regs. 5, 11. (4))
C3. S. 57 excluded (18.7.2015) by The Re-use of Public Sector Information Regulations 2015 (S.I. 2015/1415), regs. 1, 22. (7) (with regs. 5, 11. (4))
C4. S. 57 applied (with modifications) (18.7.2015) by The Re-use of Public Sector Information Regulations 2015 (S.I. 2015/1415), regs. 1, 19 (with regs. 5, 11. (4))
Commencement Information
I1. S. 57 wholly in force at 1.1.2005; s. 57 not in force at Royal Assent, see s. 87. (3); s. 57. (2) in force at 30.11.2002 by S.I. 2002/2812, art. 2. (g); s. 57. (1)(3) in force for certain purposes at 1.1.2005 by S.I. 2004/1909, art. 2; s. 57. (1)(3) otherwise in force at 1.1.2005 by S.I. 2004/3122, art. 2

Part VI Historical records and records in Public Record Office or Public Record Office of Northern Ireland

Part VI Historical records and records in Public Record Office or Public Record Office of Northern Ireland

Modifications etc. (not altering text)
C1. Pt. VI modified (1.1.2013) by The Freedom of Information (Definition of Historical Records)

(Transitional and Saving Provisions) Order 2012 (S.I. 2012/3029), arts. 1. (1), 2, Sch.

62 Interpretation of Part VI.

(1) For the purposes of this Part, a record becomes a "historical record" at the end of the period of [F1twenty years] beginning with the year following that in which it was created.

(2) Where records created at different dates are for administrative purposes kept together in one file or other assembly, all the records in that file or other assembly are to be treated for the purposes of this Part as having been created when the latest of those records was created.

[F2. (2. A)Until the end of the period of 10 years beginning with the commencement of paragraph 4 of Schedule 7 to the Constitutional Reform and Governance Act 2010, subsection (1) has effect subject to any order made under section 46. (2) of that Act.]

(3) In this Part "year" means a calendar year.

Amendments (Textual)

F1. Words in s. 62. (1) substituted (1.1.2013) by Constitutional Reform and Governance Act 2010 (c. 25), s. 52, Sch. 7 para. 4. (2); S.I. 2012/3001, art. 3. (1)(b)

F2. S. 62. (2. A) inserted (1.1.2013) by Constitutional Reform and Governance Act 2010 (c. 25), s. 52, Sch. 7 para. 4. (3); S.I. 2012/3001, art. 3. (1)(b)

Modifications etc. (not altering text)

C2. S. 62. (1): saving for the effect of 2010 c. 25, Sch. 7 para. 4. (2) (1.1.2013) by The Freedom of Information (Definition of Historical Records) (Transitional and Saving Provisions) Order 2012 (S.I. 2012/3029), arts. 1. (1), 3

Commencement Information

I1. S. 62 wholly in force at 1.1.2005; s. 62 not in force at Royal Assent, see s. 87. (3); s. 62 in force for certain purposes at 1.1.2005 by S.I. 2002/1909, art. 2 and otherwise in force at 1.1.2005 by S.I. 2004/3122, art. 2

63 Removal of exemptions: historical records generally.

(1) Information contained in a historical record cannot be exempt information by virtue of section F3... 30. (1), 32, 33, 35, [F436, 37. (1)(a), 42 or 43][F4or 42].

(2) Compliance with section 1. (1)(a) in relation to a historical record is not to be taken to be capable of having any of the effects referred to in section F5... 33. (3), [F6or 42. (2)].

[F7. (2. A)Information contained in a historical record cannot be exempt information by virtue of section 36 except—

(a) in a case falling within subsection (2)(a)(ii) of that section, or

(b) in a case falling within subsection (2)(c) of that section where the prejudice or likely prejudice relates to the effective conduct of public affairs in Northern Ireland.

(2. B)Compliance with section 1. (1)(a) in relation to a historical record is not to be taken to have any of the effects referred to in subsection (3) of section 36, except where the effect—

(a) falls within subsection (2)(a)(ii) of that section, or

(b) falls within subsection (2)(c) of that section and relates to the effective conduct of public affairs in Northern Ireland.

(2. C)Information cannot be exempt information—

(a) by virtue of section 28 or 43, or

(b) by virtue of section 36 in the excepted cases mentioned in subsection (2. A),

after the end of the period of thirty years beginning with the year following that in which the record containing the information was created.

(2. D)Compliance with section 1. (1)(a) in relation to any record is not to be taken, at any time after the end of the period of thirty years beginning with the year following that in which the record was created, to be capable—

(a) of prejudicing any of the matters referred to in section 28. (1) or 43. (2), or

51

(b) of having any of the effects referred to in section 36. (3) in the excepted cases mentioned in subsection (2. B).

(2. E)Information cannot be exempt information by virtue of any of paragraphs (a) to (ad) of section 37. (1) after whichever is the later of—

(a) the end of the period of five years beginning with the date of the relevant death, and

(b) the end of the period of twenty years beginning with the date on which the record containing the information was created.

(2. F) In subsection (2. E)(a) " the relevant death " means—

(a) for the purposes of any of paragraphs (a) to (ac) of section 37. (1), the death of the person referred to in the paragraph concerned, or

(b) for the purposes of section 37. (1)(ad), the death of the Sovereign reigning when the record containing the information was created.]

(3) Information cannot be exempt information by virtue of section 37. (1)(b) after the end of the period of sixty years beginning with the year following that in which the record containing the information was created.

(4) Information cannot be exempt information by virtue of section 31 after the end of the period of one hundred years beginning with the year following that in which the record containing the information was created.

(5) Compliance with section 1. (1)(a) in relation to any record is not to be taken, at any time after the end of the period of one hundred years beginning with the year following that in which the record was created, to be capable of prejudicing any of the matters referred to in section 31. (1).

Amendments (Textual)

F3. Word in s. 63. (1) omitted (1.1.2013) by virtue of Constitutional Reform and Governance Act 2010 (c. 25), s. 52, Sch. 7 para. 5. (2)(a); S.I. 2012/3001, art. 3. (1)(b)

F4. Words in s. 63. (1) substituted (19.1.2011 but only in so far as the words "37. (1)(a)," are omitted and otherwise prosp.) by Constitutional Reform and Governance Act 2010 (c. 25), ss. 46. (1), 52. (2), Sch. 7 para. 5. (2)(b); S.I. 2011/46, art. 3. (b)(ii) (with art. 4)

F5. Word in s. 63. (2) omitted (1.1.2013) by virtue of Constitutional Reform and Governance Act 2010 (c. 25), s. 52, Sch. 7 para. 5. (3)(a); S.I. 2012/3001, art. 3. (1)(b)

F6. Words in s. 63. (2) substituted (1.1.2013) by Constitutional Reform and Governance Act 2010 (c. 25), s. 52, Sch. 7 para. 5. (3)(b); S.I. 2012/3001, art. 3. (1)(b)

F7. S. 63. (2. A)-(2. F) inserted (19.1.2011 but only to the extent of inserting s. 63. (2. E)(2. F) and otherwise prosp.) by Constitutional Reform and Governance Act 2010 (c. 25), ss. 46. (1), 52. (2), Sch. 7 para. 5. (4); S.I. 2011/46, art. 3. (b)(iii) (with art. 4)

Modifications etc. (not altering text)

C1. Pt. VI modified (1.1.2013) by The Freedom of Information (Definition of Historical Records) (Transitional and Saving Provisions) Order 2012 (S.I. 2012/3029), arts. 1. (1), 2, Sch.

64 Removal of exemptions: historical records in public record offices.

(1) Information contained in a historical record in the Public Record Office or the Public Record Office of Northern Ireland cannot be exempt information by virtue of section 21 or 22.

(2) In relation to any information falling within section 23. (1) which is contained in a historical record in the Public Record Office or the Public Record Office of Northern Ireland, section 2. (3) shall have effect with the omission of the reference to section 23.

Modifications etc. (not altering text)

C1. Pt. VI modified (1.1.2013) by The Freedom of Information (Definition of Historical Records) (Transitional and Saving Provisions) Order 2012 (S.I. 2012/3029), arts. 1. (1), 2, Sch.

65 Decisions as to refusal of discretionary disclosure of historical

records.

(1) Before refusing a request for information relating to information which is contained in a historical record and is exempt information only by virtue of a provision not specified in section 2. (3), a public authority shall—

(a) if the historical record is a public record within the meaning of the M1. Public Records Act 1958, consult the [F8. Secretary of State], or

(b) if the historical record is a public record to which the M2. Public Records Act (Northern Ireland) 1923 applies, consult the appropriate Northern Ireland Minister.

(2) This section does not apply to information to which section 66 applies.

Amendments (Textual)

F8. Words in s. 65. (1)(a) substituted (9.12.2015) by The Transfer of Functions (Information and Public Records) Order 2015 (S.I. 2015/1897), art. 1. (2), Sch. para. 2. (5)(d)

Modifications etc. (not altering text)

C1. Pt. VI modified (1.1.2013) by The Freedom of Information (Definition of Historical Records) (Transitional and Saving Provisions) Order 2012 (S.I. 2012/3029), arts. 1. (1), 2, Sch.

C3. S. 65. (1)(a) functions transferred (9.12.2015) by The Transfer of Functions (Information and Public Records) Order 2015 (S.I. 2015/1897), arts. 1. (2), 6. (1)(b), (3)(b) (with art. 7)

Marginal Citations

M11958 c. 51.

M21923 c. 20 (N.I.).

66 Decisions relating to certain transferred public records.

(1) This section applies to any information which is (or, if it existed, would be) contained in a transferred public record, other than information which the responsible authority has designated as open information for the purposes of this section.

(2) Before determining whether—

(a) information to which this section applies falls within any provision of Part II relating to the duty to confirm or deny, or

(b) information to which this section applies is exempt information,

the appropriate records authority shall consult the responsible authority.

(3) Where information to which this section applies falls within a provision of Part II relating to the duty to confirm or deny but does not fall within any of the provisions of that Part relating to that duty which are specified in subsection (3) of section 2, any question as to the application of subsection (1)(b) of that section is to be determined by the responsible authority instead of the appropriate records authority.

(4) Where any information to which this section applies is exempt information only by virtue of any provision of Part II not specified in subsection (3) of section 2, any question as to the application of subsection (2)(b) of that section is to be determined by the responsible authority instead of the appropriate records authority.

(5) Before making by virtue of subsection (3) or (4) any determination that subsection (1)(b) or (2)(b) of section 2 applies, the responsible authority shall consult—

(a) where the transferred public record is a public record within the meaning of the M3. Public Records Act 1958, the [F9. Secretary of State], and

(b) where the transferred public record is a public record to which the M4. Public Records Act (Northern Ireland) 1923 applies, the appropriate Northern Ireland Minister.

(6) Where the responsible authority in relation to information to which this section applies is not (apart from this subsection) a public authority, it shall be treated as being a public authority for the purposes of Parts III, IV and V of this Act so far as relating to—

(a) the duty imposed by section 15. (3), and

(b) the imposition of any requirement to furnish information relating to compliance with Part I in connection with the information to which this section applies.

Amendments (Textual)
F9. Words in s. 66. (5)(a) substituted (9.12.2015) by The Transfer of Functions (Information and Public Records) Order 2015 (S.I. 2015/1897), art. 1. (2), Sch. para. 2. (5)(e)
Modifications etc. (not altering text)
C1. Pt. VI modified (1.1.2013) by The Freedom of Information (Definition of Historical Records) (Transitional and Saving Provisions) Order 2012 (S.I. 2012/3029), arts. 1. (1), 2, Sch.
C4. S. 66. (5)(a) functions transferred (9.12.2015) by The Transfer of Functions (Information and Public Records) Order 2015 (S.I. 2015/1897), arts. 1. (2), 6. (1)(b), (3)(c) (with art. 7)
Marginal Citations
M31958 c. 51.
M41923 c. 20 (N.I.).

67 Amendments of public records legislation.

Schedule 5 (which amends the M5. Public Records Act 1958 and the Public Records Act (Northern Ireland) 1923) has effect.

Modifications etc. (not altering text)
C1. Pt. VI modified (1.1.2013) by The Freedom of Information (Definition of Historical Records) (Transitional and Saving Provisions) Order 2012 (S.I. 2012/3029), arts. 1. (1), 2, Sch.
Commencement Information
I2. S. 67 wholly in force at 1.1.2005; s. 67 in force for certain purposes at Royal Assent, see s. 87. (1)(j)(3); s. 67 in force for certain further purposes at 30.11.2002 by S.I. 2002/2812, art. 2. (j); s. 67 in force for certain further purposes at 1.1.2005 by S.I. 2004/1909, art. 2 and otherwise in force at 1.1.2005 by S.I. 2004/3122, art. 2
Marginal Citations
M51958 c. 51.

Interpretation of Part VI.

62 Interpretation of Part VI.

(1) For the purposes of this Part, a record becomes a "historical record" at the end of the period of [F1twenty years] beginning with the year following that in which it was created.

(2) Where records created at different dates are for administrative purposes kept together in one file or other assembly, all the records in that file or other assembly are to be treated for the purposes of this Part as having been created when the latest of those records was created.

[F2. (2. A)Until the end of the period of 10 years beginning with the commencement of paragraph 4 of Schedule 7 to the Constitutional Reform and Governance Act 2010, subsection (1) has effect subject to any order made under section 46. (2) of that Act.]

(3) In this Part "year" means a calendar year.

Amendments (Textual)
F1. Words in s. 62. (1) substituted (1.1.2013) by Constitutional Reform and Governance Act 2010 (c. 25), s. 52, Sch. 7 para. 4. (2); S.I. 2012/3001, art. 3. (1)(b)
F2. S. 62. (2. A) inserted (1.1.2013) by Constitutional Reform and Governance Act 2010 (c. 25), s. 52, Sch. 7 para. 4. (3); S.I. 2012/3001, art. 3. (1)(b)
Modifications etc. (not altering text)
C1. Pt. VI modified (1.1.2013) by The Freedom of Information (Definition of Historical Records) (Transitional and Saving Provisions) Order 2012 (S.I. 2012/3029), arts. 1. (1), 2, Sch.
C2. S. 62. (1): saving for the effect of 2010 c. 25, Sch. 7 para. 4. (2) (1.1.2013) by The Freedom of

Information (Definition of Historical Records) (Transitional and Saving Provisions) Order 2012 (S.I. 2012/3029), arts. 1. (1), 3
Commencement Information
I1. S. 62 wholly in force at 1.1.2005; s. 62 not in force at Royal Assent, see s. 87. (3); s. 62 in force for certain purposes at 1.1.2005 by S.I. 2002/1909, art. 2 and otherwise in force at 1.1.2005 by S.I. 2004/3122, art. 2

Part VII Amendments of Data Protection Act 1998

Part VII Amendments of Data Protection Act 1998

68 Extension of meaning of "data".

(1) Section 1 of the M1. Data Protection Act 1998 (basic interpretative provisions) is amended in accordance with subsections (2) and (3).
(2) In subsection (1)—
    (a) in the definition of "data", the word "or" at the end of paragraph (c) is omitted and after paragraph (d) there is inserted "or
(e) is recorded information held by a public authority and does not fall within any of paragraphs (a) to (d);", and
    (b) after the definition of "processing" there is inserted—
""public authority" has the same meaning as in the Freedom of Information Act 2000;".
(3) After subsection (4) there is inserted—
"(5)In paragraph (e) of the definition of "data" in subsection (1), the reference to information "held" by a public authority shall be construed in accordance with section 3. (2) of the Freedom of Information Act 2000.
(6) Where section 7 of the Freedom of Information Act 2000 prevents Parts I to V of that Act from applying to certain information held by a public authority, that information is not to be treated for the purposes of paragraph (e) of the definition of "data" in subsection (1) as held by a public authority."
(4) In section 56 of that Act (prohibition of requirement as to production of certain records), after subsection (6) there is inserted—
"(6. A)A record is not a relevant record to the extent that it relates, or is to relate, only to personal data falling within paragraph (e) of the definition of "data" in section 1. (1)."
(5) In the Table in section 71 of that Act (index of defined expressions) after the entry relating to processing there is inserted—
"public authority | section 1(1).". |
Commencement Information
I1. S. 68 wholly in force at 1.1.2005; s. 68 not in force at Royal Assent, see s. 87. (3); s. 68 in force for certain purposes at 1.1.2005 by S.I. 2002/1909, art. 2 and otherwise in force at 1.1.2005 by S.I. 2004/3122, art. 2
Marginal Citations
M11998 c. 29.

69 Right of access to unstructured personal data held by public authorities.

(1) In section 7. (1) of the M2. Data Protection Act 1998 (right of access to personal data), for

"sections 8 and 9" there is substituted " sections 8, 9 and 9. A ".

F1. (2)After section 9 of that Act there is inserted—

"9. A Unstructured personal data held by public authorities.

(1) In this section "unstructured personal data" means any personal data falling within paragraph (e) of the definition of "data" in section 1. (1), other than information which is recorded as part of, or with the intention that it should form part of, any set of information relating to individuals to the extent that the set is structured by reference to individuals or by reference to criteria relating to individuals.

(2) A public authority is not obliged to comply with subsection (1) of section 7 in relation to any unstructured personal data unless the request under that section contains a description of the data.

(3) Even if the data are described by the data subject in his request, a public authority is not obliged to comply with subsection (1) of section 7 in relation to unstructured personal data if the authority estimates that the cost of complying with the request so far as relating to those data would exceed the appropriate limit.

(4) Subsection (3) does not exempt the public authority from its obligation to comply with paragraph (a) of section 7. (1) in relation to the unstructured personal data unless the estimated cost of complying with that paragraph alone in relation to those data would exceed the appropriate limit.

(5) In subsections (3) and (4) "the appropriate limit" means such amount as may be prescribed by the Secretary of State by regulations, and different amounts may be prescribed in relation to different cases.

(6) Any estimate for the purposes of this section must be made in accordance with regulations under section 12. (5) of the Freedom of Information Act 2000."

(3) In section 67. (5) of that Act (statutory instruments subject to negative resolution procedure), in paragraph (c), for "or 9. (3)" there is substituted " , 9. (3) or 9. A(5) ".

Amendments (Textual)

F1. By The Secretary of State for Constitutional Affairs Order 2003 (S.I. 2003/1887), art. 9, Sch. 2 para. 12. (1)(b), it is provided (19.8.2003) that in s. 69. (2), in the inserted s. 9. A of the Data Protection Act 1998, in each place for the words "Lord Chancellor" there be substituted the words "Secretary of State"

Commencement Information

I2. S. 69 wholly in force at 1.1.2005; s. 69 in force at Royal Assent to the extent that it confers power to make regulations, see s. 87. (1)(m)(3); s. 69 in force for certain further purposes at 1.1.2005 by S.I. 2002/1909, art. 2 and otherwise in force at 1.1.2005 by S.I. 2004/3122, art. 2

Marginal Citations

M21998 c. 29.

70 Exemptions applicable to certain manual data held by public authorities.

(1) After section 33 of the M3. Data Protection Act 1998 there is inserted—

"33. A Manual data held by public authorities.

(1) Personal data falling within paragraph (e) of the definition of "data" in section 1. (1) are exempt from—

    (a) the first, second, third, fifth, seventh and eighth data protection principles,

    (b) the sixth data protection principle except so far as it relates to the rights conferred on data subjects by sections 7 and 14,

    (c) sections 10 to 12,

    (d) section 13, except so far as it relates to damage caused by a contravention of section 7 or of the fourth data protection principle and to any distress which is also suffered by reason of that contravention,

    (e) Part III, and

(f) section 55.

(2) Personal data which fall within paragraph (e) of the definition of "data" in section 1. (1) and relate to appointments or removals, pay, discipline, superannuation or other personnel matters, in relation to—

(a) service in any of the armed forces of the Crown,

(b) service in any office or employment under the Crown or under any public authority, or

(c) service in any office or employment, or under any contract for services, in respect of which power to take action, or to determine or approve the action taken, in such matters is vested in Her Majesty, any Minister of the Crown, the National Assembly for Wales, any Northern Ireland Minister (within the meaning of the Freedom of Information Act 2000) or any public authority, are also exempt from the remaining data protection principles and the remaining provisions of Part II."

(2) In section 55 of that Act (unlawful obtaining etc. of personal data) in subsection (8) after "section 28" there is inserted " or 33. A ".

(3) In Part III of Schedule 8 to that Act (exemptions available after 23rd October 2001 but before 24th October 2007) after paragraph 14 there is inserted—

"14. A(1)This paragraph applies to personal data which fall within paragraph (e) of the definition of "data" in section 1. (1) and do not fall within paragraph 14. (1)(a), but does not apply to eligible manual data to which the exemption in paragraph 16 applies.

(2) During the second transitional period, data to which this paragraph applies are exempt from—

(a) the fourth data protection principle, and

(b) section 14. (1) to (3)."

(4) In Schedule 13 to that Act (modifications of Act having effect before 24th October 2007) in subsection (4)(b) of section 12. A to that Act as set out in paragraph 1, after "paragraph 14" there is inserted " or 14. A ".

Commencement Information

I3. S. 70 wholly in force at 1.1.2005; s. 70 not in force at Royal Assent, see s. 87. (3); s. 70 in force for certain purposes at 1.1.2005 by S.I. 2002/1909, art. 2 and otherwise in force at 1.1.2005 by S.I. 2004/3122, art. 2

Marginal Citations

M31998 c. 29.

71 Particulars registrable under Part III of Data Protection Act 1998.

In section 16. (1) of the M4. Data Protection Act 1998 (the registrable particulars), before the word "and" at the end of paragraph (f) there is inserted—

"(ff)where the data controller is a public authority, a statement of that fact,".

Commencement Information

I4. S. 71 wholly in force at 1.1.2005; s. 71 not in force at Royal Assent, see s. 87. (3); s. 71 in force for certain purposes at 1.1.2005 by S.I. 2002/1909, art. 2 and otherwise in force at 1.1.2005 by S.I. 2004/3122, art. 2

Marginal Citations

M41998 c. 29.

72 Availability under Act disregarded for purpose of exemption.

In section 34 of the M5. Data Protection Act 1998 (information available to the public by or under enactment), after the word "enactment" there is inserted " other than an enactment contained in the Freedom of Information Act 2000 ".

Marginal Citations

Other amendments

73 Further amendments of Data Protection Act 1998.

Schedule 6 (which contains further amendments of the Data Protection Act 1998) has effect.
Commencement Information
I5. S. 73 wholly in force at 1.1.2005; s. 73 in force for certain purposes at Royal Assent, see s. 87.
(1)(k)(3); s. 73 in force for certain further purposes at 14.5.2001 by S.I. 2001/1637, art. 2. (d); s.
73 in force for certain further purposes at 1.1.2005 by S.I. 2004/1909, art. 2 and otherwise in force
at 1.1.2005 by S.I. 2004/3122, art. 2

Particulars registrable under Part III of Data Protection Act 1998.

71 Particulars registrable under Part III of Data Protection Act 1998.

In section 16. (1) of the M1. Data Protection Act 1998 (the registrable particulars), before the
word "and" at the end of paragraph (f) there is inserted—
    "(ff)where the data controller is a public authority, a statement of that fact,".
Commencement Information
I1. S. 71 wholly in force at 1.1.2005; s. 71 not in force at Royal Assent, see s. 87. (3); s. 71 in
force for certain purposes at 1.1.2005 by S.I. 2002/1909, art. 2 and otherwise in force at 1.1.2005
by S.I. 2004/3122, art. 2
Marginal Citations
M11998 c. 29.

Part VIII Miscellaneous and supplemental

Part VIII Miscellaneous and supplemental

74 Power to make provision relating to environmental information.

(1) In this section "the Aarhus Convention" means the Convention on Access to Information,
Public Participation in Decision-making and Access to Justice in Environmental Matters signed at
Aarhus on 25th June 1998.
(2) For the purposes of this section "the information provisions" of the Aarhus Convention are
Article 4, together with Articles 3 and 9 so far as relating to that Article.
(3) The Secretary of State may by regulations make such provision as he considers appropriate—
    (a) for the purpose of implementing the information provisions of the Aarhus Convention or any

amendment of those provisions made in accordance with Article 14 of the Convention, and

(b) for the purpose of dealing with matters arising out of or related to the implementation of those provisions or of any such amendment.

(4) Regulations under subsection (3) may in particular—

(a) enable charges to be made for making information available in accordance with the regulations,

(b) provide that any obligation imposed by the regulations in relation to the disclosure of information is to have effect notwithstanding any enactment or rule of law,

(c) make provision for the issue by the Secretary of State of a code of practice,

(d) provide for sections 47 and 48 to apply in relation to such a code with such modifications as may be specified,

(e) provide for any of the provisions of Parts IV and V to apply, with such modifications as may be specified in the regulations, in relation to compliance with any requirement of the regulations, and

(f) contain such transitional or consequential provision (including provision modifying any enactment) as the Secretary of State considers appropriate.

(5) This section has effect subject to section 80.

75 Power to amend or repeal enactments prohibiting disclosure of information.

(1) If, with respect to any enactment which prohibits the disclosure of information held by a public authority, it appears to the [F1. Secretary of State] [F2or the [F3. Minister for the Cabinet Office]] that by virtue of section 44. (1)(a) the enactment is capable of preventing the disclosure of information under section 1, he may by order repeal or amend the enactment for the purpose of removing or relaxing the prohibition.

(2) In subsection (1)—

"enactment" means—

- any enactment contained in an Act passed before or in the same Session as this Act, or

- any enactment contained in Northern Ireland legislation or subordinate legislation passed or made before the passing of this Act;

"information" includes unrecorded information.

(3) An order under this section may do all or any of the following—

(a) make such modifications of enactments as, in the opinion of the [F1. Secretary of State] [F4or the [F5. Minister for the Cabinet Office]], are consequential upon, or incidental to, the amendment or repeal of the enactment containing the prohibition;

(b) contain such transitional provisions and savings as appear to the [F1. Secretary of State] [F4or the [F5. Minister for the Cabinet Office]] to be appropriate;

(c) make different provision for different cases.

Amendments (Textual)

F1. Words in s. 75 substituted (19.8.2003) by The Secretary of State for Constitutional Affairs Order 2003 (S.I. 2003/1887), art. 9, Sch. 2 para. 12. (1)(c)

F2. Words in s. 75. (1) inserted (9.12.2015) by The Transfer of Functions (Information and Public Records) Order 2015 (S.I. 2015/1897), art. 1. (2), Sch. para. 2. (2)(d)

F3. Words in s. 75. (1) substituted (9.11.2016) by The Transfer of Functions (Elections, Referendums, Third Sector and Information) Order 2016 (S.I. 2016/997), art. 1. (2), Sch. 2 para. 14. (2)(o) (with art. 12)

F4. Words in s. 75. (3) inserted (9.12.2015) by The Transfer of Functions (Information and Public Records) Order 2015 (S.I. 2015/1897), art. 1. (2), Sch. para. 2. (2)(d)

F5. Words in s. 75. (3) substituted (9.11.2016) by The Transfer of Functions (Elections, Referendums, Third Sector and Information) Order 2016 (S.I. 2016/997), art. 1. (2), Sch. 2 para. 14. (2)(o) (with art. 12)

Modifications etc. (not altering text)

C1. S. 75. (1) functions made exercisable concurrently (9.12.2015) by The Transfer of Functions (Information and Public Records) Order 2015 (S.I. 2015/1897), arts. 1. (2), 3. (1), (2)(d) (with art. 5)

76 Disclosure of information between Commissioner and ombudsmen.

(1) The Commissioner may disclose to a person specified in the first column of the Table below any information obtained by, or furnished to, the Commissioner under or for the purposes of this Act or the M1. Data Protection Act 1998 if it appears to the Commissioner that the information relates to a matter which could be the subject of an investigation by that person under the enactment specified in relation to that person in the second column of that Table.

TABLE

Ombudsman	Enactment
The Parliamentary Commissioner for Administration.	The Parliamentary Commissioner Act 1967 (c. 13).
The Health Service Commissioner for England.	The Health Service Commissioners Act 1993 (c. 46).
F6.	F6. . . . .
[F7The Health Service Commissioner for Scotland.]	[F7The Health Service Commissioners Act 1993 (c. 46).]
A Local Commissioner as defined by section 23(3) of the Local Government Act 1974. The Scottish Public Services Ombudsman	Part III [F8or Part 3A] of the Local Government Act 1974 (c. 7).
[F9The Scottish Public Services Ombudsman	The Scottish Public Services Ombudsman Act 2002 (asp 11)]
[F10The Commissioner for Local Administration in Scotland.]	[F10Part II of the Local Government (Scotland) Act 1975 (c. 30).]
[F10The Scottish Parliamentary Commissioner for Administration.]	[F10The Scotland Act 1998 (Transitory and Transitional Provisions)(Complaints of Maladministration) Order 1999 (S.I. 1999/1351).]
[F11The Public Services Ombudsman for Wales	Part 2 of the Public Services Ombudsman (Wales) Act 2005]
F12.	F12. . . . .
The Northern Ireland Commissioner for Complaints.	The Commissioner for Complaints (Northern Ireland) Order 1996 (S.I. 1996/1297 (N.I. 7)).
The Assembly Ombudsman for Northern Ireland.	The Ombudsman (Northern Ireland) Order 1996 (S.I. 1996/1298 (N.I. 8)).
[F13The Commissioner for Older People in Wales	The Commissioner for Older People (Wales) Act 2006]

(2) Schedule 7 (which contains amendments relating to information disclosed to ombudsmen under subsection (1) and to the disclosure of information by ombudsmen to the Commissioner) has effect.

Amendments (Textual)

F6. S. 76. (1): entry relating to Health Service Commisioner for Wales repealed (1.4.2006) by Public Services Ombudsman (Wales) Act 2005 (c. 10), ss. 39, 40, Sch. 6 para. 71. (a), Sch. 7; S.I. 2005/2800, art. 5. (1) (with art. 5. (2), Sch. 2)

F7. S. 76. (1): entry repealed (S.) (23.10.2002) by Scottish Public Services Ombudsman Act 2002 (asp 11), s. 25, Sch. 6 para. 23. (2)(a); S.S.I. 2002/467, art. 2

F8. Words in s. 76 inserted (1.10.2010) by Health Act 2009 (c. 21), ss. 35, 40, Sch. 5 para. 14; S.I. 2010/1863, art. 2

F9. S. 76. (1): entry inserted (S.) (23.10.2002) by Scottish Public Services Ombudsman Act 2002 (asp 11), s. 25, Sch. 6 para. 23. (2)(b); S.S.I. 2002/467, art. 2

F10. S. 76. (1): entry repealed (S.) (23.10.2002) by Scottish Public Services Ombudsman Act 2002 (asp 11), s. 25, Sch. 6 para. 23. (2)(a); S.S.I. 2002/467, art. 2

F11. S. 76. (1): entry substituted (1.4.2006) by Public Services Ombudsman (Wales) Act 2005 (c. 10), ss. 39. (1), 40, Sch. 6 para. 71. (b); S.I. 2005/2800, art. 5. (1) (with art. 5. (2), Sch. 2)

F12. S. 76. (1): entry relating to Social Housing Ombudsman for Wales repealed (1.4.2006) by Public Services Ombudsman (Wales) Act 2005 (c. 10), ss. 39, 40, Sch. 6 para. 71. (a), Sch. 7; S.I. 2005/2800, art. 5. (1) (with art. 5. (2), Sch. 2)

F13. S. 76. (1): entry inserted (14.10.2006 for W.) by Commissioner for Older People (Wales) Act 2006 (c. 30), ss. 1. (2), 23, Sch. 1 para. 21. (a); S.I. 2006/2699, art. 2

Modifications etc. (not altering text)

C2. S. 76. (1) applied (31.12.2009) by The INSPIRE Regulations 2009 (S.I. 2009/3157), reg. 11. (11)

Marginal Citations

M11998 c. 29.

[F1476. ADisclosure between Commissioner and Scottish Information Commissioner

The Commissioner may disclose to the Scottish Information Commissioner any information obtained or furnished as mentioned in section 76. (1) of this Act if it appears to the Commissioner that the information is of the same type that could be obtained by, or furnished to, the Scottish Information Commissioner under or for the purposes of the Freedom of Information (Scotland) Act 2002.]

Amendments (Textual)

F14. S. 76. A inserted (1.1.2005) by The Freedom of Information (Scotland) Act 2002 (Consequential Modifications) Order 2004 (S.I. 2004/3089), art. 3. (2)

77 Offence of altering etc. records with intent to prevent disclosure.

(1) Where—

   (a) a request for information has been made to a public authority, and

   (b) under section 1 of this Act or section 7 of the M2. Data Protection Act 1998, the applicant would have been entitled (subject to payment of any fee) to communication of any information in accordance with that section,

any person to whom this subsection applies is guilty of an offence if he alters, defaces, blocks, erases, destroys or conceals any record held by the public authority, with the intention of preventing the disclosure by that authority of all, or any part, of the information to the communication of which the applicant would have been entitled.

(2) Subsection (1) applies to the public authority and to any person who is employed by, is an officer of, or is subject to the direction of, the public authority.

(3) A person guilty of an offence under this section is liable on summary conviction to a fine not exceeding level 5 on the standard scale.

(4) No proceedings for an offence under this section shall be instituted—

   (a) in England or Wales, except by the Commissioner or by or with the consent of the Director of Public Prosecutions;

   (b) in Northern Ireland, except by the Commissioner or by or with the consent of the Director of Public Prosecutions for Northern Ireland.

Commencement Information

I1. S. 77 wholly in force at 1.1.2005; s. 77 not in force at Royal Assent, see s. 87. (3); s. 77 in force for certain purposes at 1.1.2005 by S.I. 2002/1909, art. 2 and otherwise in force at 1.1.2005 by S.I. 2004/3122, art. 2
Marginal Citations
M21988 c. 29.

78 Saving for existing powers.

Nothing in this Act is to be taken to limit the powers of a public authority to disclose information held by it.

79 Defamation.

Where any information communicated by a public authority to a person ("the applicant") under section 1 was supplied to the public authority by a third person, the publication to the applicant of any defamatory matter contained in the information shall be privileged unless the publication is shown to have been made with malice.

80 Scotland.

(1) No order may be made under section 4. (1) or 5 in relation to any of the bodies specified in subsection (2); and the power conferred by section 74. (3) does not include power to make provision in relation to information held by any of those bodies.
(2) The bodies referred to in subsection (1) are—
    (a) the Scottish Parliament,
    (b) any part of the Scottish Administration,
    (c) the Scottish Parliamentary Corporate Body, or
    (d) any Scottish public authority with mixed functions or no reserved functions (within the meaning of the M3. Scotland Act 1998).
[F15. (3)Section 50 of the Copyright, Designs and Patents Act 1988 and paragraph 6 of Schedule 1 to the Copyright and Rights in Databases Regulations 1997 apply in relation to the Freedom of Information (Scotland) Act 2002 as they apply in relation to this Act.]
Amendments (Textual)
F15. S. 80. (3) added (1.1.2005) by The Freedom of Information (Scotland) Act 2002 (Consequential Modifications) Order 2004 (S.I. 2004/3089), art. 3. (3)
Marginal Citations
M31998 c. 46.

F1680. AInformation held by Northern Ireland bodies

. . . .
Amendments (Textual)
F16. S. 80. A repealed (1.7.2012) by Protection of Freedoms Act 2012 (c. 9), ss. 104. (1)(a), 120, Sch. 10 Pt. 7 (with s. 97); S.I. 2012/1205, art. 3. (x)(cc)

81 Application to government departments, etc.

(1) For the purposes of this Act each government department is to be treated as a person separate from any other government department.
(2) Subsection (1) does not enable—
    (a) a government department which is not a Northern Ireland department to claim for the

purposes of section 41. (1)(b) that the disclosure of any information by it would constitute a breach of confidence actionable by any other government department (not being a Northern Ireland department), or

(b) a Northern Ireland department to claim for those purposes that the disclosure of information by it would constitute a breach of confidence actionable by any other Northern Ireland department.
(3) A government department [F17or the Welsh Assembly Government] is not liable to prosecution under this Act, but section 77 and paragraph 12 of Schedule 3 apply to a person in the public service of the Crown as they apply to any other person.
(4) The provisions specified in subsection (3) also apply to a person acting on behalf of either House of Parliament or on behalf of the Northern Ireland Assembly [F18or the National Assembly for Wales] as they apply to any other person.
Amendments (Textual)
F17. Words in s. 81. (3) inserted by The Government of Wales Act 2006 (Consequential Modifications and Transitional Provisions) Order 2007 (S.I. 2007/1388), art. 3, Sch. 1 para. 84. (2) (the amendment coming into force immediately after the end of "the initial period" (which ended with the day of the first appointment of a First Minister on 25.5.2007) in accordance with art. 1. (2)(3) of the amending S.I. and see ss. 46, 161. (5) of Government of Wales Act 2006 (c. 32))
F18. Words in s. 81. (4) inserted by The Government of Wales Act 2006 (Consequential Modifications and Transitional Provisions) Order 2007 (S.I. 2007/1388), art. 3, Sch. 1 para. 84. (3) (the amendment coming into force immediately after the end of "the initial period" (which ended with the day of the first appointment of a First Minister on 25.5.2007) in accordance with art. 1. (2)(3) of the amending S.I. and see ss. 46, 161. (5) of Government of Wales Act 2006 (c. 32))

82 Orders and regulations.

(1) Any power of the F19. . . Secretary of State [F20or the [F21. Minister for the Cabinet Office]] to make an order or regulations under this Act shall be exercisable by statutory instrument.
(2) A statutory instrument containing (whether alone or with other provisions)—
    (a) an order under section 5, 7. (3) or (8), 53. (1)(a)(iii) or 75, or
    (b) regulations under section 10. (4) or 74. (3),
shall not be made unless a draft of the instrument has been laid before, and approved by a resolution of, each House of Parliament.
(3) A statutory instrument which contains (whether alone or with other provisions)—
    (a) an order under section 4. (1) [F22or 47. (4. B)], or
    (b) regulations under any provision of this Act not specified in subsection (2)(b),
and which is not subject to the requirement in subsection (2) that a draft of the instrument be laid before and approved by a resolution of each House of Parliament, shall be subject to annulment in pursuance of a resolution of either House of Parliament.
(4) An order under section 4. (5) shall be laid before Parliament after being made.
(5) If a draft of an order under section 5 or 7. (8) would, apart from this subsection, be treated for the purposes of the Standing Orders of either House of Parliament as a hybrid instrument, it shall proceed in that House as if it were not such an instrument.
Amendments (Textual)
F19. Words in s. 82. (1) repealed (19.8.2003) by The Secretary of State for Constitutional Affairs Order 2003 (S.I. 2003/1887), art. 9, Sch. 2 para. 12. (3)
F20. Words in s. 82. (1) inserted (9.12.2015) by The Transfer of Functions (Information and Public Records) Order 2015 (S.I. 2015/1897), art. 1. (2), Sch. para. 2. (2)(e)
F21. Words in s. 82. (1) substituted (9.11.2016) by The Transfer of Functions (Elections, Referendums, Third Sector and Information) Order 2016 (S.I. 2016/997), art. 1. (2), Sch. 2 para. 14. (2)(p) (with art. 12)
F22. Words in s. 82. (3)(a) inserted (1.9.2013) by Protection of Freedoms Act 2012 (c. 9), ss. 107. (4), 120 (with s. 97); S.I. 2013/1906, art. 3. (d)

83 Meaning of "Welsh public authority".

(1) In this Act "Welsh public authority" means—
   (a) any public authority which is listed in Part II, III, IV or VI of Schedule 1 and whose functions are exercisable only or mainly in or as regards Wales, other than an excluded authority, or
   [F23. (b)any public authority which is—
(i) a subsidiary of the Welsh Ministers (as defined by section 134. (4) of the Government of Wales Act 2006), or
(ii) a subsidiary of the Assembly Commission (as defined by section 139. (4) of that Act).]
(2) In paragraph (a) of subsection (1) "excluded authority" means a public authority which is designated by the [F24. Secretary of State] [F25or the [F26. Minister for the Cabinet Office]] by order as an excluded authority for the purposes of that paragraph.
(3) Before making an order under subsection (2), the [F24. Secretary of State] [F27or the [F28. Minister for the Cabinet Office]] shall consult [F29the First Minister for Wales].
Amendments (Textual)
F23. S. 83. (1)(b) substituted by The Government of Wales Act 2006 (Consequential Modifications and Transitional Provisions) Order 2007 (S.I. 2007/1388), art. 3, Sch. 1 para. 85. (2) (the amendment coming into force immediately after the end of "the initial period" (which ended with the day of the first appointment of a First Minister on 25.5.2007) in accordance with art. 1. (2)(3) of the amending S.I. and see ss. 46, 161. (5) of Government of Wales Act 2006 (c. 32))
F24. Words in s. 83 substituted (19.8.2003) by The Secretary of State for Constitutional Affairs Order 2003 (S.I. 2003/1887), art. 9, Sch. 2 para. 12. (1)(c)
F25. Words in s. 83. (2) inserted (9.12.2015) by The Transfer of Functions (Information and Public Records) Order 2015 (S.I. 2015/1897), art. 1. (2), Sch. para. 2. (2)(f)
F26. Words in s. 83. (2) substituted (9.11.2016) by The Transfer of Functions (Elections, Referendums, Third Sector and Information) Order 2016 (S.I. 2016/997), art. 1. (2), Sch. 2 para. 14. (2)(q) (with art. 12)
F27. Words in s. 83. (3) inserted (9.12.2015) by The Transfer of Functions (Information and Public Records) Order 2015 (S.I. 2015/1897), art. 1. (2), Sch. para. 2. (2)(f)
F28. Words in s. 83. (3) substituted (9.11.2016) by The Transfer of Functions (Elections, Referendums, Third Sector and Information) Order 2016 (S.I. 2016/997), art. 1. (2), Sch. 2 para. 14. (2)(q) (with art. 12)
F29. Words in s. 83. (3) substituted by The Government of Wales Act 2006 (Consequential Modifications and Transitional Provisions) Order 2007 (S.I. 2007/1388), art. 3, Sch. 1 para. 85. (3) (the amendment coming into force immediately after the end of "the initial period" (which ended with the day of the first appointment of a First Minister on 25.5.2007) in accordance with art. 1. (2)(3) of the amending S.I. and see ss. 46, 161. (5) of Government of Wales Act 2006 (c. 32))
Modifications etc. (not altering text)
C3. S. 83. (2)(3) functions made exercisable concurrently (9.12.2015) by The Transfer of Functions (Information and Public Records) Order 2015 (S.I. 2015/1897), arts. 1. (2), 3. (1), (2)(e) (with art. 5)

84 Interpretation.

In this Act, unless the context otherwise requires—
"applicant", in relation to a request for information, means the person who made the request;
"appropriate Northern Ireland Minister" means the Northern Ireland Minister in charge of the Department of Culture, Arts and Leisure in Northern Ireland;
"appropriate records authority", in relation to a transferred public record, has the meaning given by section 15. (5);

"body" includes an unincorporated association;

F30...

"the Commissioner" means the Information Commissioner;

[F31"dataset" has the meaning given by section 11. (5);]

"decision notice" has the meaning given by section 50;

"the duty to confirm or deny" has the meaning given by section 1. (6);

"enactment" includes an enactment contained in Northern Ireland legislation;

"enforcement notice" has the meaning given by section 52;

F32. . . . .

"exempt information" means information which is exempt information by virtue of any provision of Part II;

"fees notice" has the meaning given by section 9. (1);

"government department" includes a Northern Ireland department F33. . . and any other body or authority exercising statutory functions on behalf of the Crown, but does not include—

   - any of the bodies specified in section 80. (2),

   - the Security Service, the Secret Intelligence Service or the Government Communications Headquarters, F34...

   - [F35the National Crime Agency, or]

   - [F36the Welsh Assembly Government]

"information" (subject to sections 51. (8) and 75. (2)) means information recorded in any form;

"information notice" has the meaning given by section 51;

"Minister of the Crown" has the same meaning as in the Ministers of the M4. Crown Act 1975;

"Northern Ireland Minister" includes the First Minister and deputy First Minister in Northern Ireland;

"Northern Ireland public authority" means any public authority, other than the Northern Ireland Assembly or a Northern Ireland department, whose functions are exercisable only or mainly in or as regards Northern Ireland and relate only or mainly to transferred matters;

"prescribed" means prescribed by regulations made by the [F37. Minister for the Cabinet Office];

"public authority" has the meaning given by section 3. (1);

"public record" means a public record within the meaning of the M5. Public Records Act 1958 or a public record to which the M6. Public Records Act (Northern Ireland) 1923 applies;

"publication scheme" has the meaning given by section 19;

"request for information" has the meaning given by section 8;

"responsible authority", in relation to a transferred public record, has the meaning given by section 15. (5);

"the special forces" means those units of the armed forces of the Crown the maintenance of whose capabilities is the responsibility of the Director of Special Forces or which are for the time being subject to the operational command of that Director;

"subordinate legislation" has the meaning given by subsection (1) of section 21 of the M7. Interpretation Act 1978, except that the definition of that term in that subsection shall have effect as if "Act" included Northern Ireland legislation;

"transferred matter", in relation to Northern Ireland, has the meaning given by section 4. (1) of the M8. Northern Ireland Act 1998;

"transferred public record" has the meaning given by section 15. (4);

[F38"the Tribunal", in relation to any appeal under this Act, means—

   - the Upper Tribunal, in any case where it is determined by or under Tribunal Procedure Rules that the Upper Tribunal is to hear the appeal; or

   - the First-tier Tribunal, in any other case;]

"Welsh public authority" has the meaning given by section 83.

Amendments (Textual)

F30. Words in s. 84 omitted (9.11.2016) by virtue of The Transfer of Functions (Elections, Referendums, Third Sector and Information) Order 2016 (S.I. 2016/997), art. 1. (2), Sch. 2 para. 14. (3) (with art. 12)

F31. Words in s. 84 inserted (1.9.2013) by Protection of Freedoms Act 2012 (c. 9), ss. 102. (6), 120 (with s. 97); S.I. 2013/1906, art. 3. (a)

F32. S. 84: definition of "executive committee" omitted by virtue of The Government of Wales Act 2006 (Consequential Modifications and Transitional Provisions) Order 2007 (S.I. 2007/1388), art. 3, Sch. 1 para. 86. (2) (the amendment coming into force immediately after the end of "the initial period" (which ended with the day of the first appointment of a First Minister on 25.5.2007) in accordance with art. 1. (2)(3) of the amending S.I. and see ss. 46, 161. (5) of Government of Wales Act 2006 (c. 32))

F33. Words in s. 84 omitted (N.I.) (12.4.2010) by virtue of The Northern Ireland (Abolition and Transfer of Functions) Order (Northern Ireland) 2010 (S.R. 2010/133), art. 4, Sch. para. 7 (with transitional provision in art. 5)

F34. Word in s. 84 omitted (27.5.2013) by virtue of Crime and Courts Act 2013 (c. 22), s. 61. (2), Sch. 8 para. 103; S.I. 2013/1042, art. 3. (l)

F35. Words in s. 84 inserted (27.5.2013) by Crime and Courts Act 2013 (c. 22), s. 61. (2), Sch. 8 para. 103; S.I. 2013/1042, art. 3. (l)

F36. S. 84: in definition of "government department" para. (c) substituted by The Government of Wales Act 2006 (Consequential Modifications and Transitional Provisions) Order 2007 (S.I. 2007/1388), art. 3, Sch. 1 para. 86. (3) (the amendment coming into force immediately after the end of "the initial period" (which ended with the day of the first appointment of a First Minister on 25.5.2007) in accordance with art. 1. (2)(3) of the amending S.I. and see ss. 46, 161. (5) of Government of Wales Act 2006 (c. 32))

F37. Words in s. 84 substituted (9.11.2016) by The Transfer of Functions (Elections, Referendums, Third Sector and Information) Order 2016 (S.I. 2016/997), art. 1. (2), Sch. 2 para. 14. (2)(r) (with art. 12)

F38. S. 84: definition of "the Tribunal" substituted (18.1.2010) by The Transfer of Tribunal Functions Order 2010 (S.I. 2010/22), arts. 1. (1), 5. (1), Sch. 2 para. 71

Marginal Citations

M41975 c. 26.

M51958 c. 51.

M61923 c. 20 (N.I.).

M71978 c. 30.

M81998 c. 47.

85 Expenses.

There shall be paid out of money provided by Parliament—

(a) any increase attributable to this Act in the expenses of the [F39. Secretary of State] in respect of the Commissioner, the Tribunal or the members of the Tribunal,

(b) any administrative expenses of the [F39. Secretary of State] [F40or the [F41. Minister for the Cabinet Office]] attributable to this Act,

(c) any other expenses incurred in consequence of this Act by a Minister of the Crown or government department or by either House of Parliament, and

(d) any increase attributable to this Act in the sums which under any other Act are payable out of money so provided.

Amendments (Textual)

F39. Words in s. 85 substituted (19.8.2003) by The Secretary of State for Constitutional Affairs Order 2003 (S.I. 2003/1887), art. 9, Sch. 2 para. 12. (1)(c)

F40. Words in s. 85. (b) inserted (9.12.2015) by The Transfer of Functions (Information and Public Records) Order 2015 (S.I. 2015/1897), art. 1. (2), Sch. para. 2. (2)(g)

F41. Words in s. 85. (b) substituted (9.11.2016) by The Transfer of Functions (Elections, Referendums, Third Sector and Information) Order 2016 (S.I. 2016/997), art. 1. (2), Sch. 2 para. 14. (2)(s) (with art. 12)

86 Repeals.

Schedule 8 (repeals) has effect.

Commencement Information

I2. S. 86 wholly in force at 1.1.2005; s. 86 in force for certain purposes at 30.11.2000 and in force for certain further purposes at 1.1.2001 see s. 87. (1)(2); otherwise in force at 1.1.2005 by S.I. 2004/3122, art. 2

87 Commencement.

(1) The following provisions of this Act shall come into force on the day on which this Act is passed—

(a) sections 3 to 8 and Schedule 1,

(b) section 19 so far as relating to the approval of publication schemes,

(c) section 20 so far as relating to the approval and preparation by the Commissioner of model publication schemes,

(d) section 47. (2) to (6),

(e) section 49,

(f) section 74,

(g) section 75,

(h) sections 78 to 85 and this section,

(i) paragraphs 2 and 17 to 22 of Schedule 2 (and section 18. (4) so far as relating to those paragraphs),

(j) paragraph 4 of Schedule 5 (and section 67 so far as relating to that paragraph),

(k) paragraph 8 of Schedule 6 (and section 73 so far as relating to that paragraph),

(l) Part I of Schedule 8 (and section 86 so far as relating to that Part), and

(m) so much of any other provision of this Act as confers power to make any order, regulations or code of practice.

(2) The following provisions of this Act shall come into force at the end of the period of two months beginning with the day on which this Act is passed—

(a) section 18. (1),

(b) section 76 and Schedule 7,

(c) paragraphs 1. (1), 3. (1), 4, 6, 7, 8. (2), 9. (2), 10. (a), 13. (1) and (2), 14. (a) and 15. (1) and (2) of Schedule 2 (and section 18. (4) so far as relating to those provisions), and

(d) Part II of Schedule 8 (and section 86 so far as relating to that Part).

(3) Except as provided by subsections (1) and (2), this Act shall come into force at the end of the period of five years beginning with the day on which this Act is passed or on such day before the end of that period as the [F42. Secretary of State] may by order appoint; and different days may be appointed for different purposes.

(4) An order under subsection (3) may contain such transitional provisions and savings (including provisions capable of having effect after the end of the period referred to in that subsection) as the [F42. Secretary of State] considers appropriate.

(5) During the twelve months beginning with the day on which this Act is passed, and during each subsequent complete period of twelve months in the period beginning with that day and ending with the first day on which all the provisions of this Act are fully in force, the [F42. Secretary of State] shall—

(a) prepare a report on his proposals for bringing fully into force those provisions of this Act which are not yet fully in force, and

(b) lay a copy of the report before each House of Parliament.

Subordinate Legislation Made

P1. S. 87. (3) power partly exercised: 14.5.2001 appointed for specified provisions by S.I.

2001/1637, art. 2

S. 87. (3) power partly exercised: different dates appointed for specified provisions by {S.I. 2002/2812}, arts. 2-5, Schs. 1-3 (as amended (1.4.2006) by S.I. 2005/3239, art. 9. (2), Sch. 2 para. 8, S.I. 2006/63, art. 3. (2)(b) and S.I. 2006/64, art. 3. (2)(b))

S. 87. (3) power partly exercised: different dates appointed for specified provisions by {S.I. 2003/2603}, arts. 2-4, Sch. 1

S. 87. (3) power partly exercised: 1.1.2005 appointed for specified provisions by {S.I. 2004/1909}, art. 2

S. 87. (3) power fully exercised: 1.1.2005 appointed by {S.I. 2004/3122}, art. 2

Amendments (Textual)

F42. Words in s. 87 substituted (19.8.2003) by The Secretary of State for Constitutional Affairs Order 2003 (S.I. 2003/1887), art. 9, Sch. 2 para. 12. (1)(c)

88 Short title and extent.

(1) This Act may be cited as the Freedom of Information Act 2000.

(2) Subject to subsection (3), this Act extends to Northern Ireland.

(3) The amendment or repeal of any enactment by this Act has the same extent as that enactment.

Schedules

Schedule 1. Public authorities

Section 3. (1)(a)(i).

Part I General

1. Any government department [F1other than

[F2. (a)the Competition and Markets Authority,

(b)] the Office for Standards in Education, Children's Services and Skills].

Amendments (Textual)

F1. Words in Sch. 1 para. 1 inserted (1.4.2007) by Education and Inspections Act 2006 (c. 40), ss. 157, 188. (3), Sch. 14 para. 69. (2)(a); S.I. 2007/935, art. 5. (w)(gg)

F2. Words in Sch. 1 para. 1 inserted (1.10.2013) by Enterprise and Regulatory Reform Act 2013 (c. 24), s. 103. (3), Sch. 4 para. 25. (a); S.I. 2013/2227, art. 2. (j) (with art. 3)

[F31. ZAThe Competition and Markets Authority, in respect of information held otherwise than as a tribunal.]

Amendments (Textual)

F3. Sch. 1 para. 1. ZA inserted (1.10.2013) by Enterprise and Regulatory Reform Act 2013 (c. 24), s. 103. (3), Sch. 4 para. 25. (b); S.I. 2013/2227, art. 2. (j) (with art. 3)

[F41. AThe Office for Standards in Education, Children's Services and Skills, in respect of information held for purposes other than those of the functions exercisable by Her Majesty's Chief Inspector of Education, Children's Services and Skills by virtue of section 5. (1)(a)(iii) of the Care Standards Act 2000.]

Amendments (Textual)

F4. Sch. 1 para. 1. A inserted (1.4.2007) by Education and Inspections Act 2006 (c. 40), ss. 157, 188. (3), Sch. 14 para. 69. (2)(b); S.I. 2007/935, art. 5. (w)(gg)

2. The House of Commons [F5, in respect of information other than—

(a) information relating to any residential address of a member of either House of Parliament,

(b) information relating to travel arrangements of a member of either House of Parliament, where the arrangements relate to travel that has not yet been undertaken or is regular in nature,

(c) information relating to the identity of any person who delivers or has delivered goods, or provides or has provided services, to a member of either House of Parliament at any residence of the member,

(d) information relating to expenditure by a member of either House of Parliament on security arrangements.

[F6. (e)information held by the Intelligence and Security Committee of Parliament.]

Paragraph (b) does not except information relating to the total amount of expenditure incurred on regular travel during any month.]

Amendments (Textual)

F5. Words in Sch. 1 para. 2 inserted (23.7.2008) by The Freedom of Information (Parliament and National Assembly for Wales) Order 2008 (S.I. 2008/1967), art. 2. (2)

F6. Sch. 1 para. 2. (e) inserted (25.6.2013) by Justice and Security Act 2013 (c. 18), s. 20. (1), Sch. 2 para. 5. (3)(a); S.I. 2013/1482, art. 2 (with arts. 3, 4)

3. The House of Lords [F7, in respect of information other than—

(a) information relating to any residential address of a member of either House of Parliament,

(b) information relating to travel arrangements of a member of either House of Parliament, where the arrangements relate to travel that has not yet been undertaken or is regular in nature,

(c) information relating to the identity of any person who delivers or has delivered goods, or provides or has provided services, to a member of either House of Parliament at any residence of the member,

(d) information relating to expenditure by a member of either House of Parliament on security arrangements.

[F8. (e)information held by the Intelligence and Security Committee of Parliament.]

Paragraph (b) does not except information relating to the total amount of expenditure incurred on regular travel during any month.]

Amendments (Textual)

F7. Words in Sch. 1 para. 3 inserted (23.7.2008) by The Freedom of Information (Parliament and National Assembly for Wales) Order 2008 (S.I. 2008/1967), art. 2. (3)

F8. Sch. 1 para. 3. (e) inserted (25.6.2013) by Justice and Security Act 2013 (c. 18), s. 20. (1), Sch. 2 para. 5. (3)(b); S.I. 2013/1482, art. 2 (with arts. 3, 4)

4. The Northern Ireland Assembly.

5. The National Assembly for Wales[F9, in respect of information other than—

(a) information relating to any residential address of a member of the Assembly,

(b) information relating to travel arrangements of a member of the Assembly, where the arrangements relate to travel that has not yet been undertaken or is regular in nature,

(c) information relating to the identity of any person who delivers or has delivered goods, or provides or has provided services, to a member of the Assembly at any residence of the member,

(d) information relating to expenditure by a member of the Assembly on security arrangements.

Paragraph (b) does not except information relating to the total amount of expenditure incurred on regular travel during any month.]

Amendments (Textual)

F9. Words in Sch. 1 para. 5 inserted (23.7.2008) by The Freedom of Information (Parliament and National Assembly for Wales) Order 2008 (S.I. 2008/1967), art. 2. (4)

[F105. Athe Welsh Assembly Government.]

Amendments (Textual)

F10. Sch. 1 para. 5. A inserted by The Government of Wales Act 2006 (Consequential Modifications and Transitional Provisions) Order 2007 (S.I. 2007/1388), art. 3, Sch. 1 para. 87 (the amendment coming into force immediately after the end of "the initial period" (which ended with the day of the first appointment of a First Minister on 25.5.2007) in accordance with art. 1. (2)(3) of the amending S.I. and see ss. 46, 161. (5) of Government of Wales Act 2006 (c. 32))

6. The armed forces of the Crown, except—

(a) the special forces, and

(b) any unit or part of a unit which is for the time being required by the Secretary of State to assist the Government Communications Headquarters in the exercise of its functions.

Part II Local government

England and Wales

7. A local authority within the meaning of the M1. Local Government Act 1972, namely—

(a) in England, a county council, a London borough council, a district council or a parish council,

(b) in Wales, a county council, a county borough council or a community council.

Marginal Citations

M11972 c. 70.

8. The Greater London Authority.

9. The Common Council of the City of London, in respect of information held in its capacity as a local authority, police authority or port health authority.

10. The Sub-Treasurer of the Inner Temple or the Under-Treasurer of the Middle Temple, in respect of information held in his capacity as a local authority.

11. The Council of the Isles of Scilly.

12. A parish meeting constituted under section 13 of the M2. Local Government Act 1972.

Marginal Citations

M21972 c. 70.

13. Any charter trustees constituted under section 246 of the M3. Local Government Act 1972.

Marginal Citations

M31972 c. 70.

[F1114 A fire and rescue authority constituted by a scheme under section 2 of the Fire and Rescue Services Act 2004 or a scheme to which section 4 of that Act applies.]

Amendments (Textual)

F11. Sch. 1 para. 14 substituted (E.W.) (1.10.2004 for E. and 10.11.2004 for W.) by Fire and Rescue Services Act 2004 (c. 21), ss. 53. (1), 61, Sch. 1 para. 95; S.I. 2004/2304, art. 2. (2) (subject to art. 3); S.I. 2004/2917, art. 2

[F1214. AA fire and rescue authority created by an order under section 4. A of that Act.]

Amendments (Textual)

F12. Sch. 1 para. 14. A inserted (31.1.2017 for specified purposes, 3.4.2017 in so far as not already in force) by Policing and Crime Act 2017 (c. 3), s. 183. (1)(5)(e), Sch. 1 para. 81; S.I. 2017/399, reg. 2, Sch. para. 38

15. A waste disposal authority established by virtue of an order under section 10. (1) of the M4. Local Government Act 1985.

Marginal Citations

M41985 c. 51.

F1315. A. . . . .

Amendments (Textual)

F13. Sch. 1 para. 15. A omitted (26.5.2015) by virtue of Deregulation Act 2015 (c. 20), s. 115. (7), Sch. 13 para. 6. (31); S.I. 2015/994, art. 6. (g)

16. A port health authority constituted by an order under section 2 of the M5. Public Health (Control of Disease) Act 1984.

Marginal Citations

M51984 c. 22.

17. F14. . . . .

Amendments (Textual)

F14. Sch. 1 para. 17 repealed (24.11.2005) by Licensing Act 2003 (c. 17), ss. 199, 201. (2), Sch. 7 (with ss. 2. (3), 15. (2), 195); S.I. 2005/3056, arts. 1. (2), 2. (2)

18. An internal drainage board which is continued in being by virtue of section 1 of the M6. Land Drainage Act 1991.

Marginal Citations

M61991 c. 59.

19. A joint authority established under Part IV of the M7. Local Government Act 1985 [F15. (fire and rescue services and transport)].

Amendments (Textual)

F15. Words in Sch. 1 para. 19 substituted (1.4.2005) by Civil Contingencies Act 2004 (c. 36), ss. 32. (1), 34, Sch. 2 para. 10. (3)(d); S.I. 2005/772, art. 2. (b)

Marginal Citations

M71985 c. 51.

[F1619. AAn economic prosperity board established under section 88 of the Local Democracy, Economic Development and Construction Act 2009.

Amendments (Textual)

F16. Sch. 1 paras. 19. A, 19. B inserted (17.12.2009) by Local Democracy, Economic Development and Construction Act 2009 (c. 20), ss. 119, 149, Sch. 6 para. 94; S.I. 2009/3318, art. 2. (b)

19. BA combined authority established under section 103 of that Act.]

Amendments (Textual)

F16. Sch. 1 paras. 19. A, 19. B inserted (17.12.2009) by Local Democracy, Economic Development and Construction Act 2009 (c. 20), ss. 119, 149, Sch. 6 para. 94; S.I. 2009/3318, art. 2. (b)

[F1720. The London Fire Commissioner.]

Amendments (Textual)

F17. Sch. 1 para. 20 substituted (31.1.2017 for specified purposes) by Policing and Crime Act 2017 (c. 3), s. 183. (1)(5)(e), Sch. 2 para. 108

21. A joint fire authority established by virtue of an order under section 42. (2) of the M8. Local Government Act 1985 (reorganisation of functions).

Marginal Citations

M81985 c. 51.

22. A body corporate established pursuant to an order under section 67 of the M9. Local Government Act 1985 (transfer of functions to successors of residuary bodies, etc.).

Marginal Citations

M91985 c. 51.

23. A body corporate established pursuant to an order under [F18section 17 of the Local Government and Public Involvement in Health Act 2007] (residuary bodies).

Amendments (Textual)

F18. Words in Sch. 1 para. 23 substituted (1.11.2007 with application as mentioned in art. 1. (1) of the commencing S.I.) by Local Government and Public Involvement in Health Act 2007 (c. 28), ss. 22, 245, Sch. 1 para. 20; S.I. 2007/3136, art. 2 (subject to art. 3)

24. The Broads Authority established by section 1 of the M10. Norfolk and Suffolk Broads Act 1988.

Marginal Citations

M101988 c. 4.

25. A joint committee constituted in accordance with section 102. (1)(b) of the M11. Local Government Act 1972.

Marginal Citations

M111972 c. 70.

26. A joint board which is continued in being by virtue of section 263. (1) of the M12. Local Government Act 1972.

Marginal Citations

27. A joint authority established under section 21 of the M13. Local Government Act 1992.

[F1928. A Passenger Transport Executive for an integrated transport area for the purposes of Part 2 of the Transport Act 1968.]

Amendments (Textual)

F19. Sch. 1 para. 28 substituted (E.W.) (9.2.2009) by Local Transport Act 2008 (c. 26), ss. 77, 134, Sch. 4 para. 64. (2); S.I. 2009/107, art. 2. (1), Sch. 1 Pt. 1 (subject to transitional provisions in Sch. 1 Pt. II)

[F2028. AA sub-national transport body established under section 102. E of the Local Transport Act 2008.]

Amendments (Textual)

F20. Sch. 1 para. 28. A inserted (28.1.2016 for specified purposes, 28.3.2016 in so far as not already in force) by Cities and Local Government Devolution Act 2016 (c. 1), s. 25. (2), Sch. 5 para. 16

29. Transport for London.

30. The London Transport Users Committee.

31. A joint board the constituent members of which consist of any of the public authorities described in paragraphs 8, 9, 10, 12, 15, 16, 20 to 31, 57 and 58.

32. A National Park authority established by an order under section 63 of the M14. Environment Act 1995.

33. A joint planning board constituted for an area in Wales outside a National Park by an order under section 2. (1. B) of the M15. Town and Country Planning Act 1990.

[F2133. AA strategic planning panel established under section 60. D of the Planning and Compulsory Purchase Act 2004.]

Amendments (Textual)

F21. Sch. 1 para. 33. A inserted (E.W.) (6.9.2015 for specified purposes) by Planning (Wales) Act 2015 (anaw 4), s. 58. (2)(b)(4)(b), Sch. 1 para. 5

F2234. . . . .

Amendments (Textual)

F22. Sch. 1 para. 34 repealed (1.4.2005) by Courts Act 2003 (c. 39), ss. 109. (1)(3), 110. (1), Sch. 8 para. 392, Sch. 10; S.I. 2005/910, art. 3

F2335. . . . .

Amendments (Textual)

F23. Sch. 1 para. 35 repealed (31.3.2012) by Localism Act 2011 (c. 20), s. 240. (2), Sch. 25 Pt. 32; S.I. 2012/628, art. 4. (d)

F2435. A . . . .

Amendments (Textual)

F24. Sch. 1 para. 35. A repealed (1.4.2010 for W. and 1.4.2011 otherwise) by Marine and Coastal Access Act 2009 (c. 23), ss. 321, 324, Sch. 22 Pt. 4; S.I. 2010/630, art. 3. (b); S.I. 2011/556, art. 2. (2)(o)

[F2535. BAn inshore fisheries and conservation authority for a district established under section 149 of the Marine and Coastal Access Act 2009.]

Amendments (Textual)

F25. Sch. 1 para. 35. B inserted (1.10.2010) by Marine and Coastal Access Act 2009 (c. 23), ss. 184, 324, Sch. 14 para. 19; S.I. 2010/2195, art. 3. (2)(l)

[F2635. CAn urban development corporation established under section 135 of the Local Government, Planning and Land Act 1980.]

F26. Sch. 1 para. 35. C inserted (1.10.2010) by The Freedom of Information (Additional Public Authorities) Order 2010 (S.I. 2010/937), art. 2
[F2735. DA Mayoral development corporation established under section 198 of the Localism Act 2011.]
F27. Sch. 1 para. 35. D inserted (15.1.2012) by Localism Act 2011 (c. 20), s. 240. (1)(l), Sch. 22 para. 53
[F2835. EA Local Healthwatch organisation, in respect of information held in connection with—
(a) arrangements made under section 221. (1) of the Local Government and Public Involvement in Health Act 2007, or
(b) arrangements made in pursuance of arrangements made under section 221. (1) of that Act.]
F28. Sch. 1 para. 35. E inserted (1.4.2013) by Health and Social Care Act 2012 (c. 7), ss. 189. (4), 306. (4); S.I. 2013/160, art. 2. (2) (with arts. 7-9)

Northern Ireland

36. A district council within the meaning of the M16. Local Government Act (Northern Ireland) 1972.
Marginal Citations
M161972 c. 9. (N.I.).

Part III The National Health Service

Modifications etc. (not altering text)
C1. By Care Act 2014 (c. 23), s. 127. (1), Sch. 5 para. 34; S.I. 2014/3186, art. 2. (f), it is provided (E.W.) (1.4.2015) that at the appropriate place in Sch. 1 Pt. III the words "Health Education England." shall be inserted

England and Wales

F2936. A. . . . .
F29. Sch. 1 para. 36. A omitted (1.4.2013) by virtue of Health and Social Care Act 2012 (c. 7), s. 306. (4), Sch. 5 para. 99. (a); S.I. 2013/160, art. 2. (2) (with arts. 7-9)
37. F30. . . . .
F30. Sch. 1 para. 37 repealed (1.3.2007) by National Health Service (Consequential Provisions) Act 2006 (c. 43), ss. 2, 4-6, 8, Sch. 1 para. 211. (b), Sch. 4 (with Sch.2 Pt. 1, Sch. 3 Pt. 1)
[F3137. AThe National Health Service Commissioning Board.
F31. Sch. 1 paras. 37. A, 37. B inserted (1.10.2012) by Health and Social Care Act 2012 (c. 7), s. 306. (4), Sch. 5 para. 99. (b); S.I. 2012/1831, art. 2. (2)
37. BA clinical commissioning group established under section 14. D of the National Health Service Act 2006.]
F31. Sch. 1 paras. 37. A, 37. B inserted (1.10.2012) by Health and Social Care Act 2012 (c. 7), s. 306. (4), Sch. 5 para. 99. (b); S.I. 2012/1831, art. 2. (2)
38. A special health authority established under [F32section 28 of the National Health Service Act 2006 or section 22 of the National Health Service (Wales) Act 2006].

F32. Words in Sch. 1 para. 38 substituted (1.3.2007) by National Health Service (Consequential Provisions) Act 2006 (c. 43), ss. 2, 5, 8, Sch. 1 para. 211. (c) (with Sch. 3 Pt. 1)

F3339. . . . .

F33. Sch. 1 para. 39 omitted (1.4.2013) by virtue of Health and Social Care Act 2012 (c. 7), s. 306. (4), Sch. 5 para. 99. (c); S.I. 2013/160, art. 2. (2) (with arts. 7-9)

[F3439. AA Local Health Board established under [F35section 11 of the National Health Service (Wales) Act 2006].]

F34. Sch. 1 para. 39. A inserted (10.10.2002 for W. and 1.3.2007 for E.) by National Health Service Reform and Health Care Professions Act 2002 (c. 17), s. 6. (2), Sch. 5 para. 48; S.I. 2002/2532, art. 2; S.I. 2006/1407, art. 2, Sch. 1 Pt. 2 para. 12

F35. Words in Sch. 1 para. 39. A substituted (1.3.2007) by National Health Service (Consequential Provisions) Act 2006 (c. 43), ss. 2, 5, 8, Sch. 1 para. 211. (e) (with Sch. 3 Pt. 1)

40. A National Health Service trust established under [F36section 25 of the National Health Service Act 2006 or section 18 of the National Health Service (Wales) Act 2006].

F36. Words in Sch. 1 para. 40 substituted (1.3.2007) by National Health Service (Consequential Provisions) Act 2006 (c. 43), ss. 2, 5, 8, Sch. 1 para. 211. (f) (with Sch. 3 Pt. 1)

[F3740. A An NHS foundation trust.]

F37. Sch. 1 para. 40. A inserted (1.4.2004 for E.W.) by Health and Social Care (Community Health and Standards) Act 2003 (c. 43), ss. 34, 199, Sch. 4 para. 114, S.I. 2004/759, {art. 2}

41. A Community Health Council [F38established under section 182 of the National Health Service (Wales) Act 2006].

F38. Words in Sch. 1 para. 41 substituted (1.3.2007) by National Health Service (Consequential Provisions) Act 2006 (c. 43), ss. 2, 5, 8, Sch. 1 para. 211. (g) (with Sch. 3 Pt. 1)

[F3941. AF40 . . . .]

F39. Sch. 1 para. 41. A inserted (1.9.2003) by National Health Service Reform and Health Care Professions Act 2002 (c. 17), ss. 19. (7), 42. (3); S.I. 2003/2246, art. 2

F40. Sch. 1 para. 41. A repealed (1.4.2008) by Local Government and Public Involvement in Health Act 2007 (c. 28), ss. 241, 245, Sch. 18 Pt. 18; S.I. 2008/461, art. 2. (3), Sch.

42. F41. . . . .

F41. Sch. 1 para. 42 repealed (1.4.2006) by Health and Social Care (Community Health and Standards) Act 2003 (c. 43), ss. 196, 199, Sch. 14 Pt. 4, S.I. 2005/2925, arts. 1. (3)(4)(c), {11}

43. F42. . . . .

F42. Sch. 1 para. 43 repealed (1.4.2005 for E.W.) by Health and Social Care (Community Health and Standards) Act 2003 (c. 43), ss. 190, 196, 199, Sch. 13 para. 10, Sch. 14 Pt. 7; S.I. 2005/457, art. 2. (a)(b)

[F4343. AAny person providing primary medical services [F44, primary dental services or primary ophthalmic services]—

(a) in accordance with arrangements made under [F45section 92 or 107 of the National Health Service Act 2006, or section 50 or 64 of the National Health Service (Wales) Act 2006]; or

(b) under a contract under [F46section 84 or 100 of the National Health Service Act 2006 or section 42 or 57 of the National Health Service (Wales) Act 2006];

in respect of information relating to the provision of those services.]

F43. Sch. 1 para. 43. A inserted (17.1.2005 for E., 1.4.2006 for W. for certain purposes and

1.3.2007 otherwise) by Health and Social Care (Community Health and Standards) Act 2003 (c. 43), ss. 184, 199, Sch. 11 para. 68; S.I. 2005/38, art. 2. (c) (with art. 3); S.I. 2006/345, art. 6; S.I. 2006/1407, arts. 1. (1), 2, Sch. 1 Pt. 2 para. 13. (b)

F44. Words in Sch. 1 para. 43. A substituted (1.8.2008) by Health Act 2006 (c. 28), ss. 80. (1), 83, Sch. 8 para. 45. (2)(a); S.I. 2008/1972, art. 2. (b)

F45. Words in Sch. 1 para. 43. A(a) substituted (1.3.2007) by National Health Service (Consequential Provisions) Act 2006 (c. 43), ss. 2, 5, 8, Sch. 1 para. 211. (i) (with Sch. 3 Pt. 1)

F46. Words in Sch. 1 para. 43. A(b) substituted (1.3.2007) by National Health Service (Consequential Provisions) Act 2006 (c. 43), ss. 2, 5, 8, Sch. 1 para. 211. (j) (with Sch. 3 Pt. 1)

44. Any person providing [F47general medical services, general dental services,] general ophthalmic services or pharmaceutical services under [F48the National Health Service Act 2006 or the National Health Service (Wales) Act 2006], in respect of information relating to the provision of those services.

Amendments (Textual)

F47. Words in Sch. 1 para. 44 repealed (17.1.2005 for E., 1.4.2006 for W. for certain purposes and otherwise prosp.) by Health and Social Care (Community Health and Standards) Act 2003 (c. 43), ss. 196, 199, Sch. 14 Pt. 4; S.I. 2005/38, art. 2. (d)(i) (with art. 3); S.I. 2005/2925, arts. 1. (3), 11; S.I. 2006/345, art. 7

F48. Words in Sch. 1 para. 44 substituted (1.3.2007) by National Health Service (Consequential Provisions) Act 2006 (c. 43), ss. 2, 5, 8, Sch. 1 para. 211. (k) (with Sch. 3 Pt. 1)

45.

[F49 Any person providing personal medical services or personal dental services under arrangements made under section 28. C of the M17 National Health Service Act 1977, in respect of information relating to the provision of those services.]

Amendments (Textual)

F49. Sch. 1 para. 45 repealed (17.1.2005 for E. for certain purposes, 1.4.2006 for E. otherwise, 1.4.2006 for W. for certain purposes and otherwise prosp.) by Health and Social Care (Community Health and Standards) Act 2003 (c. 43), ss. 196, 199, Sch. 14 Pt. 4; SI 2005/38, {art. 2. (d)(ii)}; S.I. 2005/2925, arts. 1. (3), 11; SI 2006/345, {art. 7}

Marginal Citations

M171977 c. 49.

[F5045. AAny person providing local pharmaceutical services under—

(a) a pilot scheme established under [F51section 134 of the National Health Service Act 2006 or section 92 of the National Health Service (Wales) Act 2006]; or

(b) an LPS scheme established under [F52 Schedule 12 to the National Health Service Act 2006 or Schedule 7 to the National Health Service (Wales) Act 2006] ,

in respect of information relating to the provision of those services.]

Amendments (Textual)

F50. Sch. 1 para. 45. A inserted (1.7.2002 for W. and 1.1.2003 for E.) by 2001 c. 15, ss. 67, 70, Sch. 5 Pt. 1 para. 14 (with ss. 64. (9), 65. (4)); S.I. 2002/1475, art. 2. (1), Sch. Pt. 1; S.I. 2003/53, art. 2. (a)

F51. Words in Sch. 1 para. 45. A(a) substituted (1.3.2007) by National Health Service (Consequential Provisions) Act 2006 (c. 43), ss. 2, 5, 8, Sch. 1 para. 211. (l) (with Sch. 3 Pt. 1)

F52. Words in Sch. 1 para. 45. A(b) substituted (1.3.2007) by virtue of National Health Service (Consequential Provisions) Act 2006 (c. 43), ss. 2, 5, 8, Sch. 1 para. 211. (m) (with Sch. 3 Pt. 1)

[F5345. BF54 . . . .]

Amendments (Textual)

F53. Sch. 1 para. 45. B inserted (1.1.2003 for E. and otherwise prosp.) by National Health Service Reform and Health Care Professions Act 2002 (c. 17), s. 20. (11), Sch. 6 para. 19; S. I. 2002/3190, art. 2

F54. Sch. 1 para. 45. B repealed (30.6.2008) by Local Government and Public Involvement in Health Act 2007 (c. 28), ss. 241, 245, Sch. 18 Pt. 18; S.I. 2008/461, art. 2. (4)(b)(c)

Northern Ireland

46.

[F55. A Health and Social Services Board established under Article 16 of the M18. Health and Personal Social Services (Northern Ireland) Order 1972.]

Amendments (Textual)

F55. Sch. 1 para. 46 repealed (N.I.) (1.4.2009) by Health and Social Care (Reform) Act (Northern Ireland) 2009 (c. 1), ss. 32, 33, 34, Sch. 6 para. 17. (2)(a), Sch. 7; S.R. 2009/114, art. 2

Marginal Citations

M18. S.I. 1972/1265 (N.I. 14).

47. A Health and Social Services Council established under Article 4 of the M19. Health and Personal Social Services (Northern Ireland) Order 1991.

Marginal Citations

M19. S.I. 1991/194 (N.I. 1).

48. A Health and Social Services Trust established under Article 10 of the M20. Health and Personal Social Services (Northern Ireland) Order 1991.

Marginal Citations

M20. S.I. 1991/194 (N.I. 1).

49. A special agency established under Article 3 of the M21. Health and Personal Social Services (Special Agencies) (Northern Ireland) Order 1990.

Marginal Citations

M21. S.I. 1990/247 (N.I. 3).

50.

[F56. The Northern Ireland Central Services Agency for the Health and Social Services established under Article 26 of the M22. Health and Personal Social Services (Northern Ireland) Order 1972.]

Amendments (Textual)

F56. Sch. 1 para. 50 repealed (N.I.) (1.4.2009) by Health and Social Care (Reform) Act (Northern Ireland) 2009 (c. 1), ss. 32, 33, 34, Sch. 6 para. 17. (2)(a), Sch. 7; S.R. 2009/114, art. 2

Marginal Citations

M22. S.I. 1972/1265 (N.I. 14).

51. Any person providing [F57primary medical services], general dental services, general ophthalmic services or pharmaceutical services under Part VI of the M23. Health and Personal Social Services (Northern Ireland) Order 1972, in respect of information relating to the provision of those services.

Amendments (Textual)

F57. Words in Sch. 1 para. 51 substituted (N.I.) (1.4.2004) by The Primary Medical Services (Northern Ireland) Order 2004 (S.I. 2004/311 (N.I. 2)), art. 10, Sch. 1 para. 18; S.R. 2004/123, art. 2. (2)

Marginal Citations

M23. S.I. 1972/1265 (N.I. 14).

[F5851. AThe Regional Business Services Organisation established under section 14 of the Health and Social Services (Reform) Act (Northern Ireland) 2009.

Amendments (Textual)

F58. Sch. 1 paras. 51. A-51. D inserted (N.I.) (1.4.2009) by Health and Social Care (Reform) Act (Northern Ireland) 2009 (c. 1), ss. 32, 34, Sch. 6 para. 17. (2)(b); S.R. 2009/114, art. 2

51. BThe Patient and Client Council established under section 16 of the Health and Social Care (Reform) Act (Northern Ireland) 2009.

Amendments (Textual)

F58. Sch. 1 paras. 51. A-51. D inserted (N.I.) (1.4.2009) by Health and Social Care (Reform) Act (Northern Ireland) 2009 (c. 1), ss. 32, 34, Sch. 6 para. 17. (2)(b); S.R. 2009/114, art. 2

51. CThe Regional Health and Social Care Board established under section 7 of the Health and

Social Care (Reform) Act (Northern Ireland) 2009.
Amendments (Textual)
F58. Sch. 1 paras. 51. A-51. D inserted (N.I.) (1.4.2009) by Health and Social Care (Reform) Act (Northern Ireland) 2009 (c. 1), ss. 32, 34, Sch. 6 para. 17. (2)(b); S.R. 2009/114, art. 2
51. DThe Regional Agency for Public Health and Social Well-being established under section 12 of the Health and Social Care (Reform) Act (Northern Ireland) 2009.]
Amendments (Textual)
F58. Sch. 1 paras. 51. A-51. D inserted (N.I.) (1.4.2009) by Health and Social Care (Reform) Act (Northern Ireland) 2009 (c. 1), ss. 32, 34, Sch. 6 para. 17. (2)(b); S.R. 2009/114, art. 2

Part IV Maintained schools and other educational institutions

England and Wales

[F5952. The governing body of—
(a) a maintained school, as defined by section 20. (7) of the School Standards and Framework Act 1998, or
(b) a maintained nursery school, as defined by section 22. (9) of that Act.]
Amendments (Textual)
F59. Sch. 1 para. 52 substituted (1.9.2003 except in relation to W. and otherwise 31.10.2005) by Education Act 2002 (c. 32), ss. 215. (1), 216, Sch. 21 para. 127 (with ss. 210. (8), 214. (4)); S.I. 2003/1667, art. 4; S.I. 2005/2910, art. 4, Sch.
[F6052. A(1)The proprietor of an Academy, in respect of information held for the purposes of the proprietor's functions under Academy arrangements.
(2) In sub-paragraph (1)—
"Academy arrangements" has the meaning given by section 1 of the Academies Act 2010;
"proprietor" has the meaning given by section 579. (1) of the Education Act 1996.]
Amendments (Textual)
F60. Sch. 1 para. 52. A inserted (1.9.2010 for certain purposes and 1.1.2011 otherwise) by Academies Act 2010 (c. 32), ss. 14, 19. (2), Sch. 2 para. 10; S.I. 2010/1937, arts. 3, 4, Schs. 2, 3 (with transitional provisions in arts. 5, 6)
53. (1)The governing body of—
(a) an institution within the further education sector,
(b) a university receiving financial support under section 65 of the M24. Further and Higher Education Act 1992,
(c) an institution conducted by a higher education corporation,
(d) a designated institution for the purposes of Part II of the M25. Further and Higher Education Act 1992 as defined by section 72. (3) of that Act, or
(e) any college, school, hall or other institution of a university which falls within paragraph (b).
(2) In sub-paragraph (1)—
(a) "governing body" is to be interpreted in accordance with subsection (1) of section 90 of the Further and Higher Education Act 1992 but without regard to subsection (2) of that section,
(b) in paragraph (a), the reference to an institution within the further education sector is to be construed in accordance with section 91. (3) of the Further and Higher Education Act 1992,
(c) in paragraph (c), "higher education corporation" has the meaning given by section 90. (1) of that Act, and
(d) in paragraph (e) "college" includes any institution in the nature of a college.
Marginal Citations
M241992 c. 13.
M251992 c. 13.

Northern Ireland

54. (1)The managers of—

(a) a controlled school, voluntary school or grant-maintained integrated school within the meaning of Article 2. (2) of the M26. Education and Libraries (Northern Ireland) Order 1986, or

(b) a pupil referral unit as defined by Article 87. (1) of the M27. Education (Northern Ireland) Order 1998.

(2) In sub-paragraph (1) "managers" has the meaning given by Article 2. (2) of the M28. Education and Libraries (Northern Ireland) Order 1986.

Marginal Citations

M26. S.I. 1986/594 (N.I. 3).

M27. S.I. 1998/1759 (N.I. 13).

M28. S.I. 1986/594 (N.I. 3).

55. (1)The governing body of—

(a) a university receiving financial support under Article 30 of the M29. Education and Libraries (Northern Ireland) Order 1993,

(b) a college of education F61. . . or in respect of which grants are paid under Article 66. (2) or (3) of the M30. Education and Libraries (Northern Ireland) Order 1986, or

(c) an institution of further education within the meaning of the M31. Further Education (Northern Ireland) Order 1997.

(2) In sub-paragraph (1) "governing body" has the meaning given by Article 30. (3) of the M32. Education and Libraries (Northern Ireland) Order 1993.

Amendments (Textual)

F61. Words in Sch. 1 para. 55. (1)(b) repealed (N.I.) (1.10.2005 or such later date as the Department may by order appoint) by The Colleges of Education (Northern Ireland) Order 2005 (S.I. 2005/1963 (N.I. 13)), arts. 1. (3), 2. (2), 14, Sch. 3 para. 4, Sch. 4

Marginal Citations

M29. S.I. 1993/2810 (N.I. 12).

M30. S.I. 1986/594 (N.I. 3).

M31. S.I. 1997/1772 (N.I. 15).

M32. S.I. 1993/2810 (N.I. 12).

56. Any person providing further education to whom grants, loans or other payments are made under Article 5. (1)(b) of the M33. Further Education (Northern Ireland) Order 1997.

Marginal Citations

M33. S.I. 1997/1772 (N.I. 15).

Part V Police

Modifications etc. (not altering text)

C2. Sch. 1 Pt. V modified (31.1.2017 for specified purposes, 3.4.2017 in so far as not already in force) by Policing and Crime Act 2017 (c. 3), ss. 50, 183. (1)(5)(e); S.I. 2017/399, reg. 2, Sch. para. 10

England and Wales

[F6257 A police and crime commissioner.]

Amendments (Textual)

F62. Sch. 1 para. 57 substituted (16.1.2012) by Police Reform and Social Responsibility Act 2011 (c. 13), s. 157. (1), Sch. 16 para. 249; S.I. 2011/3019, art. 3, Sch. 1 (with Sch. 2 para. 61)

Modifications etc. (not altering text)

C3. Sch. 1 para. 57 excluded (8.5.2017) by The Greater Manchester Combined Authority

(Transfer of Police and Crime Commissioner Functions to the Mayor) Order 2017 (S.I. 2017/470), art. 1. (2), Sch. 2 para. 18

[F6358. The Mayor's Office for Policing and Crime.]

Amendments (Textual)

F63. Sch. 1 para. 58 substituted (16.1.2012) by Police Reform and Social Responsibility Act 2011 (c. 13), s. 157. (1), Sch. 16 para. 249; S.I. 2011/3019, art. 3, Sch. 1 (with Sch. 2 para. 61)

59. A chief officer of police of a police force in England or Wales.

Northern Ireland

60. The [F64. Northern Ireland Policing Board].

Amendments (Textual)

F64. Words in entry in Sch. 1 Pt. V para. 60 substituted (4.11.2001) by virtue of 2000 c. 32, s. 74, Sch. 6 para. 25. (2)(a); S.R. 2001/396, art. 2, Sch.

61. The Chief Constable of the [F65. Police Service of Northern Ireland].

Amendments (Textual)

F65. Words in entry in Sch. 1 Pt. V para. 61 substituted (4.11.2001) by 2000 c. 32, s. 74, Sch. 6 para. 25. (2)(b); S.R. 2001/396, art. 2, Sch.

Miscellaneous

62. The British Transport Police.

63. The Ministry of Defence Police established by section 1 of the M34. Ministry of Defence Police Act 1987.

Marginal Citations

M341987 c. 4.

[F6663. AThe Civil Nuclear Police Authority.

Amendments (Textual)

F66. Sch. 1 paras. 63. A, 63. B inserted (E.W.S.) (1.3.2005) by Energy Act 2004 (c. 20), ss. 51. (2), 198. (2), Sch. 10 para. 18; S.I. 2005/442, art. 2. (1), Sch. 1

63. BThe chief constable of the Civil Nuclear Constabulary.]

Amendments (Textual)

F66. Sch. 1 paras. 63. A, 63. B inserted (E.W.S.) (1.3.2005) by Energy Act 2004 (c. 20), ss. 51. (2), 198. (2), Sch. 10 para. 18; S.I. 2005/442, art. 2. (1), Sch. 1

64. Any person who—

(a) by virtue of any enactment has the function of nominating individuals who may be appointed as special constables by justices of the peace, and

(b) is not a public authority by virtue of any other provision of this Act,

in respect of information relating to the exercise by any person appointed on his nomination of the functions of a special constable.

Part VI Other public bodies and offices: general

Modifications etc. (not altering text)

C4. Sch. 1 Pt. VI modified (temp.) (1.4.2015) by The Local Audit and Accountability Act 2014 (Commencement No. 7, Transitional Provisions and Savings) Order 2015 (S.I. 2015/841), Sch. para. 8

[F67. The Adjudication Panel for Wales.]

F68...

[F69. The adjudicators appointed under section 25 of the School Standards and Framework Act 1998.]

The Administration of Radioactive Substances Advisory Committee.

F70...

F71...

F72...

The Advisory Board on Restricted Patients.

The Advisory Board on the Registration of Homoeopathic Products.

F73...

[F74. The Advisory Committee on Clinical Excellence Awards.]

The Advisory Committee for Disabled People in Employment and Training.

The Advisory Committee for the Public Lending Right.

F72...

F68...

The Advisory Committee on Animal Feedingstuffs.

The Advisory Committee on Borderline Substances.

The Advisory Committee on Business and the Environment.

The Advisory Committee on Business Appointments.

The Advisory Committee on Conscientious Objectors.

F68...

The Advisory Committee on Dangerous Pathogens.

F75...

F76...

The Advisory Committee on the Government Art Collection

F77...

The Advisory Committee on Historic Wreck Sites.

An Advisory Committee on Justices of the Peace in England and Wales.

The Advisory Committee on the Microbiological Safety of Food.

F72...

The Advisory Committee on Novel Foods and Processes.

[F78. The Advisory Committee on Organic Standards.]

The Advisory Committee on Overseas Economic and Social Research.

The Advisory Committee on Packaging.

F79...

The Advisory Committee on Releases to the Environment.

[F80. The Advisory Committee on Statute Law.]

[F81. The Advisory Committee on Telecommunications for the Disabled and Elderly.]

F82...

The Advisory Council on the Misuse of Drugs.

The Advisory Council on Public Records.

The Advisory Group on Hepatitis.

[F83. The Advisory Council on Historical Manuscripts.]

[F84. The Advisory Council on National Records and Archives.]

[F85. The Advisory Group on Medical Countermeasures.]

[F86. The Advisory Panel on Beacon Councils.]

[F87. The Advisory Panel on Public Sector Information.]

The Advisory Panel on Standards for the Planning Inspectorate.

The Aerospace Committee.

An Agricultural Dwelling House Advisory Committee.

F88...

An Agricultural Wages Committee.

The Agriculture and Environment Biotechnology Commission.

[F89. The Agriculture and Horticulture Development Board.]
The Airborne Particles Expert Group.
[F90. The Air Quality Expert Group.]
F91...
[F92. The All-Wales Medicines Strategy Group.]
F93...
The Animal Procedures Committee.
The Animal Welfare Advisory Committee.
F72...
F94...
[F95. The Architects Registration Board.]
The Armed Forces Pay Review Body.
[F96. The Arts and Humanities Research Council.]
The Arts Council of England.
The Arts Council of Wales.
[F97. An assessor appointed for the purposes of section 133 of the Criminal Justice Act 1988 in its application to England and Wales.]
The Audit Commission for Local Authorities and the National Health Service in England and Wales.
The Auditor General for Wales.
F98...
The Bank of England [F99. (including the Bank in its capacity as the Prudential Regulation Authority)], in respect of information held for purposes other than those of its functions with respect to—
    - (a) monetary policy,
    - (b) financial operations intended to support financial institutions for the purposes of maintaining stability, and
    - (c) the provision of private banking services and related services.
The Better Regulation Task Force.
[F100. The Big Lottery Fund]
The Biotechnology and Biological Sciences Research Council.
[F101. The Board of the Pension Protection Fund.]
F102...
The Britain-Russia Centre and East-West Centre.
The British Association for Central and Eastern Europe.
The British Broadcasting Corporation, in respect of information held for purposes other than those of journalism, art or literature.
The British Coal Corporation.
The British Council.
The British Educational Communications and Technology Agency.
The British Hallmarking Council.
The British Library.
The British Museum.
The British Pharmacopoeia Commission.
F103...
F104...
The British Tourist Authority.
[F105. The British Transport Police Authority.]
F106...
The British Wool Marketing Board.
The Broadcasting Standards Commission.
F107...
[F108. The Building Regulations Advisory Committee for England.]

[F109. The Building Regulations Advisory Committee for Wales.]

F110...

[F111. Canal & River Trust, in respect of information held by it relating to functions exercisable by it by virtue of the British Waterways Board (Transfer of Functions) Order 2012 (S.I. 2012/1659).]

[F112. The Care Council for Wales.]

[F113. The Care Quality Commission.]

The Central Advisory Committee on War Pensions.

F114...

F115...

The Central Rail Users' Consultative Committee.

[F116. The Certification Officer.]

The Channel Four Television Corporation, in respect of information held for purposes other than those of journalism, art or literature.

F117...

[F118. The chief inspector of constabulary appointed under section 54. (1) of the Police Act 1996.]

[F119. The Chief Inspector of the UK Border Agency.]

F120...

F121...

The Children and Family Court Advisory and Support Service.

[F122. The Children's Commissioner.]

[F123. The Children's Commissioner for Wales.]

The Civil Aviation Authority.

The Civil Justice Council.

The Civil Procedure Rule Committee.

The Civil Service Appeal Board.

[F124. The Civil Service Commission]

The Coal Authority.

[F125. The College of Policing.]

[F126. Comisiynydd y Gymraeg (The Welsh Language Commissioner).]

The Commission for Architecture and the Built Environment.

[F127. The Commission for Equality and Human Rights.]

F128...

F129...

[F130. The Commission on Human Medicines.]

[F131. The Commission for Integrated Transport.]

The Commission for Local Administration in England.

F132...

F133...

F134...

F135...

F129...

F110...

[F136. The Commissioner for Older People in Wales]

The Commissioner for Public Appointments.

[F137. The Commissioner for Victims and Witnesses.]

[F138. The Commissioners of Northern Lighthouses.]

F139...

F140...

F141...

The Committee on Carcinogenicity of Chemicals in Food, Consumer Products and the Environment.

F68...

[F142. The Committee on Climate Change.]

F143...

The Committee on Medical Aspects of Radiation in the Environment.

The Committee on Mutagenicity of Chemicals in Food, Consumer Products and the Environment.

[F144. The Committee on Radioactive Waste Management.]

[F145. The Committee on Safety of Devices.]

The Committee on Standards in Public Life.

The Committee on Toxicity of Chemicals in Food, Consumer Products and the Environment.

The Committee on the Medical Effects of Air Pollutants.

F146...

The Commonwealth Scholarship Commission in the United Kingdom.

[F147. Communications for Business.]

The Community Development Foundation.

F148...

[F149. The Competition Service.]

[F150. Compliance Officer for the Independent Parliamentary Standards Authority.]

[F151. The Comptroller and Auditor General.]

[F152. A conservation board established under section 86 of the Countryside and Rights of Way Act 2000.]

The Construction Industry Training Board.

Consumer Communications for England.

[F153. The Consumer Council for Postal Services.]

[F154. The Consumer Council for Water]

F72...

[F155. The Consumer Panel established under section 16 of the Communications Act 2003.]

F140...

F156...

F157...

F158...

The Council for Science and Technology.

F159...

F140...

F160...

F161...

The Covent Garden Market Authority.

The Criminal Cases Review Commission.

F162...

[F163. The Criminal Injuries Compensation Authority.]

The Criminal Justice Consultative Council.

[F164. The Criminal Procedure Rule Committee.]

F165...

The Dartmoor Steering Group and Working Party.

The Darwin Advisory Committee.

The Defence Nuclear Safety Committee.

The Defence Scientific Advisory Council.

The Design Council.

F72...

The Diplomatic Service Appeal Board.

[F166. The Director of Fair Access to Higher Education.]

[F167. The Director General of the Independent Office for Police Conduct.]

[F168. Director of Labour Market Enforcement]

[F169. The Disability Employment Advisory Committee.]

F170...

F134...

The Disabled Persons Transport Advisory Committee.

[F171. The Disclosure and Barring Service.]

[F172. The Distributed Generation Co-Ordinating Group.]

[F173. The East of England Industrial Development Board.]

The Economic and Social Research Council.

F72...

[F174. The Electoral Commission.]

F72...

The Engineering Construction Industry Training Board.

The Engineering and Physical Sciences Research Council.

F175...

F140...

The English Sports Council.

The English Tourist Board.

The Environment Agency.

F176...

[F177. Equality 2025.]

[F178. The Ethnic Minority Business Forum.]

The Expert Advisory Group on AIDS.

F179...

An Expert Panel on Air Quality Standards.

The Export Guarantees Advisory Council.

[F180. The Family Justice Council.]

[F181. The Family Procedure Rule Committee.]

The Family Proceedings Rules Committee.

The Farm Animal Welfare Council.

[F182. The Film Industry Training Board for England and Wales.]

[F183. The Financial Conduct Authority.]

[F184. The Financial Reporting Advisory Board.]

F185...

The Fire Services Examination Board.

The Firearms Consultative Committee.

F186...

F187...

F188...

The Fuel Cell Advisory Panel.

[F189. The Fuel Poverty Advisory Group.]

F72...

[F190. The Gaelic Media Service, in respect of information held for purposes other than those of journalism, art or literature.]

[F191. Gambling Commission]

[F192. Gangmasters and Labour Abuse Authority]

[F193. The Gas and Electricity Consumer Council.]

F72...

The Gene Therapy Advisory Committee.

The General Chiropractic Council.

The General Dental Council.

The General Medical Council.

[F194. The General Optical Council.]

The General Osteopathic Council.

[F195. The General Pharmaceutical Council.]

F196...

F197...

[F198. The General Teaching Council for Wales.]

F199...

The Government Hospitality Advisory Committee for the Purchase of Wine.

The Government Chemist.

[F200. The Government-Industry Forum on Non-Food Use of Crops.]

The Great Britain-China Centre.

[F201. Groceries Code Adjudicator.]

F202...

The Health and Safety Executive.

[F203. The Health and Care Professions Council]

[F204. The Health and Social Care Information Centre.]

F205...

[F206. The Health Research Authority.]

The Health Service Commissioner for England.

F132...

F207...

[F208. Her Majesty's Chief Inspector of Education and Training in Wales or Prif Arolygydd Ei Mawrhydi dros Addysg a Hyfforddiant yng Nghymru].

[F209. Her Majesty's Chief Inspector of Prisons.]

[F210. Her Majesty's Commissioners for Judicial Appointments.]

[F211. Her Majesty's Inspectorate of Probation for England and Wales.]

[F212. The Herbal Medicines Advisory Committee.]

The Higher Education Funding Council for England.

The Higher Education Funding Council for Wales.

F73...

F73...

F213...

The Historic Buildings and Monuments Commission for England.

The Historic Royal Palaces Trust.

F103...

[F214. The Homes and Communities Agency.]

F72...

The Horserace Betting Levy Board.

The Horserace Totalisator Board.

F103...

Horticulture Research International.

The House of Lords Appointments Commission.

Any housing action trust established under Part III of the M35. Housing Act 1988.

F215...

The Human Fertilisation and Embryology Authority.

The Human Genetics Commission.

[F216. The Human Tissue Authority.]

The Immigration Services Commissioner.

The Imperial War Museum.

[F217. The Independent Advisory Committee on Development Impact.]

[F218. The Independent Advisory Group on Teenage Pregnancy.]

[F219. The Independent Anti-slavery Commissioner]

The Independent Board of Visitors for Military Corrective Training Centres.

The Independent Case Examiner for the Child Support Agency.

[F220. The Independent Groundwater Complaints Administrator.]

The Independent Living Funds.

[F221. Any Independent Monitoring Board established under section 6. (2) of the Prison Act 1952.]

[F167. The Independent Office for Police Conduct.]

[F222. The Independent Parliamentary Standards Authority.]

F223...

F224...

[F225. The Independent Remuneration Panel for Wales.]

[F226. The Independent Review Panel for Advertising.]

[F227. The Independent Review Panel for Borderline Products.]

F228...

[F229. The Independent Scientific Group on Cattle Tuberculosis.]

The Independent Television Commission.

F72...

The Industrial Development Advisory Board.

The Industrial Injuries Advisory Council.

The Information Commissioner.

F230...

F231...

The Insolvency Rules Committee.

[F232. The Institute for Apprenticeships.]

[F233. The Insurance Brokers Registration Council.]

[F234. The Integrated Administration and Controls System Appeals Panel.]

[F235. The Intellectual Property Advisory Committee.]

Investors in People UK.

The Joint Committee on Vaccination and Immunisation.

The Joint Nature Conservation Committee.

The Joint Prison/Probation Accreditation Panel.

[F236. The Judicial Appointments and Conduct Ombudsman.]

[F237. The Judicial Appointments Commission.]

The Judicial Studies Board.

F238...

The Land Registration Rule Committee.

The Law Commission.

F239...

[F240. The Legal Deposit Advisory Panel]

[F241. The Legal Services Board.]

F242...

F243...

F244...

F245...

F246...

F247...

[F248. The Local Government Boundary Commission for England.]

The Local Government Boundary Commission for Wales.

F249...

A local probation board established under section 4 of the Criminal Justice and Court Services Act 2000.

[F250. The London and South East Industrial Development Board.]

The London Pensions Fund Authority.

The Low Pay Commission.

F251...

[F252. The Marine Management Organisation.]

The Marshall Aid Commemoration Commission.

The Measurement Advisory Committee.

F103...

F72...

The Medical Research Council.

F72...

F253...

[F254. The Migration Advisory Committee.]

F103...

F255...

[F256. Monitor.]

The Museum of London.

The National Army Museum.

[F257. The National Assembly for Wales Remuneration Board.]

[F258. The National Association of Citizens Advice [F259. Bureaux—

 (a)] in respect of information relating to the function exercisable by virtue of article 2 of the Public Bodies (The Office of Fair Trading Transfer of Consumer Advice Scheme Function and Modification of Enforcement Functions) Order 2013 S.I. 2013/783 .]

[F260 (b) in respect of information relating to the functions transferred to it by Article 3. (1)(a), (b) or (c) of the Public Bodies (Abolition of the National Consumer Council and Transfer of the Office of Fair Trading's Functions in relation to Estate Agents etc) Order 2014 (S.I. 2014/631).]

F261. The National Audit Office.

F262...

F263...

F264...

[F265. The National Consumer Council.]

F266...

F267...

[F268. The National DNA Database Ethics Group.]

The National Employers' Liaison Committee.

[F269. The National Employment Panel.]

[F270. The National Employment Savings Trust Corporation.]

F271...

F110...

[F272. The National Forest Company.]

The National Gallery.

The National Heritage Memorial Fund.

F273...

F274...

[F275. The National Institute for Health and Care Excellence.]

The National Library of Wales.

F255...

F276...

The National Maritime Museum.

The National Museum of Science and Industry.

The National Museums and Galleries of Wales.

The National Museums and Galleries on Merseyside.

[F277. The National Non-Food Crops Centre.]

F278...

The National Portrait Gallery.

F279...

[F280. Natural England.]

The Natural Environment Research Council.

The Natural History Museum.

[F281. The Natural Resources Body for Wales.]
The New Deal Task Force.
F282...
F283 [The NHS Pay Review Body.]
[F284. The North East Industrial Development Board.]
[F285. The Northern Ireland Judicial Appointments Ombudsman.]
[F286. The North West Industrial Development Board.]
[F287. The Nuclear Decommissioning Authority.]
[F288. The Nuclear Research Advisory Council.]
[F289. The Nursing and Midwifery Council.]
F290...
[F291. The Office for Budget Responsibility.]
[F292. The Office of Communications.]
F293...
F294...
[F295. The Office for Legal Complaints.]
[F296. The Office of Manpower Economics.]
[F297. The Office for Nuclear Regulation.]
[F298. The Office of the Renewable Fuels Agency.]
[F299. The Office for Students.]
[F300. The Office of Tax Simplification.]
F301...
The Oil and Pipelines Agency.
F302...
[F303. The Olympic Lottery Distributor]
[F304. The Olympic Park Legacy Company.]
[F305. The Ombudsman for the Board of the Pension Protection Fund.]
The OSO Board.
F306...
The Panel on Standards for the Planning Inspectorate.
The Parliamentary Boundary Commission for England.
The Parliamentary Boundary Commission for Scotland.
The Parliamentary Boundary Commission for Wales.
The Parliamentary Commissioner for Administration.
The Parole Board.
F307...
F308...
[F309. The Passengers' Council.]
[F310. The Payment Systems Regulator established under section 40 of the Financial Services (Banking Reform) Act 2013.]
F311...
The Pensions Ombudsman.
[F312. The Pensions Regulator.]
F313...
[F314. The Pesticide Residues Committee.]
[F315. The Pesticides Forum.]
F110...
F72...
F316...
[F317. The Police Advisory Board for England and Wales.]
F318...
F319...
[F320. The Police Negotiating Board.]

[F321. The Police Remuneration Review Body.]
The Political Honours Scrutiny Committee.
F322...
F72...
F72...
F323...
[F324. The Prison Service Pay Review Body.]
[F325. The Prisons and Probation Ombudsman for England and Wales.]
[F326. A probation trust.]
[F327. The Professional Standards Authority for Health and Social Care]
F73...
F328...
[F329. The Public Private Partnership Agreement Arbiter.]
[F330. The Public Services Ombudsman for Wales]
[F331. Pubs Code Adjudicator.]
F332...
F333...
[F334. Qualifications Wales.]
The Race Education and Employment Forum.
The Race Relations Forum.
The Radio Authority.
The Radioactive Waste Management Advisory Committee.
F335...
F336...
A Regional Cultural Consortium.
F337... F338....
[F339. Any Regional Flood and Coastal Committee.]
[F340. The Registrar of Consultant Lobbyists]
[F341. The Registrar General for England and Wales.]
F290...
F342...
[F343. The Regulator of Community Interest Companies.]
 Remploy Ltd.
The Renewable Energy Advisory Committee.
F344...
Resource: The Council for Museums, Archives and Libraries.
F345...
F346...
The Review Body on Doctors and Dentists Remuneration.
 The Reviewing Committee on the Export of Works of Art.
The Royal Air Force Museum.
The Royal Armouries.
The Royal Botanic Gardens, Kew.
[F347. The Royal College of Veterinary Surgeons, in respect of information held by it otherwise than as a tribunal.]
The Royal Commission on Ancient and Historical Monuments of Wales.
The Royal Commission on Environmental Pollution.
The Royal Commission on Historical Manuscripts.
[F348. The Royal Hospital at Chelsea.]
F73...
The Royal Mint Advisory Committee on the Design of Coins, Medals, Seals and Decorations.
F349...
The School Teachers' Review Body.

[F350. The Science Advisory Council.]
[F351. The Science and Technology Facilities Council.]
[F352. The Scientific Advisory Committee on Nutrition.]
The Scientific Committee on Tobacco and Health.
F353...
F354...
F355...
The Sea Fish Industry Authority.
[F356. The Security Industry Authority]
The Senior Salaries Review Body.
[F357. The Sentencing Council for England and Wales.]
F358...
F358...
F359...
Sianel Pedwar Cymru, in respect of information held for purposes other than those of journalism, art or literature.
[F360. The Single Source Regulations Office.]
Sir John Soane's Museum.
F73...
[F361. Small Business Commissioner.]
[F362. The Small Business Council.]
[F363. The Small Business Investment Task Force.]
[F364. The Social Care Institute for Excellence.]
F365...
[F366. The Social Mobility and Child Poverty Commission]
The Social Security Advisory Committee.
F367...
[F368. The South West Industrial Development Board.]
F369...
The Spongiform Encephalopathy Advisory Committee.
The Sports Council for Wales.
[F370. The Sports Grounds Safety Authority.]
F371...
The Standing Advisory Committee on Industrial Property.
The Standing Advisory Committee on Trunk Road Assessment.
The Standing Dental Advisory Committee.
F110...
F110...
F110...
[F372. The Statistics Commission.]
The Steering Committee on Pharmacy Postgraduate Education.
[F373. The Strategic Investment Board.]
F374...
 The subsidence adviser appointed under section 46 of the M36 Coal Industry Act 1994.
The Substance Misuse Advisory Panel.
The Sustainable Development Commission.
F72...
[F375. The Sustainable Energy Policy Advisory Board.]
The Tate Gallery.
[F376. The TB Advisory Group]
F377...
[F378. The Technical Advisory Board.]
[F379. The Technology Strategy Board.]

The Theatres Trust.

[F380. A traffic commissioner, in respect of information held by the commissioner otherwise than as a tribunal]

F381...

The Treasure Valuation Committee.

[F382. The Tribunal Procedure Committee.]

[F383. The trustee corporation established by section 75 of the Pensions Act 2008.]

 The UK Advisory Panel for Health Care Workers Infected with Bloodborne Viruses.

[F384. The UK Chemicals Stakeholder Forum.]

[F385. The UK Commission for Employment and Skills]

 The UK Sports Council.

The United Kingdom Atomic Energy Authority.

F386...

F73...

F387...

[F388. The University for Industry.]

The Unlinked Anonymous Serosurveys Steering Group.

The Unrelated Live Transplant Regulatory Authority.

F133...

[F389. The Valuation Tribunal Service.]

[F390. The verderers of the New Forest, in respect of information held by them otherwise than as a tribunal.]

The Veterinary Products Committee.

[F391. The Veterinary Residues Committee.]

The Victoria and Albert Museum.

[F392. The Wales Audit Office.]

[F393. The Wales Centre for Health.]

F72...

F394...

The Wallace Collection.

The War Pensions Committees.

F395...

F396...

F397...

The Welsh Committee for Professional Development of Pharmacy.

F398...

The Welsh Dental Committee.

F399...

The Welsh Industrial Development Advisory Board.

F400...

The Welsh Medical Committee.

F401...

The Welsh Nursing and Midwifery Committee.

The Welsh Optometric Committee.

The Welsh Pharmaceutical Committee.

The Welsh Scientific Advisory Committee.

The Westminster Foundation for Democracy.

[F402. The West Midlands Industrial Development Board.]

The Wilton Park Academic Council.

F403...

The Women's National Commission.

[F404. The Yorkshire and the Humber and the East Midlands Industrial Development Board.]

F405...

The Youth Justice Board for England and Wales.

The Zoos Forum.

Amendments (Textual)

F67. Sch. 1 Pt. VI: entry added (11.11.2002) by The Freedom of Information (Additional Public Authorities) Order 2002 (S.I. 2002/2623), art. 2, Sch. 1

F68. Sch. 1 Pt. VI: entry omitted (1.10.2010) by virtue of The Freedom of Information (Removal of References to Public Authorities) Order 2010 (S.I. 2010/939), arts. 1. (2), 2, Sch. Pt. 1

F69. Sch. 1 Pt. VI: entry inserted (1.10.2011) by The Freedom of Information (Additional Public Authorities) Order 2011 (S.I. 2011/1041), art. 2. (1), Sch. 1 Pt. 1

F70. Sch. 1 Pt. VI: entry omitted (19.9.2013) by virtue of The Public Bodies (Abolition of Administrative Justice and Tribunals Council) Order 2013 (S.I. 2013/2042), art. 1. (2), Sch. para. 22. (a)

F71. Sch. 1 Pt. VI: entry repealed (1.4.2007) by Education and Inspections Act 2006 (c. 40), ss. 157, 184, 188. (3), Sch. 14 para. 69. (3), Sch. 18 Pt. 5; S.I. 2007/935, art. 5. (w)(z)(gg)(ii)

F72. Sch. 1 Pt. VI: entry removed (11.8.2003) by virtue of The Freedom of Information (Removal of References to Public Authorities) Order 2003 (S.I. 2003/1883), art. 2, Sch.

F73. Sch. 1 Pt. VI: entries removed (29.6.2004) by virtue of The Freedom of Information (Removal of References to Public Authorities) Order 2004 (S.I. 2004/1641), art. 2, Sch. 1

F74. Sch. 1 Pt. VI: entry inserted (1.10.2011) by The Freedom of Information (Additional Public Authorities) Order 2011 (S.I. 2011/1041), art. 2. (1), Sch. 1 Pt. 1

F75. Sch. 1 Pt. VI: entry omitted (1.10.2011) by virtue of The Freedom of Information (Removal of References to Public Authorities) Order 2011 (S.I. 2011/1042), art. 2. (1), Sch. Pt. 1

F76. Sch. 1 Pt. VI: entry omitted (1.4.2009) by virtue of The Transfer of Tribunal Functions and Revenue and Customs Appeals Order 2009 (S.I. 2009/56), art. 3, Sch. 1 para. 296. (a)

F77. Words in Sch. 1 Pt. VI repealed (22.7.2012) by The Advisory Committee on Hazardous Substances (Abolition) Order 2012 (S.I. 2012/1923), art. 1. (2), Sch.

F78. Sch. 1 Pt. VI: entry added (19.4.2004) by The Freedom of Information (Additional Public Authorities) Order 2004 (S.I. 2004/938), art. 3, Sch. 2

F79. Words in Sch. 1 Pt. VI repealed (27.3.2015) by The Public Bodies (Abolition of the Advisory Committees on Pesticides) Order 2015 (S.I. 2015/978), art. 1. (2), Sch. Pt. 1

F80. Sch. 1 Pt. VI: entry added (19.4.2004) by The Freedom of Information (Additional Public Authorities) Order 2004 (S.I. 2004/938), art. 3, Sch. 2

F81. Sch. 1 Pt. VI: entry inserted (11.8.2003) by The Freedom of Information (Additional Public Authorities) Order 2003 (S.I. 2003/1882), art. 2, Sch. 1

F82. Words in Sch. 1 Pt. VI omitted (17.3.2015) by virtue of The Public Bodies (Abolition of the Library Advisory Council for England) Order 2015 (S.I. 2015/850), arts. 1. (2), 3. (3)

F83. Sch. 1 Pt. VI: entry inserted (11.8.2003) by The Freedom of Information (Additional Public Authorities) Order 2003 (S.I. 2003/1882), art. 2, Sch. 1

F84. Sch. 1 Pt. VI: entry inserted (11.8.2003) by The Freedom of Information (Additional Public Authorities) Order 2003 (S.I. 2003/1882), art. 2, Sch. 1

F85. Sch. 1 Pt. VI: entry inserted (11.8.2003) by The Freedom of Information (Additional Public Authorities) Order 2003 (S.I. 2003/1882), art. 2, Sch. 1

F86. Sch. 1 Pt. VI: entry inserted (11.8.2003) by The Freedom of Information (Additional Public Authorities) Order 2003 (S.I. 2003/1882), art. 2, Sch. 1

F87. Sch. 1 Pt. VI: entry inserted (7.2.2006) by The Freedom of Information (Additional Public Authorities) Order 2005 (S.I. 2005/3593), art. 2, Sch. 1

F88. Words in Sch. 1 Pt. VI repealed (25.6.2013) by Enterprise and Regulatory Reform Act 2013 (c. 24), s. 103. (3), Sch. 20 para. 2; S.I. 2013/1455, art. 2. (c), Sch. 1 (with art. 4. (2))

F89. Sch. 1 Pt. VI: entry inserted (29.2.2008) by The Agriculture and Horticulture Development Board Order 2008 (S.I. 2008/576), art. 18, Sch. 5 para. 5

F90. Sch. 1 Pt. VI: entry inserted (11.8.2003) by The Freedom of Information (Additional Public Authorities) Order 2003 (S.I. 2003/1882), art. 2, Sch. 1

F91. Words in Sch. 1 Pt. VI omitted (1.7.2012) by virtue of Health and Social Care Act 2012 (c.

7), s. 306. (4), Sch. 20 para. 1. (b) (with Sch. 20 para. 4); S.I. 2012/1319, art. 2. (3)

F92. Sch. 1 Pt. VI: entry added (11.11.2002) by The Freedom of Information (Additional Public Authorities) Order 2002 (S.I. 2002/2623), art. 2, Sch. 1

F93. Sch. 1 Pt. VI: entry repealed (1.4.2006) by The Ancient Monuments Board for Wales (Abolition) Order 2006 (S.I. 2006/64), art. 3. (1)(b)(iii)

F94. Words in Sch. 1 Pt. VI omitted (31.10.2012) by virtue of Health and Social Care Act 2012 (c. 7), s. 306. (4), Sch. 20 para. 5. (1)(c); S.I. 2012/1831, art. 2. (3)

F95. Sch. 1 Pt. VI: entry added (19.4.2004) by The Freedom of Information (Additional Public Authorities) Order 2004 (S.I. 2004/938), art. 3, Sch. 2

F96. Sch. 1 Pt. VI: entry inserted (16.12.2004) by Higher Education Act 2004 (c. 8), ss. 49, 52. (2), Sch. 6 para. 10; S.I. 2004/3255, art. 2

F97. Sch. 1 Pt. VI: entry inserted (1.10.2011) by The Freedom of Information (Additional Public Authorities) Order 2011 (S.I. 2011/1041), art. 2. (1), Sch. 1 Pt. 1

F98. Sch. 1 Pt. VI: entry repealed (31.3.2009) by Legal Services Act 2007 (c. 29), ss. 210, 211. (2), Sch. 23 (with ss. 29, 192, 193); S.I. 2009/503, art. 2. (f)(vii)

F99. Words in Sch. 1 Pt. VI inserted (1.3.2017) by The Bank of England and Financial Services (Consequential Amendments) Regulations 2017 (S.I. 2017/80), reg. 1, Sch. para. 10. (b)

F100. Sch. 1 Pt. VI: entry inserted (2.6.2008) by The Freedom of Information (Additional Public Authorities) Order 2008 (S.I. 2008/1271), art. 2, Sch.

F101. Sch. 1 Pt. VI: entry inserted (6.4.2005) by Pensions Act 2004 (c. 35), ss. 319. (1), 322, Sch. 12 para. 79; S.I. 2005/275, art. 2. (7), Sch. Pt. 7 (subject to art. 2. (12))

F102. Sch. 1 Pt. VI: entry repealed (1.11.2007) by Offender Management Act 2007 (c. 21), ss. 39, 41. (1), Sch. 5 Pt. 2; S.I. 2007/3001, art. 2. (1)(p)(t)(v)

F103. Sch. 1 Pt. VI: entries repealed (1.4.2008) by The Agriculture and Horticulture Development Board Order 2008 (S.I. 2008/576), art. 18, Sch. 5 para. 7 (with Sch. 4 para. 10)

F104. Sch. 1 Pt. VI: entry omitted (22.3.2013) by virtue of The Public Bodies (Abolition of British Shipbuilders) Order 2013 (S.I. 2013/687), art. 1. (2), Sch. 1 para. 14

F105. Sch. 1 Pt. VI: entry inserted (7.2.2006) by The Freedom of Information (Additional Public Authorities) Order 2005 (S.I. 2005/3593), art. 2, Sch. 1

F106. Sch. 1 Pt. VI: entry omitted (2.7.2012) by virtue of The British Waterways Board (Transfer of Functions) Order 2012 (S.I. 2012/1659), art. 1. (2), Sch. 3 para. 15. (2)(a) (with arts. 4-6)

F107. Sch. 1 Pt. VI: entry omitted (31.12.2011) by virtue of The Freedom of Information (Removal of References to Public Authorities) Order 2010 (S.I. 2010/939), arts. 1. (3), 2, Sch. Pt. 2

F108. Sch. 1 Pt. VI: entry inserted (31.12.2011) by The Freedom of Information (Additional Public Authorities) Order 2010 (S.I. 2010/937), arts. 1. (2), 3, Sch. Pt. 2

F109. Sch. 1 Pt. VI: entry inserted (31.12.2011) by The Freedom of Information (Additional Public Authorities) Order 2010 (S.I. 2010/937), arts. 1. (2), 3, Sch. Pt. 2

F110. Sch. 1 Pt. VI: entry removed (7.2.2006) by virtue of The Freedom of Information (Removal of References to Public Authorities) Order 2005 (S.I. 2005/3594), art. 2, Sch. 1

F111. Words in Sch. 1 Pt. VI inserted (2.7.2012) by The British Waterways Board (Transfer of Functions) Order 2012 (S.I. 2012/1659), art. 1. (2), Sch. 3 para. 15. (2)(b) (with arts. 4-6)

F112. Sch. 1 Pt. VI: entry added (11.11.2002) by The Freedom of Information (Additional Public Authorities) Order 2002 (S.I. 2002/2623), art. 2, Sch. 1

F113. Sch. 1 Pt. VI: entry inserted (1.10.2008) by Health and Social Care Act 2008 (c. 14), ss. 95, 170, Sch. 5 para. 73. (b); S.I. 2008/2497, art. 2. (q)(viii)

F114. Sch. 1 Pt. VI: entry repealed (1.4.2002) by The Abolition of the Central Council for Education and Training in Social Work Order 2002 (S.I. 2002/797), art. 2. (c)

F115. Sch. 1 Pt. VI: entry repealed (1.4.2007) by Police and Justice Act 2006 (c. 48), ss. 52, 53, Sch. 15 Pt. 1. (A); S.I. 2007/709, art. 3. (o)(q) (subject to arts. 6, 7)

F116. Sch. 1 Pt. VI: entry added (11.11.2002) by The Freedom of Information (Additional Public Authorities) Order 2002 (S.I. 2002/2623), art. 2, Sch. 1

F117. Sch. 1 Pt. VI: entry omitted (1.10.2011) by virtue of The Freedom of Information (Removal of References to Public Authorities) Order 2011 (S.I. 2011/1042), art. 2. (1), Sch. Pt. 1

F118. Words in Sch. 1 Pt. VI inserted (16.1.2012) by Police Reform and Social Responsibility Act 2011 (c. 13), ss. 87, 157. (1); S.I. 2011/3019, art. 3, Sch. 1

F119. Sch. 1 Pt. VI: entry inserted (1.10.2011) by The Freedom of Information (Additional Public Authorities) Order 2011 (S.I. 2011/1041), art. 2. (1), Sch. 1 Pt. 1

F120. Words in Sch. 1 Pt. VI omitted (1.8.2012) by virtue of The Public Bodies (Child Maintenance and Enforcement Commission: Abolition and Transfer of Functions) Order 2012 (S.I. 2012/2007), art. 1. (2), Sch. para. 109. (d)

F121. Words in Sch. 1 Pt. VI repealed (8.5.2012) by Welfare Reform Act 2012 (c. 5), s. 150. (2)(j), Sch. 13 para. 17. (a)

F122. Sch. 1 Pt. VI: entry inserted (1.6.2006) by The Freedom of Information (Additional Public Authorities) Order 2005 (S.I. 2005/3593), art. 3, Sch. 2

F123. Sch. 1 Pt. VI: entry added (11.11.2002) by The Freedom of Information (Additional Public Authorities) Order 2002 (S.I. 2002/2623), art. 2, Sch. 1

F124. Sch. 1 Pt. VI: entry substituted (11.11.2010) by Constitutional Reform and Governance Act 2010 (c. 25), ss. 19, 52. (2), Sch. 2 para. 12; S.I. 2010/2703, art. 2. (a)

F125. Words in Sch. 1 Pt. VI inserted (13.5.2014) by Anti-social Behaviour, Crime and Policing Act 2014 (c. 12), s. 185. (1), Sch. 11 para. 92 (with ss. 21, 33, 42, 58, 75, 93); S.I. 2014/949, art. 3, Sch. para. 23. (g)

F126. Words in Sch. 1 Pt. VI inserted (1.4.2012) by The Welsh Language (Wales) Measure 2011 (Transfer of functions, Transitional and Consequential Provisions) Order 2012 (S.I. 2012/990), arts. 1. (2), 8

F127. Sch. 1 Pt. VI: entry inserted (18.4.2006) by Equality Act 2006 (c. 3), ss. 2, 93, Sch. 1 para. 48 (with s. 92); S.I. 2006/1082, art. 2. (a)(l)

F128. Sch. 1 Pt. VI: entry repealed (1.4.2004 for E.W.) by Health and Social Care (Community Health and Standards) Act 2003 (c. 43), ss. 196, 199, Sch. 14 Pt. 2; S.I. 2004/759, art. 13

F129. Sch. 1 Pt. VI: entry repealed (1.4.2009) by Health and Social Care Act 2008 (c. 14), ss. 95, 166, 170, Sch. 5 para. 73. (a), Sch. 15 Pt. 1; S.I. 2009/462, art. 2, Sch. 1 para. 36

F130. Sch. 1 Pt. VI: entry inserted (1.10.2010) by The Freedom of Information (Additional Public Authorities) Order 2010 (S.I. 2010/937), arts. 1. (2), 3, Sch. Pt. 1

F131. Sch. 1 Pt. VI: entry inserted (7.2.2006) by The Freedom of Information (Additional Public Authorities) Order 2005 (S.I. 2005/3593), art. 2, Sch. 1

F132. Sch. 1 Pt. VI: entry repealed (1.4.2006) by Public Services Ombudsman (Wales) Act 2005 (c. 10), ss. 39, 40, Sch. 6 para. 71. (a), Sch. 7; S.I. 2005/2800, art. 5. (1) (with art. 5. (2), Sch. 2)

F133. Sch. 1 Pt. VI: entry repealed (1.4.2009) by Housing and Regeneration Act 2008 (c. 17), ss. 56, 321. (1), 325, Sch. 8 para. 77. (3), Sch. 16; S.I. 2009/803, arts. 1. (2), 3. (2)(3), 10

F134. Sch. 1 Pt. VI: entry repealed (1.10.2007) by Equality Act 2006 (c. 3), ss. 40, 91, 93. (1), Sch. 3 para. 60, Sch. 4 (with s. 92); S.I. 2007/2603, art. 2. (a)(d) (subject to art. 3)

F135. Words in Sch. 1 Pt. VI repealed (1.4.2013) by The Public Bodies (Abolition of the Commission for Rural Communities) Order 2012 (S.I. 2012/2654), art. 1. (4), Sch.

F136. Sch. 1 Pt. VI: entry inserted (14.10.2006) by Commissioner for Older People (Wales) Act 2006 (c. 30), ss. 1. (2), 23, Sch. 1 para. 21. (b); S.I. 2006/2699, art. 2

F137. Sch. 1 Pt. VI: entry inserted (1.10.2011) by The Freedom of Information (Additional Public Authorities) Order 2011 (S.I. 2011/1041), art. 2. (1), Sch. 1 Pt. 1

F138. Sch. 1 Pt. VI: entry added (11.11.2002) by The Freedom of Information (Additional Public Authorities) Order 2002 (S.I. 2002/2623), art. 2, Sch. 1

F139. Sch. 1 Pt. VI: entry omitted (1.10.2011) by virtue of The Freedom of Information (Removal of References to Public Authorities) Order 2011 (S.I. 2011/1042), art. 2. (1), Sch. Pt. 1

F140. Sch. 1 Pt. VI: entry repealed (1.10.2006) by Natural Environment and Rural Communities Act 2006 c. 16), ss. 105, 107, Sch. 11 para. 153. (3), {Sch. 12}; S.I. 2006/2541, art. 2

F141. Words in Sch. 1 Pt. VI repealed (23.4.2014) by The Public Bodies (Abolition of the Committee on Agricultural Valuation) Order 2014 (S.I. 2014/1068), arts. 1. (2), 3. (2)

F142. Sch. 1 Pt. VI: entry inserted (26.11.2008) by Climate Change Act 2008 (c. 27), ss. 32, 100,

F143. Sch. 1 Pt. VI: entry omitted (1.10.2010) by virtue of The Freedom of Information (Removal of References to Public Authorities) Order 2010 (S.I. 2010/939), arts. 1. (2), 2, Sch. Pt. 1

F144. Sch. 1 Pt. VI: entry added (19.4.2004) by The Freedom of Information (Additional Public Authorities) Order 2004 (S.I. 2004/938), art. 3, Sch. 2

F145. Sch. 1 Pt. VI: entry inserted (11.8.2003) by The Freedom of Information (Additional Public Authorities) Order 2003 (S.I. 2003/1882), art. 2, Sch. 1

F146. Sch. 1 Pt. VI: entry omitted (1.10.2011) by virtue of The Freedom of Information (Removal of References to Public Authorities) Order 2011 (S.I. 2011/1042), art. 2. (1), Sch. Pt. 1

F147. Sch. 1 Pt. VI: entry inserted (11.8.2003) by The Freedom of Information (Additional Public Authorities) Order 2003 (S.I. 2003/1882), art. 2, Sch. 1

F148. Words in Sch. 1 Pt. VI omitted (1.4.2014) by virtue of The Enterprise and Regulatory Reform Act 2013 (Competition) (Consequential, Transitional and Saving Provisions) Order 2014 (S.I. 2014/892), art. 1. (1), Sch. 1 para. 147 (with art. 3)

F149. Sch. 1 Pt. VI: entry inserted (11.8.2003) by The Freedom of Information (Additional Public Authorities) Order 2003 (S.I. 2003/1882), art. 2, Sch. 1

F150. Sch. 1 Pt. VI: entry inserted (19.4.2010) by Parliamentary Standards Act 2009 (c. 13), Sch. 2 para. 11 (as substituted by Constitutional Reform and Governance Act 2010 (c. 25), ss. 26, 52. (2), Sch. 3; S.I. 2010/1277, art. 2. (c))

F151. Words in Sch. 1 Pt. VI inserted (1.4.2012) by Budget Responsibility and National Audit Act 2011 (c. 4), s. 29, Sch. 5 para. 23. (1)(a); S.I. 2011/2576, art. 5

F152. Sch. 1 Pt. VI: entry inserted (1.6.2006) by The Freedom of Information (Additional Public Authorities) Order 2005 (S.I. 2005/3593), art. 3, Sch. 2

F153. Sch. 1 Pt. VI: entry added (11.11.2002) by The Freedom of Information (Additional Public Authorities) Order 2002 (S.I. 2002/2623), art. 2, Sch. 1

F154. Sch. 1 Pt. VI: entry inserted (2.6.2008) by The Freedom of Information (Additional Public Authorities) Order 2008 (S.I. 2008/1271), art. 2, Sch.

F155. Sch. 1 Pt. VI: entry inserted (29.12.2003) by Communications Act 2003 (c. 21), ss. 406. (1)(7), 411. (2), Sch. 17 para. 164 (with Sch. 18); S.I. 2003/3142, art. 3. (1), Sch. 1 (subject to art. 3. (3) and with art. 11)

F156. Sch. 1 Pt. VI: entry omitted by virtue of The Health Professions Order 2001 (S.I. 2002/254), art. 48. (3), Sch. 4 para. 9 (with art. 3. (19)) (the amendment coming into force in accordance with art. 1. (2)(3) of the amending S.I.)

F157. Sch. 1 Pt. VI: entry omitted (1.10.2011) by virtue of The Freedom of Information (Removal of References to Public Authorities) Order 2011 (S.I. 2011/1042), art. 2. (1), Sch. Pt. 1

F158. Words in Sch. 1 Pt. VI omitted (1.12.2012) by virtue of Health and Social Care Act 2012 (c. 7), s. 306. (4), Sch. 15 para. 69. (1)(d); S.I. 2012/2657, art. 2. (3)

F159. Sch. 1 Pt. VI: entry repealed (1.11.2007) by Tribunals, Courts and Enforcement Act 2007 (c. 15), ss. 146, 148, Sch. 23 Pt. 1; S.I. 2007/2709, art. 3. (d)(vii)

F160. Words in Sch. 1 Pt. VI omitted (1.4.2013) by virtue of The Natural Resources Body for Wales (Functions) Order 2013 (S.I. 2013/755), art. 1. (2), Sch. 2 para. 399. (2) (with Sch. 7)

F161. Words in Sch. 1 Pt. VI repealed (2.5.2012) by The Public Bodies (Abolition of Courts Boards) Order 2012 (S.I. 2012/1206), art. 1. (2), Sch. para. 2

F162. Sch. 1 Pt. VI: entry omitted (3.11.2008) by virtue of The Transfer of Tribunal Functions Order 2008 (S.I. 2008/2833), art. 9. (1), Sch. 3 para. 188

F163. Sch. 1 Pt. VI: entry added (11.11.2002) by The Freedom of Information (Additional Public Authorities) Order 2002 (S.I. 2002/2623), art. 2, Sch. 1

F164. Sch. 1 Pt. VI: entry inserted (7.2.2006) by The Freedom of Information (Additional Public Authorities) Order 2005 (S.I. 2005/3593), art. 2, Sch. 1

F165. Sch. 1 Pt. VI: entry repealed (18.9.2012) by The Public Bodies (Abolition of Crown Court Rule Committee and Magistrates' Courts Rule Committee) Order 2012 (S.I. 2012/2398), art. 1. (2), Sch. 1 para. 8

F166. Sch. 1 Pt. VI: entry inserted (1.7.2004) by Higher Education Act 2004 (c. 8), ss. 49, 52. (1),

Sch. 6 para. 10

F167. Sch. 1 Pt. VI: entries inserted (31.1.2017 for specified purposes, 8.1.2018 in so far as not already in force) by Policing and Crime Act 2017 (c. 3), s. 183. (1)(5)(e), Sch. 9 para. 66; S.I. 2017/1249, reg. 2 (with reg. 3)

F168. Words in Sch. 1 Pt. VI inserted (12.7.2016) by Immigration Act 2016 (c. 19), s. 94. (1), Sch. 3 para. 9. (a); S.I. 2016/603, reg. 3. (u)

F169. Sch. 1 Pt. VI: entry inserted (11.8.2003) by The Freedom of Information (Additional Public Authorities) Order 2003 (S.I. 2003/1882), art. 2, Sch. 1

F170. Words in Sch. 1 Pt. VI repealed (7.2.2013) by The Public Bodies (Abolition of the Disability Living Allowance Advisory Board) Order 2013 (S.I. 2013/252), art. 1. (2), Sch. Pt. 1

F171. Words in Sch. 1 Pt. VI inserted (15.10.2012) by Protection of Freedoms Act 2012 (c. 9), s. 120, Sch. 9 para. 133 (with s. 97); S.I. 2012/2521, art. 2. (e)

F172. Sch. 1 Pt. VI: entry added (19.4.2004) by The Freedom of Information (Additional Public Authorities) Order 2004 (S.I. 2004/938), art. 3, Sch. 2

F173. Sch. 1 Pt. VI: entry added (19.4.2004) by The Freedom of Information (Additional Public Authorities) Order 2004 (S.I. 2004/938), art. 3, Sch. 2

F174. Sch. 1 Pt. VI: entry added (11.11.2002) by The Freedom of Information (Additional Public Authorities) Order 2002 (S.I. 2002/2623), art. 2, Sch. 1

F175. Sch. 1 Pt. VI: entry omitted (coming into force in accordance with art. 1. (2)(3) of the amending S.I.) by virtue of The Nursing and Midwifery Order 2001 (S.I. 2002/253), art. 54. (3), Sch. 5 para. 17. (a) (with art. 3. (18))

F176. Sch. 1 Pt. VI: entry repealed (1.10.2007) by Equality Act 2006 (c. 3), ss. 40, 91, 93. (1), Sch. 3 para. 60, Sch. 4 (with s. 92); S.I. 2007/2603, art. 2. (a)(d) (subject to art. 3)

F177. Sch. 1 Pt. VI: entry inserted (1.10.2011) by The Freedom of Information (Additional Public Authorities) Order 2011 (S.I. 2011/1041), art. 2. (1), Sch. 1 Pt. 1

F178. Sch. 1 Pt. VI: entry inserted (11.8.2003) by The Freedom of Information (Additional Public Authorities) Order 2003 (S.I. 2003/1882), art. 2, Sch. 1

F179. Sch. 1 Pt. VI: entry omitted (1.10.2010) by virtue of The Freedom of Information (Removal of References to Public Authorities) Order 2010 (S.I. 2010/939), arts. 1. (2), 2, Sch. Pt. 1

F180. Sch. 1 Pt. VI: entry inserted (7.2.2006) by The Freedom of Information (Additional Public Authorities) Order 2005 (S.I. 2005/3593), art. 2, Sch. 1

F181. Sch. 1 Pt. VI: entry inserted (7.2.2006) by The Freedom of Information (Additional Public Authorities) Order 2005 (S.I. 2005/3593), art. 2, Sch. 1

F182. Sch. 1 Pt. VI: entry inserted (1.10.2010) by The Freedom of Information (Additional Public Authorities) Order 2010 (S.I. 2010/937), arts. 1. (2), 3, Sch. Pt. 1

F183. Sch. 1 Pt. VI: entries inserted (1.4.2013) by Financial Services Act 2012 (c. 21), s. 122. (3), Sch. 18 para. 91. (b) (with Sch. 20); S.I. 2013/423, art. 3, Sch.

F184. Sch. 1 Pt. VI: entry inserted (11.8.2003) by The Freedom of Information (Additional Public Authorities) Order 2003 (S.I. 2003/1882), art. 2, Sch. 1

F185. Sch. 1 Pt. VI entry omitted (1.4.2013) by virtue of Financial Services Act 2012 (c. 21), s. 122. (3), Sch. 18 para. 91. (a) (with Sch. 20); S.I. 2013/423, art. 3, Sch.

F186. Sch. 1 Pt. VI: entry omitted (1.10.2010) by virtue of The Freedom of Information (Removal of References to Public Authorities) Order 2010 (S.I. 2010/939), arts. 1. (2), 2, Sch. Pt. 1

F187. Sch. 1 Pt. VI: entry repealed (18.7.2014) by The Public Bodies (Abolition of Food from Britain) Order 2014 (S.I. 2014/1924), art. 1. (3), Sch.

F188. Sch. 1 Pt. VI: entry repealed (1.11.2011) by Sports Grounds Safety Authority Act 2011 (c. 6), ss. 6, 8. (1), Sch. 2 para. 8, Sch. 3; S.I. 2011/2597, art. 2

F189. Sch. 1 Pt. VI: entry added (19.4.2004) by The Freedom of Information (Additional Public Authorities) Order 2004 (S.I. 2004/938), art. 3, Sch. 2

F190. Sch. 1 Pt. VI: entry inserted (7.2.2006) by The Freedom of Information (Additional Public Authorities) Order 2005 (S.I. 2005/3593), art. 2, Sch. 1

F191. Sch. 1 Pt. VI: entry for "Gambling Commission" substituted (1.10.2005) for entry for "Gaming Board of Great Britain" by Gambling Act 2005 (c. 19), ss. 356. (1), 358. (1), Sch. 16

para. 16 (with ss. 352, 354, Sch. 16 para. 21); S.I. 2005/2455, art. 2. (1), Sch.

F192. Words in Sch. 1 Pt. VI substituted (12.7.2016) by Immigration Act 2016 (c. 19), s. 94. (1), Sch. 3 para. 9. (b); S.I. 2016/603, reg. 3. (u)

F193. Sch. 1 Pt. VI: entry added (11.11.2002) by The Freedom of Information (Additional Public Authorities) Order 2002 (S.I. 2002/2623), art. 2, Sch. 1

F194. Sch. 1 Pt. VI: entry inserted (7.2.2006) by The Freedom of Information (Additional Public Authorities) Order 2005 (S.I. 2005/3593), art. 2, Sch. 1

F195. Sch. 1 Pt. VI: entry inserted (27.9.2010) by The Pharmacy Order 2010 (S.I. 2010/231), arts. 1. (5), 68, Sch. 4 para. 9. (a); S.I. 2010/1621, art. 2. (1), Sch.

F196. Words in Sch. 1 Pt. VI omitted (1.8.2012) by virtue of Health and Social Care Act 2012 (c. 7), s. 306. (4), Sch. 15 para. 50. (e); S.I. 2012/1319, art. 2. (4)

F197. Words in Sch. 1 Pt. VI omitted (1.4.2012) by virtue of Education Act 2011 (c. 21), s. 82. (3), Sch. 2 para. 25; S.I. 2012/924, art. 2

F198. Sch. 1 Pt. VI: entry added (11.11.2002) by The Freedom of Information (Additional Public Authorities) Order 2002 (S.I. 2002/2623), art. 2, Sch. 1

F199. Sch. 1 Pt. VI: entry omitted (1.10.2011) by virtue of The Freedom of Information (Removal of References to Public Authorities) Order 2011 (S.I. 2011/1042), art. 2. (1), Sch. Pt. 1

F200. Sch. 1 Pt. VI: entry inserted (11.8.2003) by The Freedom of Information (Additional Public Authorities) Order 2003 (S.I. 2003/1882), art. 2, Sch. 1

F201. Words in Sch. 1 Pt. VI inserted (25.6.2013) by Groceries Code Adjudicator Act 2013 (c. 19), ss. 21. (3), 25; S.I. 2013/1236, art. 2

F202. Sch. 1 Pt. VI: entry omitted (1.4.2008) by virtue of The Legislative Reform (Health and Safety Executive) Order 2008 (S.I. 2008/960), art. 22, Sch. 3

F203. Words in Sch. 1 Pt. VI substituted (1.8.2012) by Health and Social Care Act 2012 (c. 7), s. 306. (4), Sch. 15 para. 56. (a); S.I. 2012/1319, art. 2. (4)

F204. Words in Sch. 1 Pt. VI inserted (1.4.2013) by Health and Social Care Act 2012 (c. 7), s. 306. (4), Sch. 19 para. 8; S.I. 2013/160, art. 2. (2) (with arts. 7-9)

F205. Words in Sch. 1 Pt. VI omitted (1.4.2013) by virtue of Health and Social Care Act 2012 (c. 7), s. 306. (4), Sch. 7 para. 10; S.I. 2013/160, art. 2. (2) (with arts. 7-9)

F206. Words in Sch. 1 Pt. VI inserted (1.1.2015) by Care Act 2014 (c. 23), s. 127. (1), Sch. 7 para. 26; S.I. 2014/2473, art. 5. (m)

F207. Sch. 1 Pt. VI: entry repealed (1.8.2010) by Health and Social Care Act 2008 (c. 14), ss. 166, 170, Sch. 15 Pt. 2; S.I. 2010/708, art. 4. (2)(d)(vii)

F208. Sch. 1 Pt. VI: entry substituted (1.1.2001) by virtue of 2000 c. 21, s. 73. (3)(a); S.I. 2000/3230, art. 2, Sch.

F209. Sch. 1 Pt. VI: entry inserted (1.10.2011) by The Freedom of Information (Additional Public Authorities) Order 2011 (S.I. 2011/1041), art. 2. (1), Sch. 1 Pt. 1

F210. Sch. 1 Pt. VI: entry added (19.4.2004) by The Freedom of Information (Additional Public Authorities) Order 2004 (S.I. 2004/938), art. 3, Sch. 2

F211. Sch. 1 Pt. VI: entry inserted (1.10.2011) by The Freedom of Information (Additional Public Authorities) Order 2011 (S.I. 2011/1041), art. 2. (1), Sch. 1 Pt. 1

F212. Sch. 1 Pt. VI: entry inserted (1.10.2010) by The Freedom of Information (Additional Public Authorities) Order 2010 (S.I. 2010/937), arts. 1. (2), 3, Sch. Pt. 1

F213. Sch. 1 Pt. VI: entry repealed (1.4.2006) by The Historic Buildings Council for Wales (Abolition) Order 2006 (S.I. 2006/63), art. 3. (1)(c)(iii)

F214. Sch. 1 Pt. VI: entry inserted (8.9.2008) by Housing and Regeneration Act 2008 (c. 17), ss. 56, 325, Sch. 8 para. 77. (2); S.I. 2008/2358, art. 2. (1)(2)

F215. Sch. 1 Pt. VI: entry repealed (1.4.2009) by Housing and Regeneration Act 2008 (c. 17), ss. 277, 321. (1), 325, Sch. 9 para. 28. (3), Sch. 16; S.I. 2009/803, arts. 1. (2), 8. (1)(2), 10

F216. Sch. 1 Pt. VI: entry inserted (1.4.2005) by Human Tissue Act 2004 (c. 30), ss. 13. (2), 60. (2), Sch. 2 para. 27 (with s. 37. (7)); S.I. 2005/919, art. 3, Sch. (with art. 2)

F217. Sch. 1 Pt. VI: entry inserted (1.10.2010) by The Freedom of Information (Additional Public Authorities) Order 2010 (S.I. 2010/937), arts. 1. (2), 3, Sch. Pt. 1

F218. Sch. 1 Pt. VI: entry inserted (11.8.2003) by The Freedom of Information (Additional Public Authorities) Order 2003 (S.I. 2003/1882), art. 2, Sch. 1

F219. Words in Sch. 1 Pt. VI inserted (31.7.2015) by Modern Slavery Act 2015 (c. 30), ss. 40. (9), 61. (1); S.I. 2015/1476, reg. 2. (c)

F220. Sch. 1 Pt. VI: entry inserted (7.2.2006) by The Freedom of Information (Additional Public Authorities) Order 2005 (S.I. 2005/3593), art. 2, Sch. 1

F221. Sch. 1 Pt. VI: entry inserted (1.11.2007) by Offender Management Act 2007 (c. 21), ss. 39, 41. (1), Sch. 3 para. 10; S.I. 2007/3001, art. 2. (1)(p)(r)

F222. Sch. 1 Pt. VI: entry inserted (12.10.2009) by Parliamentary Standards Act 2009 (c. 13), ss. 3, 14. (2)(3), Sch. 1 para. 27. (1) (with ss. 1, 2. (1)); S.I. 2009/2500, art. 2. (d)

F223. Sch. 1 Pt. VI: entry omitted (31.1.2017 for specified purposes, 8.1.2018 in so far as not already in force) by virtue of Policing and Crime Act 2017 (c. 3), s. 183. (1)(5)(e), Sch. 9 para. 66; S.I. 2017/1249, reg. 2 (with reg. 3)

F224. Words in Sch. 1 Pt. VI omitted (1.7.2012) by virtue of Health and Social Care Act 2012 (c. 7), s. 306. (4), Sch. 13 para. 7. (b); S.I. 2012/1319, art. 2. (3)

F225. Sch. 1 Pt. VI: entry inserted (1.10.2010) by The Freedom of Information (Additional Public Authorities) Order 2010 (S.I. 2010/937), arts. 1. (2), 3, Sch. Pt. 1

F226. Sch. 1 Pt. VI: entry added (19.4.2004) by The Freedom of Information (Additional Public Authorities) Order 2004 (S.I. 2004/938), art. 3, Sch. 2

F227. Sch. 1 Pt. VI: entry added (19.4.2004) by The Freedom of Information (Additional Public Authorities) Order 2004 (S.I. 2004/938), art. 3, Sch. 2

F228. Words in Sch. 1 Pt. VI omitted (1.12.2012) by virtue of The Protection of Freedoms Act 2012 (Disclosure and Barring Service Transfer of Functions) Order 2012 (S.I. 2012/3006), arts. 1. (1), 17 (with Pt. 4)

F229. Sch. 1 Pt. VI: entry inserted (11.8.2003) by The Freedom of Information (Additional Public Authorities) Order 2003 (S.I. 2003/1882), art. 2, Sch. 1

F230. Sch. 1 Pt. VI: entry repealed (1.4.2012) by Localism Act 2011 (c. 20), s. 240. (2), Sch. 13 para. 78, Sch. 25 Pt. 20; S.I. 2012/628, art. 7

F231. Words in Sch. 1 Pt. VI repealed (2.7.2012) by The Inland Waterways Advisory Council (Abolition) Order 2012 (S.I. 2012/1658), arts. 1. (b), 5, Sch.

F232. Words in Sch. 1 Pt. VI inserted (1.4.2017) by Enterprise Act 2016 (c. 12), s. 44. (5), Sch. 4 para. 11; S.I. 2017/346, reg. 2. (a)

F233. Sch. 1 Pt. VI: entry omitted (30.4.2001) by virtue of S.I. 2001/1283, art. 3. (7)

F234. Sch. 1 Pt. VI: entry inserted (11.8.2003) by The Freedom of Information (Additional Public Authorities) Order 2003 (S.I. 2003/1882), art. 2, Sch. 1

F235. Sch. 1 Pt. VI: entry inserted (11.8.2003) by The Freedom of Information (Additional Public Authorities) Order 2003 (S.I. 2003/1882), art. 2, Sch. 1

F236. Sch. 1 Pt. VI: entry inserted (3.4.2006) by Constitutional Reform Act 2005 (c. 4), ss. 62. (2), 148, Sch. 13 para. 17. (3); S.I. 2006/1014, art. 2. (a), Sch. 1 para. 16

F237. Sch. 1 Pt. VI: entry inserted (3.4.2006) by Constitutional Reform Act 2005 (c. 4), ss. 61. (2), 148, Sch. 12 para. 36. (3); S.I. 2006/1014, art. 2. (a), Sch. 1 para. 15

F238. Sch. 1 Pt. VI: entry omitted (1.10.2010) by virtue of The Freedom of Information (Removal of References to Public Authorities) Order 2010 (S.I. 2010/939), arts. 1. (2), 2, Sch. Pt. 1

F239. Sch. 1 Pt. VI: entry repealed (1.4.2010) by The Apprenticeships, Skills, Children and Learning Act 2009 (Consequential Amendments) (England and Wales) Order 2010 (S.I. 2010/1080), arts. 1. (2)(a), 2, Sch. 1 para. 43. (a), Sch. 2 Pt. 1

F240. Sch. 1 Pt. VI: entry inserted (2.6.2008) by The Freedom of Information (Additional Public Authorities) Order 2008 (S.I. 2008/1271), art. 2, Sch.

F241. Sch. 1 Pt. VI: entry inserted (7.3.2008) by Legal Services Act 2007 (c. 29), ss. 2. (2), 211. (2), Sch. 1 para. 31 (with ss. 29, 192, 193); S.I. 2008/222, art. 2. (h)

F242. Words in Sch. 1 Pt. VI omitted (1.4.2013) by virtue of Legal Aid, Sentencing and Punishment of Offenders Act 2012 (c. 10), s. 151. (1), Sch. 5 para. 55; S.I. 2013/453, art. 3. (h) (with savings and transitional provisions in S.I. 2013/534, art. 6)

F243. Sch. 1 Pt. VI: entry repealed (6.4.2010) by Legal Services Act 2007 (c. 29), ss. 210, 211. (2), Sch. 23 (with ss. 29, 192, 193); S.I. 2010/2089, art. 2. (e)(viii)

F244. Sch. 1 Pt. VI: entry repealed (6.10.2010) by Legal Services Act 2007 (c. 29), ss. 210, 211. (2), Sch. 23 (with ss. 29, 192, 193); S.I. 2010/2089, art. 2. (e)(viii)

F245. Sch. 1 Pt. VI: entry repealed (31.12.2011) by Legal Services Act 2007 (c. 29), ss. 210, 211. (2), Sch. 23 (with ss. 29, 192, 193); S.I. 2010/2089, art. 4. (b)(vii)

F246. Sch. 1 Pt. VI: entry repealed (W.) (1.4.2004) by The Library Advisory Council for Wales Abolition and Consequential Amendments Order 2004 (S.I. 2004/803), art. 3. (3)

F247. Words in Sch. 1 Pt. VI repealed (2.2.2012) by The Local Better Regulation Office (Dissolution and Transfer of Functions, Etc.) Order 2012 (S.I. 2012/246), arts. 1. (2), 2, 4. (2), Sch. 1 para. 20 (with Sch. 2)

F248. Sch. 1 Pt. VI: entry inserted (1.4.2010) by Local Democracy, Economic Development and Construction Act 2009 (c. 20), ss. 55, 148, Sch. 1 para. 21; S.I. 2009/3318, art. 4. (d)(dd)

F249. Sch. 1 Pt. VI: entry repealed (1.4.2010) by Local Democracy, Economic Development and Construction Act 2009 (c. 20), ss. 146, 148, Sch. 7 Pt. 3; S.I. 2009/3318, art. 4. (hh)

F250. Sch. 1 Pt. VI: entry added (19.4.2004) by The Freedom of Information (Additional Public Authorities) Order 2004 (S.I. 2004/938), art. 3, Sch. 2

F251. Words in Sch. 1 Pt. VI repealed (18.9.2012) by The Public Bodies (Abolition of Crown Court Rule Committee and Magistrates' Courts Rule Committee) Order 2012 (S.I. 2012/2398), art. 1. (2), Sch. 2 para. 3

F252. Sch. 1 Pt. VI: entry inserted (12.1.2010) by Marine and Coastal Access Act 2009 (c. 23), ss. 1, 324, Sch. 2 para. 6; S.I. 2009/3345, art. 2, Sch. para. 1

F253. Sch. 1 Pt. VI: entry omitted (1.10.2010) by virtue of The Freedom of Information (Removal of References to Public Authorities) Order 2010 (S.I. 2010/939), arts. 1. (2), 2, Sch. Pt. 1

F254. Sch. 1 Pt. VI: entry inserted (1.10.2011) by The Freedom of Information (Additional Public Authorities) Order 2011 (S.I. 2011/1041), art. 2. (1), Sch. 1 Pt. 1

F255. Sch. 1 Pt. VI: entry repealed (1.12.2006) by National Lottery Act 2006 (c. 23), ss. 21, 22, Sch. 3; S.I. 2006/3201, art. 2. (e)

F256. Word in Sch. 1 Pt. VI inserted (1.7.2012) by Health and Social Care Act 2012 (c. 7), s. 306. (4), Sch. 13 para. 7. (a); S.I. 2012/1319, art. 2. (3)

F257. Sch. 1 Pt. VI: entry inserted (22.7.2010) by National Assembly for Wales (Remuneration) Measure 2010 (nawm 4), ss. 17. (2), 20. (2)

F258. Words in Sch. 1 Pt. VI inserted (28.3.2013) by The Public Bodies (The Office of Fair Trading Transfer of Consumer Advice Scheme Function and Modification of Enforcement Functions) Order 2013 (S.I. 2013/783), arts. 1. (2), 7

F259. Words in Sch. 1 Pt. VI substituted (1.4.2014) by The Public Bodies (Abolition of the National Consumer Council and Transfer of the Office of Fair Trading's Functions in relation to Estate Agents etc) Order 2014 (S.I. 2014/631), art. 1. (3), Sch. 1 para. 10. (2)(a) (with Sch. 1 para. 28, Sch. 2 paras. 13-15)

F260. Words in Sch. 1 Pt. VI inserted (1.4.2014) by The Public Bodies (Abolition of the National Consumer Council and Transfer of the Office of Fair Trading's Functions in relation to Estate Agents etc) Order 2014 (S.I. 2014/631), art. 1. (3), Sch. 1 para. 10. (2)(b) (with Sch. 1 para. 28, Sch. 2 paras. 13-15)

F261. Sch. 1 Pt. VI: reference to old NAO to be read as a reference to NAO (1.4.2012) by Budget Responsibility and National Audit Act 2011 (c. 4), s. 29, Sch. 5 para. 23. (1)(b); S.I. 2011/2576, art. 5

F262. Sch. 1 Pt. VI: entry repealed (1.4.2009) by Health and Social Care Act 2008 (c. 14), ss. 166, 170, Sch. 15 Pt. 7; S.I. 2009/270, art. 2. (2)(b)

F263. Sch. 1 Pt. VI: entry omitted (1.10.2010) by virtue of The Freedom of Information (Removal of References to Public Authorities) Order 2010 (S.I. 2010/939), arts. 1. (2), 2, Sch. Pt. 1

F264. Words in Sch. 1 Pt. VI omitted (1.4.2014) by virtue of The Public Bodies (Abolition of the National Consumer Council and Transfer of the Office of Fair Trading's Functions in relation to Estate Agents etc) Order 2014 (S.I. 2014/631), art. 1. (3), Sch. 1 para. 10. (3) (with Sch. 1 para.

28, Sch. 2 paras. 13-15)

F265. Sch. 1 Pt. VI: entry inserted (21.12.2007) by Consumers, Estate Agents and Redress Act 2007 (c. 17), ss. 1. (4), 66. (2), Sch. 1 para. 35 (with s. 6. (9)); S.I. 2007/3546, art. 3, Sch. and expressed to be inserted (1.10.2010) by The Freedom of Information (Additional Public Authorities) Order 2010 (S.I. 2010/937), arts. 1. (2), 3, Sch. Pt. 1

F266. Sch. 1 Pt. VI: entry omitted (1.4.2006) by virtue of The National Council for Education and Training for Wales (Transfer of Functions to the National Assembly for Wales and Abolition) Order 2005 (S.I. 2005/3238), art. 9. (1), Sch. 1 para. 85 (with art. 7)

F267. Sch. 1 Pt. VI: entry repealed (1.4.2006) by Serious Organised Crime and Police Act 2005 (c. 15), ss. 59, 174. (2), 178, Sch. 4 para. 160, Sch. 17 Pt. 2; S.I. 2006/378, art. 4. (1), Sch. para. 13. (kk) (subject to art. 4. (2)-(7))

F268. Sch. 1 Pt. VI: entry inserted (1.10.2011) by The Freedom of Information (Additional Public Authorities) Order 2011 (S.I. 2011/1041), art. 2. (1), Sch. 1 Pt. 1

F269. Sch. 1 Pt. VI: entry inserted (11.8.2003) by The Freedom of Information (Additional Public Authorities) Order 2003 (S.I. 2003/1882), art. 2, Sch. 1

F270. Sch. 1 Pt. VI: entry inserted (1.10.2011) by The Freedom of Information (Additional Public Authorities) Order 2011 (S.I. 2011/1041), art. 2. (1), Sch. 1 Pt. 1

F271. Words in Sch. 1 Pt. VI omitted (1.4.2012) by virtue of The Public Bodies (Abolition of the National Endowment for Science, Technology and the Arts) Order 2012 (S.I. 2012/964), arts. 1. (2), 3. (1), Sch.

F272. Sch. 1 Pt. VI: entry inserted (11.8.2003) by The Freedom of Information (Additional Public Authorities) Order 2003 (S.I. 2003/1882), art. 2, Sch. 1

F273. Sch. 1 Pt. VI: entry omitted (21.1.2011) by virtue of Identity Documents Act 2010 (c. 40), ss. 12, 14. (2), Sch. para. 11

F274. Words in Sch. 1 Pt. VI omitted (1.4.2013) by virtue of Health and Social Care Act 2012 (c. 7), s. 306. (4), Sch. 20 para. 9. (1)(c); S.I. 2013/160, art. 2. (2) (with arts. 7-9)

F275. Words in Sch. 1 Pt. VI inserted (1.4.2013) by Health and Social Care Act 2012 (c. 7), s. 306. (4), Sch. 17 para. 8; S.I. 2013/160, art. 2. (2) (with arts. 7-9)

F276. Sch. 1 Pt. VI: entry omitted (1.10.2013) by virtue of The Public Bodies (Merger of the Gambling Commission and the National Lottery Commission) Order 2013 (S.I. 2013/2329), art. 1. (2), Sch. para. 26 (with art. 8, Sch. para. 43)

F277. Sch. 1 Pt. VI: entry inserted (1.10.2010) by The Freedom of Information (Additional Public Authorities) Order 2010 (S.I. 2010/937), arts. 1. (2), 3, Sch. Pt. 1

F278. Words in Sch. 1 Pt. VI omitted (7.10.2013) by virtue of Crime and Courts Act 2013 (c. 22), s. 61. (2), Sch. 8 para. 104; S.I. 2013/1682, art. 3. (v)

F279. Sch. 1 Pt. VI: entry repealed (1.4.2005) by Health Protection Agency Act 2004 (c. 17), ss. 11. (2), 12, Sch. 4; S.I. 2005/121, art. 2. (2)

F280. Sch. 1 Pt. VI: entry inserted (2.5.2006 for E.W. and 1.10.2006 otherwise) by Natural Environment and Rural Communities Act 2006 (c. 16), ss. 105. (1), 107, Sch. 11 para. 153. (2); S.I. 2006/1176, art. 4; S.I. 2006/2541, art. 2

F281. Words in Sch. 1 Pt. VI inserted (1.4.2013) by The Natural Resources Body for Wales (Functions) Order 2013 (S.I. 2013/755), art. 1. (2), Sch. 2 para. 399. (3) (with Sch. 7)

F282. Sch. 1 Pt. VI: entry repealed (1.12.2006) by National Lottery Act 2006 (c. 23), ss. 21, 22, Sch. 3; S.I. 2006/3201, art. 2. (e)

F283. Sch. 1 Pt. VI: entry inserted (1.10.2011) by The Freedom of Information (Additional Public Authorities) Order 2011 (S.I. 2011/1041), art. 2. (1), Sch. 1 Pt. 1

F284. Sch. 1 Pt. VI: entry added (19.4.2004) by The Freedom of Information (Additional Public Authorities) Order 2004 (S.I. 2004/938), art. 3, Sch. 2

F285. Sch. 1 Pt. VI: entry inserted by Justice (Northern Ireland) Act 2002 (c. 26), Sch. 3. A para. 17. (3) (as inserted (25.9.2006) by Constitutional Reform Act 2005 (c. 4), ss. 124. (3), 148, Sch. 15; S.I. 2006/1537, art. 3. (d))

F286. Sch. 1 Pt. VI: entry added (19.4.2004) by The Freedom of Information (Additional Public Authorities) Order 2004 (S.I. 2004/938), art. 3, Sch. 2

F287. Sch. 1 Pt. VI: entry inserted (27.7.2004) by Energy Act 2004 (c. 20), ss. 2. (10), 198. (2), Sch. 1 para. 18; S.I. 2004/1973, art. 2, Sch.

F288. Sch. 1 Pt. VI: entry inserted (11.8.2003) by The Freedom of Information (Additional Public Authorities) Order 2003 (S.I. 2003/1882), art. 2, Sch. 1

F289. Sch. 1 Pt. VI: entry inserted (coming into force in accordance with art. 1. (2)(3) of the amending S.I.) by The Nursing and Midwifery Order 2001 (S.I. 2002/253), art. 54. (3), Sch. 5 para. 17. (b) (with art. 3. (18))

F290. Sch. 1 Pt. VI: entry repealed (6.4.2005) by Pensions Act 2004 (c. 35), ss. 320, 322, Sch. 13 Pt. 1; S.I. 2005/275, art. 2. (7), Sch. Pt. 7 (subject to art. 2. (12))

F291. Sch. 1 Pt. VI: entry inserted (4.4.2011) by Budget Responsibility and National Audit Act 2011 (c. 4), ss. 3. (2), 29. (3), Sch. 1 para. 27; S.I. 2011/892, art. 3, Sch. 2 para. 1

F292. Sch. 1 Pt. VI: entry inserted (1.7.2002) by Office of Communications Act 2002 (c. 11), s. 1. (10), Sch. para. 22; S.I. 2002/1483, art. 2

F293. Words in Sch. 1 Pt. VI omitted (1.7.2012) by virtue of Health and Social Care Act 2012 (c. 7), s. 306. (4), Sch. 15 para. 71. (1)(c); S.I. 2012/1319, art. 2. (3)

F294. Sch. 1 Pt. VI: entry omitted (1.10.2011) by virtue of The Freedom of Information (Removal of References to Public Authorities) Order 2011 (S.I. 2011/1042), art. 2. (1), Sch. Pt. 1

F295. Sch. 1 Pt. VI: entry inserted (1.1.2009) by Legal Services Act 2007 (c. 29), ss. 114. (2), 211. (2), Sch. 15 para. 32 (with ss. 29, 192, 193); S.I. 2008/3149, art. 2. (e)(ii)

F296. Sch. 1 Pt. VI: entry inserted (11.8.2003) by The Freedom of Information (Additional Public Authorities) Order 2003 (S.I. 2003/1882), art. 2, Sch. 1

F297. Words in Sch. 1 Pt. VI inserted (10.3.2014) by Energy Act 2013 (c. 32), s. 156. (1), Sch. 12 para. 75; S.I. 2014/251, art. 3. (f)(iv)

F298. Sch. 1 Pt. VI: entry inserted (1.10.2010) by The Freedom of Information (Additional Public Authorities) Order 2010 (S.I. 2010/937), arts. 1. (2), 3, Sch. Pt. 1

F299. Sch. 1 Pt. VI: entry inserted (1.1.2018) by Higher Education and Research Act 2017 (c. 29), s. 124. (5), Sch. 1 para. 20; S.I. 2017/788, reg. 2. (b)

F300. Words in Sch. 1 Pt. VI inserted (28.11.2016) by Finance Act 2016 (c. 24), s. 189, Sch. 25 para. 14; S.I. 2016/1133, reg. 2

F301. Sch. 1 Pt. VI: entry repealed (1.4.2012) by Localism Act 2011 (c. 20), s. 240. (2), Sch. 16 para. 58, Sch. 25 Pt. 26; S.I. 2012/628, art. 6. (i)(j) (with arts. 9, 11, 14, 15, 17)

F302. Words in Sch. 1 Pt. VI omitted (2.12.2014) by virtue of The Olympic Delivery Authority (Dissolution) Order 2014 (S.I. 2014/3184), art. 1. (2), Sch. para. 14

F303. Sch. 1 Pt. VI: entry inserted (2.6.2008) by The Freedom of Information (Additional Public Authorities) Order 2008 (S.I. 2008/1271), art. 2, Sch.

F304. Sch. 1 Pt. VI: entry inserted (1.10.2011) by The Freedom of Information (Additional Public Authorities) Order 2011 (S.I. 2011/1041), art. 2. (1), Sch. 1 Pt. 1

F305. Sch. 1 Pt. VI: entry inserted (6.4.2005) by Pensions Act 2004 (c. 35), ss. 319. (1), 322, Sch. 12 para. 79; S.I. 2005/275, art. 2. (7), Sch. Pt. 7 (subject to art. 2. (12))

F306. Sch. 1 Pt. VI: entry omitted (1.10.2010) by virtue of The Freedom of Information (Removal of References to Public Authorities) Order 2010 (S.I. 2010/939), arts. 1. (2), 2, Sch. Pt. 1

F307. Sch. 1 Pt. VI: entry omitted (1.10.2011) by virtue of The Freedom of Information (Removal of References to Public Authorities) Order 2011 (S.I. 2011/1042), art. 2. (1), Sch. Pt. 1

F308. Sch. 1 Pt. VI: entry repealed (1.1.2009) by Health and Social Care Act 2008 (c. 14), ss. 166, 170, Sch. 15 Pt. 6; S.I. 2008/2497, art. 7. (2)(d)

F309. Words in Sch. 1 Pt. VI inserted (5.3.2015) by Infrastructure Act 2015 (c. 7), ss. 9. (8), 57. (1); S.I. 2015/481, reg. 2. (a)

F310. Words in Sch. 1 Pt. VI inserted (1.3.2014) by Financial Services (Banking Reform) Act 2013 (c. 33), s. 148. (5), Sch. 4 para. 15; S.I. 2014/377, art. 2. (1)(a), Sch. Pt. 1

F311. Sch. 1 Pt. VI: entry repealed (1.9.2005) by Pensions Act 2004 (c. 35), ss. 320, 322, Sch. 13 Pt. 1; S.I. 2005/1720, art. 2. (16), Sch. Pt. 3 (with arts. 4, 5)

F312. Sch. 1 Pt. VI: entry inserted (6.4.2005) by Pensions Act 2004 (c. 35), ss. 319. (1), 322, Sch. 12 para. 79; S.I. 2005/275, art. 2. (7), Sch. Pt. 7 (subject to art. 2. (12))

F313. Sch. 1 Pt. VI: entry omitted (1.10.2011) by virtue of The Freedom of Information (Removal of References to Public Authorities) Order 2011 (S.I. 2011/1042), art. 2. (1), Sch. Pt. 1

F314. Sch. 1 Pt. VI: entry inserted (11.8.2003) by The Freedom of Information (Additional Public Authorities) Order 2003 (S.I. 2003/1882), art. 2, Sch. 1

F315. Sch. 1 Pt. VI: entry added (19.4.2004) by The Freedom of Information (Additional Public Authorities) Order 2004 (S.I. 2004/938), art. 3, Sch. 2

F316. Words in Sch. 1 Pt. VI omitted (26.3.2015 for specified purposes, 20.4.2015 for specified purposes, 26.5.2015 in so far as not already in force) by virtue of Deregulation Act 2015 (c. 20), s. 115. (2)(e), Sch. 21 para. 1. (2)(b); S.I. 2015/994, arts. 5, 6. (p)

F317. Sch. 1 Pt. VI: entry added (19.4.2004) by The Freedom of Information (Additional Public Authorities) Order 2004 (S.I. 2004/938), art. 3, Sch. 2

F318. Sch. 1 Pt. VI: entry repealed (1.4.2004) by Police Reform Act 2002 (c. 30), ss. 107, 108. (2), Sch. 7 para. 23. (b), Sch. 8; S.I. 2004/913, art. 2. (c)(e)(f)(ix)

F319. Sch. 1 Pt. VI: entry repealed (1.4.2007) by Police and Justice Act 2006 (c. 48), ss. 52, 53, Sch. 15 Pt. 1. (A); S.I. 2007/709, art. 3. (o)(q) (subject to arts. 6, 7)

F320. Sch. 1 Pt. VI: entry repealed (1.9.2014 for E.W.N.I.) by Anti-social Behaviour, Crime and Policing Act 2014 (c. 12), s. 185. (1), Sch. 11 para. 102 (with ss. 21, 33, 42, 58, 75, 93); S.I. 2014/2125, art. 4. (d)(i)

F321. Words in Sch. 1 Pt. VI inserted (1.9.2014) by Anti-social Behaviour, Crime and Policing Act 2014 (c. 12), s. 185. (1), Sch. 11 para. 92 (with ss. 21, 33, 42, 58, 75, 93); ; S.I. 2014/2125, art. 2. (f)(v)

F322. Sch. 1 Pt. VI: entry omitted (1.10.2011) by virtue of Postal Services Act 2011 (c. 5), ss. 91. (1), 93. (3), Sch. 12 para. 157; S.I. 2011/2329, art. 3. (1)

F323. Sch. 1 Pt. VI: entry omitted (1.4.2010) by virtue of The General and Specialist Medical Practice (Education, Training and Qualifications) Order 2010 (S.I. 2010/234), arts. 1. (4), 7. (1), Sch. 3 para. 1. (2)(c); S.I. 2010/478, art. 2. (c)

F324. Sch. 1 Pt. VI: entry added (19.4.2004) by The Freedom of Information (Additional Public Authorities) Order 2004 (S.I. 2004/938), art. 3, Sch. 2

F325. Sch. 1 Pt. VI: entry inserted (1.10.2011) by The Freedom of Information (Additional Public Authorities) Order 2011 (S.I. 2011/1041), art. 2. (1), Sch. 1 Pt. 1

F326. Sch. 1 Pt. VI: entry inserted (1.4.2008) by The Offender Management Act 2007 (Consequential Amendments) Order 2008 (S.I. 2008/912), art. 3, Sch. 1 para. 17. (2)

F327. Words in Sch. 1 Pt. VI inserted (1.12.2012) by Health and Social Care Act 2012 (c. 7), s. 306. (4), Sch. 15 para. 69. (2); S.I. 2012/2657, art. 2. (3)

F328. Sch. 1 Pt. VI entry omitted (1.3.2017) by virtue of The Bank of England and Financial Services (Consequential Amendments) Regulations 2017 (S.I. 2017/80), reg. 1, Sch. para. 10. (a)

F329. Sch. 1 Pt. VI: entry added (19.4.2004) by The Freedom of Information (Additional Public Authorities) Order 2004 (S.I. 2004/938), art. 3, Sch. 2

F330. Sch. 1 Pt. VI: entry inserted (1.4.2006) by Public Services Ombudsman (Wales) Act 2005 (c. 10), ss. 39. (1), 40, Sch. 6 para. 71. (b); S.I. 2005/2800, art. 5. (1) (with art. 5. (2), Sch. 2)

F331. Words in Sch. 1 Pt. VI inserted (2.5.2016) by Small Business, Enterprise and Employment Act 2015 (c. 26), s. 164. (1), Sch. 1 para. 25; S.I. 2016/532, reg. 2. (a)

F332. Sch. 1 Pt. VI: entry omitted (1.4.2006) by virtue of The Qualifications, Curriculum and Assessment Authority for Wales (Transfer of Functions to the National Assembly for Wales and Abolition) Order 2005 (S.I. 2005/3239), art. 9. (1), Sch. 1 para. 31 (with art. 7)

F333. Words in Sch. 1 Pt. VI omitted (1.4.2012) by virtue of Education Act 2011 (c. 21), s. 82. (3), Sch. 8 para. 10; S.I. 2012/924, art. 2

F334. Words in Sch. 1 Pt. VI inserted (6.8.2015) by Qualifications Wales Act 2015 (anaw 5), s. 60. (2), Sch. 1 para. 37; S.I. 2015/1591, art. 2. (d)

F335. Sch. 1 Pt. VI: entry repealed (24.7.2005) by Railways Act 2005 (c. 14), ss. 59. (6)(7), 60, Sch. 13 (with s. 14. (4)(5), Sch. 11 para. 11. (2)); S.I. 2005/1909, art. 2, Sch.

F336. Sch. 1 Pt. VI: entry repealed (1.4.2013) by The Public Bodies (Abolition of the Railway Heritage Committee) Order 2013 (S.I. 2013/64), arts. 1. (2), 4 (with art. 8)

F337. Words in Sch. 1 Pt. VI repealed (1.7.2012 at 0.02 a.m.) by Public Bodies Act 2011 (c. 24), s. 38. (3), Sch. 6 (with Sch. 6 Note 1); S.I. 2012/1662, art. 2. (2)(b)

F338. Words in Sch. 1 Pt. VI repealed (31.3.2012) by Localism Act 2011 (c. 20), s. 240. (2), Sch. 25 Pt. 32; S.I. 2012/628, art. 4. (d)

F339. Words in Sch. 1 Pt. VI substituted (14.7.2014) by Water Act 2014 (c. 21), s. 94. (2)(r), Sch. 10 para. 17

F340. Words in Sch. 1 Pt. VI inserted (23.5.2014) by Transparency of Lobbying, Non-Party Campaigning and Trade Union Administration Act 2014 (c. 4), s. 45. (1)(a), Sch. 2 para. 13; S.I. 2014/1236, art. 2. (1)(k)

F341. Sch. 1 Pt. VI: entry inserted (7.2.2006) by The Freedom of Information (Additional Public Authorities) Order 2005 (S.I. 2005/3593), art. 2, Sch. 1

F342. Words in Sch. 1 Pt. VI omitted (1.10.2013) by virtue of The Public Bodies (Abolition of the Registrar of Public Lending Right) Order 2013 (S.I. 2013/2352), art. 1. (2), Sch. 1 para. 13 (with art. 8)

F343. Sch. 1 Pt. VI: entry inserted (1.10.2010) by The Freedom of Information (Additional Public Authorities) Order 2010 (S.I. 2010/937), arts. 1. (2), 3, Sch. Pt. 1

F344. Sch. 1 Pt. VI: entry omitted (1.10.2011) by virtue of The Freedom of Information (Removal of References to Public Authorities) Order 2011 (S.I. 2011/1042), art. 2. (1), Sch. Pt. 1

F345. Words in Sch. 1 Pt. VI omitted (31.3.2015) by virtue of Defence Reform Act 2014 (c. 20), s. 50. (1), Sch. 4 para. 21. (b); S.I. 2015/791, art. 3

F346. Sch. 1 Pt. VI: entry omitted (1.10.2011) by virtue of The Freedom of Information (Removal of References to Public Authorities) Order 2011 (S.I. 2011/1042), art. 2. (1), Sch. Pt. 1

F347. Sch. 1 Pt. VI: entry inserted (1.6.2006) by The Freedom of Information (Additional Public Authorities) Order 2005 (S.I. 2005/3593), art. 3, Sch. 2

F348. Sch. 1 Pt. VI: entry added (19.4.2004) by The Freedom of Information (Additional Public Authorities) Order 2004 (S.I. 2004/938), art. 3, Sch. 2

F349. Sch. 1 Pt. VI: entry omitted (27.9.2010) by virtue of The Pharmacy Order 2010 (S.I. 2010/231), arts. 1. (5), 68, Sch. 4 para. 9. (b); S.I. 2010/1621, art. 2. (1), Sch.

F350. Sch. 1 Pt. VI: entry inserted (1.10.2010) by The Freedom of Information (Additional Public Authorities) Order 2010 (S.I. 2010/937), arts. 1. (2), 3, Sch. Pt. 1

F351. Sch. 1 Pt. VI: entry inserted (1.10.2011) by The Freedom of Information (Additional Public Authorities) Order 2011 (S.I. 2011/1041), art. 2. (1), Sch. 1 Pt. 1

F352. Sch. 1 Pt. VI: entry inserted (11.8.2003) by The Freedom of Information (Additional Public Authorities) Order 2003 (S.I. 2003/1882), art. 2, Sch. 1

F353. Sch. 1 Pt. VI: entry repealed (29.12.2003) by Communications Act 2003 (c. 21), ss. 406. (6)(7), 411. (2), Sch. 19. (1) (with Sch. 18, Sch. 19. (1) Note 1); S.I. 2003/3142, art. 3. (1), Sch. 1 (subject to art. 3. (3) and with art. 11)

F354. Sch. 1 Pt. VI: entry omitted (19.9.2013) by virtue of The Public Bodies (Abolition of Administrative Justice and Tribunals Council) Order 2013 (S.I. 2013/2042), art. 1. (2), Sch. para. 22. (b)

F355. Sch. 1 Pt. VI: entry repealed (1.11.2007) by Tribunals, Courts and Enforcement Act 2007 (c. 15), ss. 146, 148. (5), Sch. 23 Pt. 1; S.I. 2007/2709, art. 3. (d)(vii)

F356. Sch. 1 Pt. VI: entry inserted (1.4.2003) by 2001 c. 12, ss. 1, 26, Sch. 1 para. 23; S.I. 2002/3125, art. 3. (d)

F357. Sch. 1 Pt. VI: entry inserted (6.4.2010) by Coroners and Justice Act 2009 (c. 25), ss. 177, 182, Sch. 21 para. 82; S.I. 2010/816, art. 2, Sch. para. 20. (b)

F358. Sch. 1 Pt. VI: entry repealed (6.4.2010) by Coroners and Justice Act 2009 (c. 25), ss. 178, 182, Sch. 23 Pt. 4; S.I. 2010/816, art. 2, Sch. para. 22. (b)(iii)

F359. Sch. 1 Pt. VI: entry repealed (1.4.2006) by Serious Organised Crime and Police Act 2005 (c. 15), ss. 59, 174. (2), 178, Sch. 4 para. 160, Sch. 17 Pt. 2; S.I. 2006/378, art. 4. (1), Sch. para. 13. (kk) (subject to art. 4. (2)-(7))

F360. Words in Sch. 1 Pt. VI inserted (14.7.2014) by Defence Reform Act 2014 (c. 20), s. 50. (1), Sch. 4 para. 21. (a); S.I. 2014/1751, art. 3. (g)

F361. Words in Sch. 1 Pt. VI inserted (6.4.2017) by Enterprise Act 2016 (c. 12), s. 44. (5), Sch. 1 para. 21; S.I. 2017/473, reg. 2

F362. Sch. 1 Pt. VI: entry inserted (11.8.2003) by The Freedom of Information (Additional Public Authorities) Order 2003 (S.I. 2003/1882), art. 2, Sch. 1

F363. Sch. 1 Pt. VI: entry inserted (11.8.2003) by The Freedom of Information (Additional Public Authorities) Order 2003 (S.I. 2003/1882), art. 2, Sch. 1

F364. Sch. 1 Pt. VI: entry inserted (11.8.2003) by The Freedom of Information (Additional Public Authorities) Order 2003 (S.I. 2003/1882), art. 2, Sch. 1

F365. Words in Sch. 1 Pt. VI repealed (1.8.2013) by Welfare Reform Act 2012 (c. 5), s. 150. (3), Sch. 14 Pt. 8; S.I. 2012/3090, art. 2. (2)(c)

F366. Words in Sch. 1 Pt. VI inserted (8.5.2012) by Welfare Reform Act 2012 (c. 5), s. 150. (2)(j), Sch. 13 para. 17. (b)

F367. Sch. 1 Pt. VI: entry omitted (1.10.2010) by virtue of The Freedom of Information (Removal of References to Public Authorities) Order 2010 (S.I. 2010/939), arts. 1. (2), 2, Sch. Pt. 1

F368. Sch. 1 Pt. VI: entry added (19.4.2004) by The Freedom of Information (Additional Public Authorities) Order 2004 (S.I. 2004/938), art. 3, Sch. 2

F369. Sch. 1 Pt. VI: entry omitted (1.10.2010) by virtue of The Freedom of Information (Removal of References to Public Authorities) Order 2010 (S.I. 2010/939), arts. 1. (2), 2, Sch. Pt. 1

F370. Sch. 1 Pt. VI: entry inserted (1.11.2011) by Sports Grounds Safety Authority Act 2011 (c. 6), ss. 6. (1), 8. (1), Sch. 2 para. 8; S.I. 2011/2597, art. 2

F371. Sch. 1 Pt. VI: entry repealed (1.4.2012) by Localism Act 2011 (c. 20), s. 240. (2), Sch. 4 para. 54, Sch. 25 Pt. 5; S.I. 2012/628, art. 6. (h) (with arts. 9, 11, 14, 15, 17)

F372. Sch. 1 Pt. VI: entry inserted (11.8.2003) by The Freedom of Information (Additional Public Authorities) Order 2003 (S.I. 2003/1882), art. 2, Sch. 1

F373. Sch. 1 Pt. VI: entry inserted (11.8.2003) by The Freedom of Information (Additional Public Authorities) Order 2003 (S.I. 2003/1882), art. 2, Sch. 1

F374. Sch. 1 Pt. VI: entry repealed (1.12.2006) by Railways Act 2005 (c. 14), ss. 59. (6)(7), 60, Sch. 13 (with s. 14. (4)(5), Sch. 11 para. 11. (2)); S.I. 2006/2911, art. 2, Sch. (subject to arts. 3-7)

F375. Sch. 1 Pt. VI: entry added (19.4.2004) by The Freedom of Information (Additional Public Authorities) Order 2004 (S.I. 2004/938), art. 3, Sch. 2

F376. Sch. 1 Pt. VI: entry inserted (2.6.2008) by The Freedom of Information (Additional Public Authorities) Order 2008 (S.I. 2008/1271), art. 2, Sch.

F377. Sch. 1 Pt. VI: entry repealed (1.9.2005) by Education Act 2005 (c. 18), ss. 123, 125. (3)(b), Sch. 19 Pt. 3

F378. Sch. 1 Pt. VI: entry inserted (11.8.2003) by The Freedom of Information (Additional Public Authorities) Order 2003 (S.I. 2003/1882), art. 2, Sch. 1

F379. Sch. 1 Pt. VI: entry inserted (1.10.2011) by The Freedom of Information (Additional Public Authorities) Order 2011 (S.I. 2011/1041), art. 2. (1), Sch. 1 Pt. 1

F380. Words in Sch. 1 Pt. VI substituted (3.7.2013) by The Local Transport Act 2008 (Traffic Commissioners) (Consequential Amendments) Order 2013 (S.I. 2013/1644), art. 1. (1), Sch. 1 (with arts. 1. (3), 2, 7)

F381. Words in Sch. 1 Pt. VI omitted (1.4.2012) by virtue of Education Act 2011 (c. 21), s. 82. (3), Sch. 5 para. 16; S.I. 2012/924, art. 2

F382. Sch. 1 Pt. VI: entry inserted (1.10.2011) by The Freedom of Information (Additional Public Authorities) Order 2011 (S.I. 2011/1041), art. 2. (1), Sch. 1 Pt. 1

F383. Sch. 1 Pt. VI: entry inserted (5.7.2010) by Pensions Act 2008 (c. 30), ss. 75, 149, Sch. 1 para. 24; S.I. 2010/10, art. 2. (a)

F384. Sch. 1 Pt. VI: entry inserted (11.8.2003) by The Freedom of Information (Additional Public Authorities) Order 2003 (S.I. 2003/1882), art. 2, Sch. 1

F385. Sch. 1 Pt. VI: entry inserted (2.6.2008) by The Freedom of Information (Additional Public Authorities) Order 2008 (S.I. 2008/1271), art. 2, Sch.

F386. Sch. 1 Pt. VI: entry omitted by virtue of The Nursing and Midwifery Order 2001 (S.I. 2002/253), art. 54. (3), Sch. 5 para. 17. (b) (with art. 3. (18)) (the amendment coming into force in accordance with art. 1. (2)(3) of the amending S.I.)

F387. Sch. 1 Pt. VI: entry omitted (1.10.2011) by virtue of The Freedom of Information (Removal of References to Public Authorities) Order 2011 (S.I. 2011/1042), art. 2. (1), Sch. Pt. 1

F388. Sch. 1 Pt. VI: entry inserted (1.6.2006) by The Freedom of Information (Additional Public Authorities) Order 2005 (S.I. 2005/3593), art. 3, Sch. 2

F389. Sch. 1 Pt. VI: entry inserted (1.4.2004) by Local Government Act 2003 (c. 26), ss. 105. (9), 128, Sch. 4 para. 24; S.I. 2003/2938, art. 6. (a) (subject to art. 8, Sch.)

F390. Sch. 1 Pt. VI: entry inserted (1.6.2006) by The Freedom of Information (Additional Public Authorities) Order 2005 (S.I. 2005/3593), art. 3, Sch. 2

F391. Sch. 1 Pt. VI: entry inserted (11.8.2003) by The Freedom of Information (Additional Public Authorities) Order 2003 (S.I. 2003/1882), art. 2, Sch. 1

F392. Words in Sch. 1 Pt. VI inserted (1.4.2014) by Public Audit (Wales) Act 2013 (anaw 3), s. 35. (2), Sch. 4 para. 19 (with Sch. 3 para. 3); S.I. 2013/1466, art. 3. (1)

F393. Sch. 1 Pt. VI: entry inserted (1.4.2005) by Health (Wales) Act 2003 (c. 4), ss. 7. (1), 10. (2), Sch. 3 para. 15; S.I. 2003/2660, art. 3. (2)

F394. Sch. 1 Pt. VI: entry omitted (1.4.2006) by virtue of The Wales Tourist Board (Transfer of Functions to the National Assembly for Wales and Abolition) Order 2005 (S.I. 2005/3225), arts. 1. (2), 2, 6. (2), Sch. 2 Pt. 1 para. 5 (with art. 3. (1))

F395. Sch. 1 Pt. VI: entry omitted (1.10.2010) by virtue of The Freedom of Information (Removal of References to Public Authorities) Order 2010 (S.I. 2010/939), arts. 1. (2), 2, Sch. Pt. 1

F396. Sch. 1 Pt. VI: entry repealed (1.4.2006) by Public Services Ombudsman (Wales) Act 2005 (c. 10), ss. 39, 40, Sch. 6 para. 71. (a), Sch. 7; S.I. 2005/2800, art. 5. (1) (with art. 5. (2), Sch. 2)

F397. Sch. 1 Pt. VI: entry repealed (29.12.2003) by Communications Act 2003 (c. 21), ss. 406. (6)(7), 411. (2), Sch. 19. (1) (with Sch. 18, Sch. 19. (1) Note 1); S.I. 2003/3142, art. 3. (1), Sch. 1 (subject to art. 3. (3) and with art. 11)

F398. Sch. 1 Pt. VI: entry omitted (19.9.2013) by virtue of The Public Bodies (Abolition of Administrative Justice and Tribunals Council) Order 2013 (S.I. 2013/2042), art. 1. (2), Sch. para. 22. (c)

F399. Sch. 1 Pt. VI: entry repealed (1.4.2006) by The Welsh Development Agency (Transfer of Functions to the National Assembly for Wales and Abolition) Order 2005 (S.I. 2005/3226), arts. 1. (2), 2, 7. (1)(b), Sch. 2 Pt. 1 para. 13 (with art. 3. (1))

F400. Words in Sch. 1 Pt. VI omitted (1.4.2012) by virtue of The Welsh Language (Wales) Measure 2011 (Transfer of functions, Transitional and Consequential Provisions) Order 2012 (S.I. 2012/990), arts. 1. (2), 8

F401. Sch. 1 Pt. VI: entry omitted by virtue of The Nursing and Midwifery Order 2001 (S.I. 2002/253), art. 54. (3), Sch. 5 para. 17 (with art. 3. (18)) (the amendment coming into force in accordance with art. 1. (2)(3) of the amending S.I.)

F402. Sch. 1 Pt. VI: entry added (19.4.2004) by The Freedom of Information (Additional Public Authorities) Order 2004 (S.I. 2004/938), art. 3, Sch. 2

F403. Sch. 1 Pt. VI: entry omitted (1.10.2010) by virtue of The Freedom of Information (Removal of References to Public Authorities) Order 2010 (S.I. 2010/939), arts. 1. (2), 2, Sch. Pt. 1

F404. Sch. 1 Pt. VI: entry added (19.4.2004) by The Freedom of Information (Additional Public Authorities) Order 2004 (S.I. 2004/938), art. 3, Sch. 2

F405. Words in Sch. 1 Pt. VI omitted (1.4.2012) by virtue of Education Act 2011 (c. 21), s. 82. (3), Sch. 16 para. 17; S.I. 2012/924, art. 2

Marginal Citations

M351988 c. 50.

M361994 c. 21.

Part VII Other public bodies and offices: Northern Ireland

[F406. An advisory committee established under paragraph 25 of the Health and Personal Social Services (Northern Ireland) Order 1972.]

F407...

The Advisory Committee on Justices of the Peace in Northern Ireland.

F408...

F409...

F410...

The Agricultural Wages Board for Northern Ireland.

[F411. The Agri-food and Biosciences Institute]

The Arts Council of Northern Ireland.

The Assembly Ombudsman for Northern Ireland.

[F412. The Attorney General for Northern Ireland.]

[F413. The Belfast Harbour Commissioners.]

The Board of Trustees of National Museums and Galleries of Northern Ireland.

F414...

The Boundary Commission for Northern Ireland.

[F415. A central advisory committee established under paragraph 24 of the Health and Personal Social Services (Northern Ireland) Order 1972.]

[F416. The Certification Officer for Northern Ireland.]

The Charities Advisory Committee.

[F417. The Charity Commission for Northern Ireland]

The Chief Electoral Officer for Northern Ireland.

[F418. The Chief Inspector of Criminal Justice in Northern Ireland.]

The Civil Service Commissioners for Northern Ireland.

[F419. Comhairle na Gaelscolaíochta.]

[F420. The Commission for Victims and Survivors for Northern Ireland]

[F421. The Commissioner for Children and Young People for Northern Ireland]

[F422. The Commissioner for Older People for Northern Ireland]

The Commissioner for Public Appointments for Northern Ireland.

F423...

The Construction Industry Training Board.

The consultative Civic Forum referred to in section 56. (4) of the M37. Northern Ireland Act 1998.

The Council for Catholic Maintained Schools.

The Council for Nature Conservation and the Countryside.

The County Court Rules Committee (Northern Ireland).

[F424. The Criminal Injuries Compensation Appeals Panel for Northern Ireland, in relation to information held by it otherwise than as a tribunal.]

[F425. A development corporation established under Part III of the Strategic Investment and Regeneration of Sites (Northern Ireland) Order 2003]

F426...

The Distinction and Meritorious Service Awards Committee.

F427...

The Drainage Council for Northern Ireland.

[F428. The Education Authority]

F429...

The Equality Commission for Northern Ireland.

The Family Proceedings Rules Committee (Northern Ireland).

F430...

F431...

The General Consumer Council for Northern Ireland.

[F432. The General Teaching Council for Northern Ireland.]

[F433. The Governors of the Armargh Observatory and Planetarium.]
[F434. The Harbour of Donaghadee Commissioners.]
The Health and Safety Agency for Northern Ireland.
The Historic Buildings Council.
The Historic Monuments Council.
The Independent Assessor of Military Complaints Procedures in Northern Ireland.
The Independent Commissioner for Holding Centres.
[F435. The Independent Financial Review Panel]
[F436. An independent monitoring board appointed under section 10 of the Prison Act (Northern Ireland) 1953.]
The Independent Reviewer of the Northern Ireland (Emergency Provisions) Act.
F437...
F437...
[F438. Invest Northern Ireland]
F439...
The Labour Relations Agency.
F440...
F441...
The Lay Observer for Northern Ireland.
F439...
F442...
F443...
The Livestock & Meat Commission for Northern Ireland.
F437...
The Local Government Staff Commission.
[F444. The Londonderry Port and Harbour Commissioners.]
The Magistrates' Courts Rules Committee (Northern Ireland).
F445...
F446...
The Northern Ireland Audit Office.
[F447. The Northern Ireland Authority for Utility Regulation.]
The Northern Ireland Building Regulations Advisory Committee.
The Northern Ireland Civil Service Appeal Board.
The Northern Ireland Commissioner for Complaints.
The Northern Ireland Community Relations Council.
F439...
The Northern Ireland Council for the Curriculum, Examinations and Assessment.
F439...
[F448. The Northern Ireland Court of Judicature Rules Committee.]
The Northern Ireland Crown Court Rules Committee.
F449...
[F450. The Northern Ireland Events Company.]
[F451. The Northern Ireland Fire and Rescue Service Board]
The Northern Ireland Fishery Harbour Authority.
[F452. The Northern Ireland Health and Personal Social Services Regulation and Improvement Authority.]
The Northern Ireland Higher Education Council.
The Northern Ireland Housing Executive.
The Northern Ireland Human Rights Commission.
The Northern Ireland Insolvency Rules Committee.
[F453. The Northern Ireland Judicial Appointments Commission.]
[F454. The Northern Ireland Law Commission.]
F455...

[F456. The Northern Ireland Library Authority]

The Northern Ireland Local Government Officers' Superannuation Committee.

The Northern Ireland Museums Council.

F457...

[F458. The Northern Ireland Practice and Education Council for Nursing and Midwifery.]

[F459. The Northern Ireland Social Care Council.]

F460...

The Northern Ireland Tourist Board.

The Northern Ireland Transport Holding Company.

F461...

F449...

The Parades Commission.

[F462. Parole Commissioners for Northern Ireland]

[F463. The Pharmaceutical Society of Northern Ireland, in respect of information held by it otherwise than as a tribunal.]

[F464. The Poisons Board (Northern Ireland).]

The Police Ombudsman for Northern Ireland.

[F465. A policing and community safety partnership or a district policing and community safety partnership established under Part 3 of the Justice (Northern Ireland) Act 2011.]

[F466. The Prisoner Ombudsman for Northern Ireland.]

The Probation Board for Northern Ireland.

[F467. The Royal Ulster Constabulary George Cross Foundation.]

The Rural Development Council for Northern Ireland.

[F468. The Safeguarding Board for Northern Ireland]

The Sentence Review Commissioners appointed under section 1 of the M38. Northern Ireland (Sentences) Act 1998.

F469...

[F470. The discretionary support Commissioner appointed under Article 136 of the Welfare Reform (Northern Ireland) Order 2015.]

The Sports Council for Northern Ireland.

The Staff Commission for Education and Library Boards.

The Statistics Advisory Committee.

The Statute Law Committee for Northern Ireland.

F427...

[F439. The Training and Employment Agency.]

Ulster Supported Employment Ltd.

[F471. The Warrenpoint Harbour Authority.]

[F472. The Waste Management Advisory Board.]

The Youth Council for Northern Ireland.

Amendments (Textual)

F406. Sch. 1 Pt. VII: entry added (19.4.2004) by The Freedom of Information (Additional Public Authorities) Order 2004 (S.I. 2004/938), art. 4, Sch. 3

F407. Sch. 1 Pt. VII: entry omitted (1.4.2009) by virtue of The Transfer of Tribunal Functions and Revenue and Customs Appeals Order 2009 (S.I. 2009/56), art. 3, Sch. 1 para. 296. (b)

F408. Sch. 1 Pt. VII: entry repealed (1.4.2005) by Justice (Northern Ireland) Act 2002 (c. 26), ss. 86, 87. (1), Sch. 13; S.R. 2005/109, art. 2, Sch.

F409. Words in Sch. 1 Pt. VII repealed (27.3.2015) by The Public Bodies (Abolition of the Advisory Committees on Pesticides) Order 2015 (S.I. 2015/978), art. 1. (2), Sch. Pt. 1

F410. Sch. 1 Pt. VII: entry repealed (N.I.) (1.4.2006) by The Agriculture (Northern Ireland) Order 2004 (S.I. 2004/3327 (N.I. 23)), arts. 1. (3), 13, Sch. 4; S.R. 2006/172, art. 2

F411. Sch. 1 Pt. VII: entry inserted (N.I.) (1.4.2006) by The Agriculture (Northern Ireland) Order 2004 (S.I. 2004/3327 (N.I. 23)), arts. 1. (3), 3. (5), Sch. 1 para. 21; S.R. 2006/172, art. 2

F412. Sch. 1 Pt. VII: entry inserted (12.4.2010) by Justice (Northern Ireland) Act 2002 (c. 26), ss.

23. (9), 87. (1); S.R. 2010/113, art. 2, Sch. para. 3

F413. Sch. 1 Pt. VII: entry added (11.11.2002) by The Freedom of Information (Additional Public Authorities) Order 2002 (S.I. 2002/2623), art. 3, Sch. 2

F414. Sch. 1. Pt. VII: entry repealed (19.8.2005) by The Criminal Justice (Northern Ireland) Order 2005 (S.I. 2005/1965 (N.I. 15)), arts. 1. (4), 10. (2), 27, Sch. 1 para. 10. (a), Sch. 2

F415. Sch. 1 Pt. VII: entry added (19.4.2004) by The Freedom of Information (Additional Public Authorities) Order 2004 (S.I. 2004/938), art. 4, Sch. 3

F416. Sch. 1 Pt. VII: entry added (11.11.2002) by The Freedom of Information (Additional Public Authorities) Order 2002 (S.I. 2002/2623), art. 3, Sch. 2

F417. Sch. 1 Pt. VII: entry inserted (N.I.) (27.3.2009) by Charities Act (Northern Ireland) 2008 (c. 12), ss. 6. (7), 185, Sch. 1 para. 14; S.R. 2009/138, art. 2, Sch.

F418. Sch. 1 Pt. VII: entry inserted (26.5.2003) by Justice (Northern Ireland) Act 2002 (c. 26), ss. 45. (3), 87, Sch. 8 para. 16; S.R. 2003/265, art. 2

F419. Sch. 1 Pt. VII: entry inserted (11.8.2003) by The Freedom of Information (Additional Public Authorities) Order 2003 (S.I. 2003/1882), art. 3, Sch. 2

F420. Sch. 1 Pt. VII: entry inserted (N.I.) by The Victims and Survivors (Northern Ireland) Order 2006 (S.I. 2006/2953 (N.I. 17)), Sch. para. 19 (as substituted (23.5.2008) by Commission for Victims and Survivors Act (Northern Ireland) 2008 (c. 6), s. 1. (2), Sch. 1)

F421. Sch. 1 Pt. VII: entry inserted (N.I.) (14.3.2003) by The Commissioner for Children and Young People (Northern Ireland) Order 2003 (S.I. 2003/439 (N.I. 11)), arts. 1. (2)(b), 5. (3), Sch. 2 para. 15

F422. Sch. 1 Pt. 7: entry inserted (9.2.2011) by Commissioner for Older People Act (Northern Ireland) 2011 (c. 1 (N.I.)), s. 28. (1)(a), Sch. 1 para. 15

F423. Sch. 1 Pt. VII: entry repealed (N.I.) (23.5.2008) by Commission for Victims and Survivors Act (Northern Ireland) 2008 (c. 6), s. 1, Sch. 2

F424. Sch. 1 Pt. VII: entry inserted (11.8.2003) by The Freedom of Information (Additional Public Authorities) Order 2003 (S.I. 2003/1882), art. 3, Sch. 2

F425. Sch. 1 Pt. VII: entry inserted (N.I.) (7.3.2003) by The Strategic Investment and Regeneration of Sites (Northern Ireland) Order 2003 (S.I. 2003/410 (N.I. 1)), arts. 1. (2), 15. (3), Sch. 1 para. 23

F426. Words in Sch. 1 Pt. VII repealed (1.5.2015) by Public Authorities (Reform) Act (Northern Ireland) 2009 (c. 3), s. 7. (1), Sch. 3 (with Sch. 1 para. 4. (3)); S.R. 2015/230, art. 2. (c)

F427. Words in Sch. 1 Pt. VII repealed (1.4.2012) by Justice Act (Northern Ireland) 2011 (c. 24), s. 111. (3), Sch. 8 Pt. 2; S.R. 2012/142, art. 2. (e)

F428. Words in Sch. 1 Pt. VII substituted (12.12.2014) by Education Act (Northern Ireland) 2014 (c. 12), s. 7, Sch. 1 para. 19 (with Sch. 2 para. 4. (3))

F429. Sch. 1 Pt. VII: entry repealed (N.I.) (prosp.) by Public Authorities (Reform) Act (Northern Ireland) 2009 (c. 3), ss. 6, 7, Sch. 3; and omitted (1.10.2010) by virtue of The Freedom of Information (Removal of References to Public Authorities) Order 2010 (S.I. 2010/939), art. 3, Sch. Pt. 3

F430. Sch. 1 Pt. VII: entry repealed (N.I.) (1.7.2006) by The Fire and Rescue Services (Northern Ireland) Order 2006 (S.I. 2006/1254 (N.I. 9)), arts. 1. (3), 63. (2), Sch. 4 (with art. 49); S.R. 2006/257, art. 2. (b)(e)(v)

F431. Sch. 1 Pt. VII: entry repealed (N.I.) (1.6.2009) by Public Authorities (Reform) Act (Northern Ireland) 2009 (c. 3), ss. 1, 7, Sch. 1 para. 13, Sch. 3; S.R. 2009/172, art. 2. (e)

F432. Sch. 1 Pt. VII: entry inserted (11.8.2003) by The Freedom of Information (Additional Public Authorities) Order 2003 (S.I. 2003/1882), art. 3, Sch. 2

F433. Sch. 1 Pt. VII: entry inserted (11.8.2003) by The Freedom of Information (Additional Public Authorities) Order 2003 (S.I. 2003/1882), art. 3, Sch. 2

F434. Sch. 1 Pt. VII: entry inserted (11.8.2003) by The Freedom of Information (Additional Public Authorities) Order 2003 (S.I. 2003/1882), art. 3, Sch. 2

F435. Sch. 1 Pt. 7: entry inserted (N.I.) (29.3.2011) by Assembly Members (Independent Financial Review and Standards) Act (Northern Ireland) 2011 (c. 17), ss. 36, 38. (1)(c), Sch. 5 para. 3

F436. Sch. 1. Pt. VII: entry inserted (19.8.2005) by The Criminal Justice (Northern Ireland) Order 2005 (S.I. 2005/1965 (N.I. 15)), arts. 1. (4), 10. (2), Sch. 1 para. 10. (b)

F437. Sch. 1 Pt. VII: entries repealed (N.I.) (1.4.2002) by Industrial Development Act (Northern Ireland) 2002 (c. 1 (N.I.)), s. 5. (4), Sch. 4 (with Sch. 2 paras. 1. (4), 4. (4), 6. (4)); S.R. 2002/134, art. 2

F438. Sch. 1 Pt. VII: entry inserted (N.I.) (1.4.2002) by Industrial Development Act (Northern Ireland) 2002 (c. 1 (N.I.)), s. 1. (2), Sch. 1 para. 21 (with Sch. 2 paras. 1. (4), 4. (4), 6. (4)); S.R. 2002/134, art. 2

F439. Sch. 1 Pt. VII: entries removed (29.6.2004) by virtue of The Freedom of Information (Removal of References to Public Authorities) Order 2004 (S.I. 2004/1641), art. 3, Sch. 2

F440. Sch. 1 Pt. VII: entry repealed (N.I.) (1.6.2009) by Public Authorities (Reform) Act (Northern Ireland) 2009 (c. 3), ss. 5. (1)(a)(iii), 6, 7, Sch. 3; S.R. 2009/172, art. 2. (e)

F441. Sch. 1 Pt. 7: entry omitted (1.10.2011) by virtue of The Freedom of Information (Removal of References to Public Authorities) Order 2011 (S.I. 2011/1042), art. 2. (2), Sch. Pt. 2

F442. Sch. 1 Pt. 7: entry omitted (1.10.2011) by virtue of The Freedom of Information (Removal of References to Public Authorities) Order 2011 (S.I. 2011/1042), art. 2. (2), Sch. Pt. 2

F443. Sch. 1 Pt. VII: entry omitted (15.5.2008) by virtue of The Criminal Justice (Northern Ireland Consequential Amendments) Order 2008 (S.I. 2008/1241), art. 4. (a)

F444. Sch. 1 Pt. VII: entry added (11.11.2002) by The Freedom of Information (Additional Public Authorities) Order 2002 (S.I. 2002/2623), art. 3, Sch. 2

F445. Sch. 1 Pt. VII: entry repealed (N.I.) (1.4.2009) by Health and Social Care (Reform) Act (Northern Ireland) 2009 (c. 1), ss. 32, 33, 34, Sch. 6 para. 17. (3), Sch. 7; S.R. 2009/114, art. 2

F446. Sch. 1 Pt. VII: entry repealed (29.12.2003) by Communications Act 2003 (c. 21), ss. 406. (6)(7), 411. (2), Sch. 19. (1) (with Sch 18, Sch. 19. (1) Note 1); S.I. 2003/3142, art. 3. (1), Sch. 1 (subject to art. 3. (3) and with art. 11)

F447. Sch. 1 Pt. VII: entry inserted (N.I.) (1.4.2007) by The Water and Sewerage Services (Northern Ireland) Order 2006 (S.I. 2006/3336 (N.I. 21)), arts. 1. (2), 308. (1), Sch. 12 para. 43 (with art. 307); S.R. 2007/194, art. 2. (2), Sch. 1 Pt. 2 (subject to art. 3)

F448. Sch. 1 Pt. VII: entry inserted (1.10.2009) by Constitutional Reform Act 2005 (c. 4), ss. 59. (5), 148. (1), Sch. 11 para. 34. (b); S.I. 2009/1604, art. 2. (d)

F449. Sch. 1 Pt. VII: entries removed (7.2.2006) by virtue of The Freedom of Information (Removal of References to Public Authorities) Order 2005 (S.I. 2005/3594), art. 2, Sch. 1

F450. Sch. 1 Pt. VII: entry added (1.6.2006) by The Freedom of Information (Additional Public Authorities) Order 2005 (S.I. 2005/3593), art. 5, Sch. 4

F451. Sch. 1 Pt. VII: entry inserted (N.I.) (1.7.2006) by The Fire and Rescue Services (Northern Ireland) Order 2006 (S.I. 2006/1254 (N.I. 9)), arts. 1. (3), 3. (3), Sch. 1 para. 19 (with art. 49); S.R. 2006/257, art. 2. (a)(c)

F452. Sch. 1 Pt. VII: entry added (7.2.2006) by The Freedom of Information (Additional Public Authorities) Order 2005 (S.I. 2005/3593), art. 4, Sch. 3

F453. Sch. 1 Pt. VII: entry inserted (15.6.2005) by Justice (Northern Ireland) Act 2002 (c. 26), ss. 3. (3), 87. (1), Sch. 2 para. 20; S.R. 2005/281, art. 3. (1), Sch. 2 paras. 2, 6 (subject to art. 3. (2)(3))

F454. Sch. 1 Pt. VII: entry inserted (16.4.2007) by Justice (Northern Ireland) Act 2002 (c. 26), ss. 50. (7), 87. (1), Sch. 9 para. 15; S.R. 2007/237, art. 2, Sch. paras. 1, 5

F455. Words in Sch. 1 Pt. VII repealed (1.4.2015) by Legal Aid and Coroners' Courts Act (Northern Ireland) 2014 (c. 11), s. 12. (1), Sch. 2 para. 3, Sch. 3 Pt. 1 (with ss. 2. (3), 9, Sch. 1 para. 3. (3)); S.R. 2015/193, art. 2. (e)(f)

F456. Sch. 1 Pt. VII: entry inserted (N.I.) (1.10.2008) by Libraries Act (Northern Ireland) 2008 (c. 8), ss. 10, 12, Sch. 3 para. 6; S.R. 2008/396, art. 2. (h)

F457. Sch. 1 Pt. VII: entry repealed (N.I.) (1.6.2009) by Public Authorities (Reform) Act (Northern Ireland) 2009 (c. 3), ss. 6, 7, Sch. 3; S.R. 2009/172, art. 2. (e); and expressed to be omitted (1.10.2010) by virtue of The Freedom of Information (Removal of References to Public Authorities) Order 2010 (S.I. 2010/939), art. 3, Sch. Pt. 3

F458. Sch. 1 Pt. VII: entry inserted (11.8.2003) by The Freedom of Information (Additional Public

Authorities) Order 2003 (S.I. 2003/1882), art. 3, Sch. 2

F459. Sch. 1 Pt. VII: entry inserted (11.8.2003) by The Freedom of Information (Additional Public Authorities) Order 2003 (S.I. 2003/1882), art. 3, Sch. 2

F460. Sch. 1 Pt. VII: entry repealed (1.10.2009) by Constitutional Reform Act 2005 (c. 4), ss. 59. (5), 148. (1), Sch. 11 para. 34. (a), Sch. 18 Pt. 5; S.I. 2009/1604, art. 2. (f)

F461. Sch. 1 Pt. VII: entry repealed (N.I.) (1.4.2007) by The Water and Sewerage Services (Northern Ireland) Order 2006 (S.I. 2006/3336 (N.I. 21)), arts. 1. (2), 308. (2), Sch. 13 (with art. 307); S.R. 2007/194, art. 2. (2), Sch. 1 Pt. 2 (subject to art. 3)

F462. Sch. 1 Pt. VII: entry inserted (15.5.2008) by virtue of The Criminal Justice (Northern Ireland Consequential Amendments) Order 2008 (S.I. 2008/1241), art. 4. (b)

F463. Sch. 1 Pt. VII: entry added (1.6.2006) by The Freedom of Information (Additional Public Authorities) Order 2005 (S.I. 2005/3593), art. 5, Sch. 4

F464. Sch. 1 Pt. VII: entry added (7.2.2006) by The Freedom of Information (Additional Public Authorities) Order 2005 (S.I. 2005/3593), art. 4, Sch. 3

F465. Words in Sch. 1 Pt. VII inserted (1.4.2012) by Justice Act (Northern Ireland) 2011 (c. 24), s. 111. (3), Sch. 7 para. 9; S.R. 2012/142, art. 2. (d)

F466. Sch. 1 Pt. 7: entry inserted (1.10.2011) by The Freedom of Information (Additional Public Authorities) Order 2011 (S.I. 2011/1041), art. 2. (2), Sch. 1 Pt. 2

F467. Sch. 1 Pt. 7: entry inserted (1.10.2011) by The Freedom of Information (Additional Public Authorities) Order 2011 (S.I. 2011/1041), art. 2. (2), Sch. 1 Pt. 2

F468. Words in Sch. 1 Pt. VII inserted (14.9.2012) by Safeguarding Board Act (Northern Ireland) 2011 (c. 7), ss. 13. (3), 17. (2); S.R. 2012/338, art. 2. (1)

F469. Words in Sch. 1 Pt. VII repealed (N.I.) (31.3.2017) by The Welfare Reform (Northern Ireland) Order 2015 (S.I. 2015/2006), art. 2. (2), Sch. 12 Pt. 7; S.R. 2016/411, art. 3. (3)(c)

F470. Words in Sch. 1 Pt. VII inserted (17.2.2016) by The Welfare Reform (Northern Ireland) Order 2015 (S.I. 2015/2006 (N.I. 1)), arts. 2. (2), 136. (9); S.R. 2016/46, art. 3. (5)(f)

F471. Sch. 1 Pt. VII: entry added (11.11.2002) by The Freedom of Information (Additional Public Authorities) Order 2002 (S.I. 2002/2623), art. 3, Sch. 2

F472. Sch. 1 Pt. VII: entry inserted (11.8.2003) by The Freedom of Information (Additional Public Authorities) Order 2003 (S.I. 2003/1882), art. 3, Sch. 2

Marginal Citations

M371998 c. 47.

M381998 c. 35.

Schedule 2. The Commissioner and the Tribunal

Section 18. (4).

Part I Provision consequential on s. 18(1) and (2)

General

1. (1)Any reference in any enactment, instrument or document to the Data Protection Commissioner or the Data Protection Registrar shall be construed, in relation to any time after the commencement of section 18. (1), as a reference to the Information Commissioner.

(2) F1. . . . .

Amendments (Textual)

F1. Sch. 2 para. 1. (2) repealed (18.1.2010) by The Transfer of Tribunal Functions Order 2010 (S.I. 2010/22), arts. 1. (1), 5. (3), Sch. 4 Pt. 1

I1. Sch. 2 para. 1 wholly in force at 14.5.2001; Sch. 2 para. 1. (1) in force at 30.1.2001, see s. 87. (2)(c)(3); Sch. 1 para. 1. (2) in force at 14.5.2001 by S.I. 2001/1637, art. 2. (b)

[F21. AThe Office for Standards in Education, Children's Services and Skills, in respect of information held for purposes other than those of the functions exercisable by Her Majesty's Chief Inspector of Education, Children's Services and Skills by virtue of section 5. (1)(a)(iii) of the Care Standards Act 2000.]

Amendments (Textual)
F2. Sch. 1 Pt. 1 para. 1. A inserted (1.4.2007) by Education and Inspections Act 2006 (c. 40), ss. 157, 188, Sch. 14 para. 69. (2)(b); S.I. 2007/935, art. 5. (gg)

2. (1)Any reference in this Act or in any instrument under this Act to the Commissioner shall be construed, in relation to any time before the commencement of section 18. (1), as a reference to the Data Protection Commissioner.

(2) F3. . . . .

Amendments (Textual)
F3. Sch. 2 para. 2. (2) repealed (18.1.2010) by The Transfer of Tribunal Functions Order 2010 (S.I. 2010/22), arts. 1. (1), 5. (3), Sch. 4 Pt. 1

Public Records Act 1958 (c. 51)

3. (1)In Part II of the Table in paragraph 3 of Schedule 1 to the Public Records Act 1958 (definition of public records), the entry relating to the Data Protection Commissioner is omitted and there is inserted at the appropriate place—
"Information Commissioner."

(2) F4. . . . .

Amendments (Textual)
F4. Sch. 2 para. 3. (2) repealed (18.1.2010) by The Transfer of Tribunal Functions Order 2010 (S.I. 2010/22), arts. 1. (1), 5. (3), Sch. 4 Pt. 1

I2. Sch. 2 para. 3 wholly in force at 14.5.2001; Sch. 2 para. 3. (1) in force at 30.1.2001, see s. 87. (2)(c)(3); Sch. 2 para. 3. (2) in force at 14.5.2001 by S.I. 2001/1637, art. 2. (b)

Parliamentary Commissioner Act 1967 (c. 13)

4. In Schedule 2 to the Parliamentary Commissioner Act 1967 (departments etc. subject to investigation), the entry relating to the Data Protection Commissioner is omitted and there is inserted at the appropriate place—
"Information Commissioner".

5. F5. . . . .

Amendments (Textual)
F5. Sch. 2 para. 5 repealed (18.1.2010) by The Transfer of Tribunal Functions Order 2010 (S.I. 2010/22), arts. 1. (1), 5. (3), Sch. 4 Pt. 1

Superannuation Act 1972 (c. 11)

6. In Schedule 1 to the Superannuation Act 1972 (employment with superannuation scheme), for "Data Protection Commissioner" there is substituted " Information Commissioner ".

Consumer Credit Act 1974 (c. 39)

7. In section 159 of the Consumer Credit Act 1974 (correction of wrong information), in

subsections (7) and (8)(b), for "Data Protection Commissioner", in both places where it occurs, there is substituted " Information Commissioner ".

House of Commons Disqualification Act 1975 (c. 24)

8. (1)In Part II of Schedule 1 to the House of Commons Disqualification Act 1975 (bodies whose members are disqualified), the entry relating to the Data Protection Tribunal is omitted and there is inserted at the appropriate place—
"The Information Tribunal".
(2) In Part III of that Schedule (disqualifying offices), the entry relating to the Data Protection Commissioner is omitted and there is inserted at the appropriate place—
"The Information Commissioner".
Commencement Information
I3. Sch. 2 para. 8 wholly in force at 14.5.2001; Sch. 2 para. 8. (2) in force at 30.1.2001, see s. 87. (2)(c)(3); Sch. 2 para. 8. (1) in force at 14.5.2001 by S.I. 2001/1637, art. 2. (b)

Northern Ireland Assembly Disqualification Act 1975 (c. 25)

9. (1)In Part II of Schedule 1 to the Northern Ireland Assembly Disqualification Act 1975 (bodies whose members are disqualified), the entry relating to the Data Protection Tribunal is omitted and there is inserted at the appropriate place—
"The Information Tribunal".
(2) In Part III of that Schedule (disqualifying offices), the entry relating to the Data Protection Commissioner is omitted and there is inserted at the appropriate place—
"The Information Commissioner".
Commencement Information
I4. Sch. 2 para. 9 wholly in force at 14.5.2001; Sch. 2 para. 9. (2) in force at 30.1.2001, see s. 87. (2)(c)(3); Sch. 2 para. 9. (1) in force at 14.5.2001 by S.I. 2001/1637, art. 2. (b)

Tribunals and Inquiries Act 1992 (c. 53)

10. In paragraph 14 of Part I of Schedule 1 to the Tribunals and Inquiries Act 1992 (tribunals under direct supervision of Council on Tribunals)—
(a) in sub-paragraph (a), for "The Data Protection Commissioner" there is substituted " The Information Commissioner ", and
(b) F6. . . . .
Amendments (Textual)
F6. Sch. 2 para. 10. (b) repealed (18.1.2010) by The Transfer of Tribunal Functions Order 2010 (S.I. 2010/22), arts. 1. (1), 5. (3), Sch. 4 Pt. 1
Commencement Information
I5. Sch. 2 para. 10 wholly in force at 30.11.2002; Sch. 2 para. 10. (a) in force at 30.1.2001, see s. 87. (2)(c)(3); Sch. 2 para. 10. (b) in force at 30.11.2002 by S.I. 2002/2812, art. 2. (h)

Judicial Pensions and Retirement Act 1993 (c. 8)

11. F7. . . . .
Amendments (Textual)
F7. Sch. 2 para. 11 repealed (18.1.2010) by The Transfer of Tribunal Functions Order 2010 (S.I. 2010/22), arts. 1. (1), 5. (3), Sch. 4 Pt. 1
12. In Schedule 7 to that Act (retirement dates: transitional provisions), in paragraph 5. (5)(xxvi) for "the Data Protection Tribunal" there is substituted " the Information Tribunal ".

Data Protection Act 1998 (c. 29)

13. (1)Section 6 of the Data Protection Act 1998 (the Data Protection Commissioner and the Data Protection Tribunal) is amended as follows.

(2) For subsection (1) there is substituted—

"(1)For the purposes of this Act and of the Freedom of Information Act 2000 there shall be an officer known as the Information Commissioner (in this Act referred to as "the Commissioner")."

(3) F8. . . . .

Amendments (Textual)

F8. Sch. 2 para. 13. (3) repealed (18.1.2010) by The Transfer of Tribunal Functions Order 2010 (S.I. 2010/22), arts. 1. (1), 5. (3), Sch. 4 Pt. 1

Commencement Information

I6. Sch. 2 para. 13 wholly in force at 14.5.2001; Sch. 2 para. 13. (1)(2) in force at 30.1.2001, see s. 87. (2)(c)(3); Sch. 2 para. 13. (3) in force at 14.5.2001 by S.I. 2001/1637, art. 2. (b)

14. In section 70. (1) of that Act (supplementary definitions)—

(a) in the definition of "the Commissioner", for "the Data Protection Commissioner" there is substituted " the Information Commissioner ", and

(b) F9. . . . .

Amendments (Textual)

F9. Sch. 2 para. 14. (b) repealed (18.1.2010) by The Transfer of Tribunal Functions Order 2010 (S.I. 2010/22), arts. 1. (1), 5. (3), Sch. 4 Pt. 1

Commencement Information

I7. Sch. 2 para. 14 wholly in force at 14.5.2001; Sch. 2 para. 14. (a) in force at 30.1.2001, see s. 87. (2)(c)(3); Sch. 2 para. 14. (b) in force at 14.5.2001 by S.I. 2001/1637, art. 2. (b)

15. (1)Schedule 5 to that Act (the Data Protection Commissioner and the Data Protection Tribunal) is amended as follows.

(2) In paragraph 1. (1), for "Data Protection Commissioner" there is substituted " Information Commissioner ".

(3) Part III shall cease to have effect.

Commencement Information

I8. Sch. 2 para. 15 wholly in force at 14.5.2001; Sch. 2 para. 15. (1)(2) in force at 30.1.2001, see s. 87. (2)(c)(3); Sch. 2 para. 15. (3) in force at 14.5.2001 by S.I. 2001/1637, art. 2. (b)

Part II Amendments relating to extension of functions of Commissioner and Tribunal

Interests represented by lay members of Tribunal

16. F10. . . . .

Amendments (Textual)

F10. Sch. 2 para. 16 repealed (18.1.2010) by The Transfer of Tribunal Functions Order 2010 (S.I. 2010/22), arts. 1. (1), 5. (3), Sch. 4 Pt. 1

Expenses incurred under this Act excluded in calculating fees

17. F11. . . . .

Amendments (Textual)

F11. Sch. 2 para. 17 repealed (18.1.2010) by The Transfer of Tribunal Functions Order 2010 (S.I. 2010/22), arts. 1. (1), 5. (3), Sch. 4 Pt. 1

Information provided to Commissioner or Tribunal

18. In section 58 of that Act (disclosure of information to Commissioner or Tribunal), after "this Act" there is inserted " or the Freedom of Information Act 2000 ".

19. (1)Section 59 of that Act (confidentiality of information) is amended as follows.

(2) In subsections (1) and (2), for "this Act", wherever occurring, there is substituted " the information Acts ".

(3) After subsection (3) there is inserted—

"(4)In this section "the information Acts" means this Act and the Freedom of Information Act 2000."

Deputy commissioners

20. (1)Paragraph 4 of Schedule 5 to that Act (officers and staff) is amended as follows.

(2) In sub-paragraph (1)(a), after "a deputy commissioner" there is inserted " or two deputy commissioners ".

(3) After sub-paragraph (1) there is inserted—

"(1. A)The Commissioner shall, when appointing any second deputy commissioner, specify which of the Commissioner's functions are to be performed, in the circumstances referred to in paragraph 5. (1), by each of the deputy commissioners."

Exercise of Commissioner's functions by others

21. (1)Paragraph 5 of Schedule 5 to that Act (exercise of functions of Commissioner during vacancy etc.) is amended as follows.

(2) In sub-paragraph (1)—

(a) after "deputy commissioner" there is inserted " or deputy commissioners ", and

(b) after "this Act" there is inserted " or the Freedom of Information Act 2000 ".

(3) In sub-paragraph (2) after "this Act" there is inserted " or the Freedom of Information Act 2000 ".

Money

22. In paragraph 9. (1) of Schedule 5 to that Act (money) for "or section 159 of the Consumer Credit Act 1974" there is substituted " , under section 159 of the Consumer Credit Act 1974 or under the Freedom of Information Act 2000 ".

Schedule 3. Powers of entry and inspection

Section 55.
Modifications etc. (not altering text)
C1. Sch. 3 applied (with modifications) (31.12.2009) by The INSPIRE Regulations 2009 (S.I. 2009/3157), {reg. 11. (1)-(3)(9)}

Issue of warrants

1. (1)If a circuit judge [F1or a District Judge (Magistrates' Courts)] is satisfied by information on oath supplied by the Commissioner that there are reasonable grounds for suspecting—

(a) that a public authority has failed or is failing to comply with—

(i) any of the requirements of Part I of this Act,

(ii) so much of a decision notice as requires steps to be taken, or

(iii) an information notice or an enforcement notice, or

(b) that an offence under section 77 has been or is being committed,

and that evidence of such a failure to comply or of the commission of the offence is to be found on any premises specified in the information, he may, subject to paragraph 2, grant a warrant to the Commissioner.

(2) A warrant issued under sub-paragraph (1) shall authorise the Commissioner or any of his officers or staff at any time within seven days of the date of the warrant—

(a) to enter and search the premises,

(b) to inspect and seize any documents or other material found there which may be such evidence as is mentioned in that sub-paragraph, and

(c) to inspect, examine, operate and test any equipment found there in which information held by the public authority may be recorded.

Amendments (Textual)

F1. Words in Sch. 3 para. 1. (1) inserted (1.4.2005) by Courts Act 2003 (c. 39), ss. 65. (2), 110. (1), Sch. 4 para. 13; S.I. 2005/910, art. 3. (u)

Modifications etc. (not altering text)

C2. Sch. 3 para. 1: powers of seizure extended (1.4.2003) by 2001 c. 16, ss. 50, 52-54, 68, 138. (2), Sch. 1 Pt. 1 para. 73; S.I. 2003/708, art. 2

Commencement Information

I1. Sch. 3 para. 1 wholly in force at 1.1.2005; Sch. 3 para. 1 not in force at Royal Assent, see s. 87. (3); Sch. 3 para. 1 in force for certain purposes at 30.11.2002 by S.I. 2002/2812, art. 2. (d)(e); Sch. 3 para. 1 in force for certain further purposes at 1.1.2005 by S.I. 2004/1909, art. 2 and otherwise in force at 1.1.2005 by S.I. 2004/3122, art. 2

2. (1)A judge shall not issue a warrant under this Schedule unless he is satisfied—

(a) that the Commissioner has given seven days' notice in writing to the occupier of the premises in question demanding access to the premises, and

(b) that either—

(i) access was demanded at a reasonable hour and was unreasonably refused, or

(ii) although entry to the premises was granted, the occupier unreasonably refused to comply with a request by the Commissioner or any of the Commissioner's officers or staff to permit the Commissioner or the officer or member of staff to do any of the things referred to in paragraph 1. (2), and

(c) that the occupier, has, after the refusal, been notified by the Commissioner of the application for the warrant and has had an opportunity of being heard by the judge on the question whether or not it should be issued.

(2) Sub-paragraph (1) shall not apply if the judge is satisfied that the case is one of urgency or that compliance with those provisions would defeat the object of the entry.

Commencement Information

I2. Sch. 3 para. 2 wholly in force at 1.1.2005; Sch. 3 para. 2 not in force at Royal Assent, see s. 87. (3); Sch. 3 para. 2 in force for certain purposes at 30.11.2002 by S.I. 2002/2812, art. 2. (d)(e); Sch. 3 para. 2 in force for certain further purposes at 1.1.2005 by S.I. 2004/1909, art. 2 and otherwise in force at 1.1.2005 by S.I. 2004/3122, art. 2

3. A judge who issues a warrant under this Schedule shall also issue two copies of it and certify them clearly as copies.

Commencement Information

I3. Sch. 3 para. 3 wholly in force at 1.1.2005; Sch. 3 para. 3 not in force at Royal Assent, see s. 87. (3); Sch. 3 para. 3 in force for certain purposes at 30.11.2002 by S.I. 2002/2812, art. 2. (d)(e); Sch. 3 para. 3 in force for certain further purposes at 1.1.2005 by S.I. 2004/1909, art. 2 and otherwise in force at 1.1.2005 by S.I. 2004/3122, art. 2

Execution of warrants

4. A person executing a warrant issued under this Schedule may use such reasonable force as may be necessary.

Commencement Information

I4. Sch. 3 para. 4 wholly in force at 1.1.2005; Sch. 3 para. 4 not in force at Royal Assent, see s. 87. (3); Sch. 3 para. 4 in force for certain purposes at 30.11.2002 by S.I. 2002/2812, art. 2. (d)(e); Sch. 3 para. 4 in force for certain further purposes at 1.1.2005 by S.I. 2004/1909, art. 2 and otherwise in force at 1.1.2005 by S.I. 2004/3122, art. 2

5. A warrant issued under this Schedule shall be executed at a reasonable hour unless it appears to the person executing it that there are grounds for suspecting that the evidence in question would not be found if it were so executed.

Commencement Information

I5. Sch. 3 para. 5 wholly in force at 1.1.2005; Sch. 3 para. 5 not in force at Royal Assent, see s. 87. (3); Sch. 3 para. 5 in force for certain purposes at 30.11.2002 by S.I. 2002/2812, art. 2. (d)(e); Sch. 3 para. 5 in force for certain further purposes at 1.1.2005 by S.I. 2004/1909, art. 2 and otherwise in force at 1.1.2005 by S.I. 2004/3122, art. 2

6. (1)If the premises in respect of which a warrant is issued under this Schedule are occupied by a public authority and any officer or employee of the authority is present when the warrant is executed, he shall be shown the warrant and supplied with a copy of it; and if no such officer or employee is present a copy of the warrant shall be left in a prominent place on the premises.

(2) If the premises in respect of which a warrant is issued under this Schedule are occupied by a person other than a public authority and he is present when the warrant is executed, he shall be shown the warrant and supplied with a copy of it; and if that person is not present a copy of the warrant shall be left in a prominent place on the premises.

Commencement Information

I6. Sch. 3 para. 6 wholly in force at 1.1.2005; Sch. 3 para. 6 not in force at Royal Assent, see s. 87. (3); Sch. 3 para. 6 in force for certain purposes at 30.11.2002 by S.I. 2002/2812, art. 2. (d)(e); Sch. 3 para. 6 in force for certain further purposes at 1.1.2005 by S.I. 2004/1909, art. 2 and otherwise in force at 1.1.2005 by S.I. 2004/3122, art. 2

7. (1)A person seizing anything in pursuance of a warrant under this Schedule shall give a receipt for it if asked to do so.

(2) Anything so seized may be retained for so long as is necessary in all the circumstances but the person in occupation of the premises in question shall be given a copy of anything that is seized if he so requests and the person executing the warrant considers that it can be done without undue delay.

Modifications etc. (not altering text)

C3. Sch. 3 para. 7. (2) applied (1.4.2003) by 2001 c. 16, ss. 57. (1)(p), 138. (2) (with s. 57. (2)-(4)); S.I. 2003/708, art. 2

Commencement Information

I7. Sch. 3 para. 7 wholly in force at 1.1.2005; Sch. 3 para. 7 not in force at Royal Assent, see s. 87. (3); Sch. 3 para. 7 in force for certain purposes at 30.11.2002 by S.I. 2002/2812, art. 2. (d)(e); Sch. 3 para. 7 in force for certain further purposes at 1.1.2005 by S.I. 2004/1909, art. 2 and otherwise in force at 1.1.2005 by S.I. 2004/3122, art. 2

Matters exempt from inspection and seizure

8. The powers of inspection and seizure conferred by a warrant issued under this Schedule shall not be exercisable in respect of information which is exempt information by virtue of section 23. (1) or 24. (1).

Commencement Information

I8. Sch. 3 para. 8 wholly in force at 1.1.2005; Sch. 3 para. 8 not in force at Royal Assent, see s. 87.

(3); Sch. 3 para. 8 in force for certain purposes at 30.11.2002 by S.I. 2002/2812, art. 2. (d)(e); Sch. 3 para. 8 in force for certain further purposes at 1.1.2005 by S.I. 2004/1909, art. 2 and otherwise in force at 1.1.2005 by S.I. 2004/3122, art. 2

9. (1)Subject to the provisions of this paragraph, the powers of inspection and seizure conferred by a warrant issued under this Schedule shall not be exercisable in respect of—

(a) any communication between a professional legal adviser and his client in connection with the giving of legal advice to the client with respect to his obligations, liabilities or rights under this Act, or

(b) any communication between a professional legal adviser and his client, or between such an adviser or his client and any other person, made in connection with or in contemplation of proceedings under or arising out of this Act (including proceedings before the Tribunal) and for the purposes of such proceedings.

(2) Sub-paragraph (1) applies also to—

(a) any copy or other record of any such communication as is there mentioned, and

(b) any document or article enclosed with or referred to in any such communication if made in connection with the giving of any advice or, as the case may be, in connection with or in contemplation of and for the purposes of such proceedings as are there mentioned.

(3) This paragraph does not apply to anything in the possession of any person other than the professional legal adviser or his client or to anything held with the intention of furthering a criminal purpose.

(4) In this paragraph references to the client of a professional legal adviser include references to any person representing such a client.

Commencement Information

I9. Sch. 3 para. 9 wholly in force at 1.1.2005; Sch. 3 para. 9 not in force at Royal Assent, see s. 87. (3); Sch. 3 para. 9 in force for certain purposes at 30.11.2002 by S.I. 2002/2812, art. 2. (d)(e); Sch. 3 para. 9 in force for certain further purposes at 1.1.2005 by S.I. 2004/1909, art. 2 and otherwise in force at 1.1.2005 by S.I. 2004/3122, art. 2

10. If the person in occupation of any premises in respect of which a warrant is issued under this Schedule objects to the inspection or seizure under the warrant of any material on the grounds that it consists partly of matters in respect of which those powers are not exercisable, he shall, if the person executing the warrant so requests, furnish that person with a copy of so much of the material in relation to which the powers are exercisable.

Commencement Information

I10. Sch. 3 para. 10 wholly in force at 1.1.2005; Sch. 3 para. 10 not in force at Royal Assent, see s. 87. (3); Sch. 3 para. 10 in force for certain purposes at 30.11.2002 by S.I. 2002/2812, art. 2. (d)(e); Sch. 3 para. 10 in force for certain further purposes at 1.1.2005 by S.I. 2004/1909, art. 2 and otherwise in force at 1.1.2005 by S.I. 2004/3122, art. 2

Return of warrants

11. A warrant issued under this Schedule shall be returned to the court from which it was issued—

(a) after being executed, or

(b) if not executed within the time authorised for its execution;

and the person by whom any such warrant is executed shall make an endorsement on it stating what powers have been exercised by him under the warrant.

Commencement Information

I11. Sch. 3 para. 11 wholly in force at 1.1.2005; Sch. 3 para. 11 not in force at Royal Assent, see s. 87. (3); Sch. 3 para. 11 in force for certain purposes at 30.11.2002 by S.I. 2002/2812, art. 2. (d)(e); Sch. 3 para. 11 in force for certain further purposes at 1.1.2005 by S.I. 2004/1909, art. 2 and otherwise in force at 1.1.2005 by S.I. 2004/3122, art. 2

Offences

12. Any person who—

(a) intentionally obstructs a person in the execution of a warrant issued under this Schedule, or

(b) fails without reasonable excuse to give any person executing such a warrant such assistance as he may reasonably require for the execution of the warrant,

is guilty of an offence.

Modifications etc. (not altering text)

C4. Sch. 3 para. 12 extended (31.12.2009) by The INSPIRE Regulations 2009 (S.I. 2009/3157), reg. 11. (13)

Commencement Information

I12. Sch. 3 para. 12 wholly in force at 1.1.2005; Sch. 3 para. 12 not in force at Royal Assent, see s. 87. (3); Sch. 3 para. 12 in force for certain purposes at 30.11.2002 by S.I. 2002/2812, art. 2. (d)(e); Sch. 3 para. 12 in force for certain further purposes at 1.1.2005 by S.I. 2004/1909, art. 2 and otherwise in force at 1.1.2005 by S.I. 2004/3122, art. 2

Vessels, vehicles etc.

13. In this Schedule "premises" includes any vessel, vehicle, aircraft or hovercraft, and references to the occupier of any premises include references to the person in charge of any vessel, vehicle, aircraft or hovercraft.

Commencement Information

I13. Sch. 3 para. 13 wholly in force at 1.1.2005; Sch. 3 para. 13 not in force at Royal Assent, see s. 87. (3); Sch. 3 para. 13 in force for certain purposes at 30.11.2002 by S.I. 2002/2812, art. 2. (d)(e); Sch. 3 para. 13 in force for certain further purposes at 1.1.2005 by S.I. 2004/1909, art. 2 and otherwise in force at 1.1.2005 by S.I. 2004/3122, art. 2

Scotland and Northern Ireland

14. In the application of this Schedule to Scotland—

(a) for any reference to a circuit judge there is substituted a reference to the sheriff, and

(b) for any reference to information on oath there is substituted a reference to evidence on oath.

Commencement Information

I14. Sch. 3 para. 14 wholly in force at 1.1.2005; Sch. 3 para. 14 not in force at Royal Assent, see s. 87. (3); Sch. 3 para. 14 in force for certain purposes at 30.11.2002 by S.I. 2002/2812, art. 2. (d)(e); Sch. 3 para. 14 in force for certain further purposes at 1.1.2005 by S.I. 2004/1909, art. 2 and otherwise in force at 1.1.2005 by S.I. 2004/3122, art. 2

15. In the application of this Schedule to Northern Ireland—

(a) for any reference to a circuit judge there is substituted a reference to a county court judge, and

(b) for any reference to information on oath there is substituted a reference to a complaint on oath.

Commencement Information

I15. Sch. 3 para. 15 wholly in force at 1.1.2005; Sch. 3 para. 15 not in force at Royal Assent, see s. 87. (3); Sch. 3 para. 15 in force for certain purposes at 30.11.2002 by S.I. 2002/2812, art. 2. (d)(e); Sch. 3 para. 15 in force for certain further purposes at 1.1.2005 by S.I. 2004/1909, art. 2 and otherwise in force at 1.1.2005 by S.I. 2004/3122, art. 2

Schedule 4. Amendments of public records legislation

Section 67.

Part I Amendments of Public Records Act 1958

Functions of Advisory Council on Public Records

1. In section 1 of the M1. Public Records Act 1958 (general responsibility of the Lord Chancellor for public records), after subsection (2) there is inserted—

"(2. A)The matters on which the Advisory Council on Public Records may advise the Lord Chancellor include matters relating to the application of the Freedom of Information Act 2000 to information contained in public records which are historical records within the meaning of Part VI of that Act."

Marginal Citations

M11958 c. 51.

Access to public records

2. (1)Section 5 of that Act (access to public records) is amended in accordance with this paragraph.

(2) Subsections (1) and (2) are omitted.

(3) For subsection (3) there is substituted—

"(3)It shall be the duty of the Keeper of Public Records to arrange that reasonable facilities are available to the public for inspecting and obtaining copies of those public records in the Public Record Office which fall to be disclosed in accordance with the Freedom of Information Act 2000."

(4) Subsection (4) and, in subsection (5), the words from "and subject to" to the end are omitted.

3. Schedule 2 of that Act (enactments prohibiting disclosure of information obtained from the public) is omitted.

Power to extend meaning of "public records"

4. In Schedule 1 to that Act (definition of public records) after the Table at the end of paragraph 3 there is inserted—

"3. A(1)Her Majesty may by Order in Council amend the Table at the end of paragraph 3 of this Schedule by adding to either Part of the Table an entry relating to any body or establishment—

(a) which, at the time when the Order is made, is specified in Schedule 2 to the Parliamentary Commissioner Act 1967 (departments, etc. subject to investigation), or

(b) in respect of which an entry could, at that time, be added to Schedule 2 to that Act by an Order in Council under section 4 of that Act (which confers power to amend that Schedule).

(2) An Order in Council under this paragraph may relate to a specified body or establishment or to bodies or establishments falling within a specified description.

(3) An Order in Council under this paragraph shall be subject to annulment in pursuance of a resolution of either House of Parliament."

Part II Amendment of Public Records Act (Northern Ireland) 1923

5. After section 5 of the M2. Public Records Act (Northern Ireland) 1923 (deposit of documents in Record Office by trustees or other persons) there is inserted—

"5. A Access to public records

It shall be the duty of the Deputy Keeper of the Records of Northern Ireland to arrange that reasonable facilities are available to the public for inspecting and obtaining copies of those public records in the Public Record Office of Northern Ireland which fall to be disclosed in accordance with the Freedom of Information Act 2000."
Marginal Citations
M21923 c.20. (N.I.).

Schedule 5. Further amendments of Data Protection Act 1998

Section 73.

Request by data controller for further information

1. In section 7 of the M1. Data Protection Act 1998 (right of access to personal data), for subsection (3) there is substituted—
"(3)Where a data controller—

(a) reasonably requires further information in order to satisfy himself as to the identity of the person making a request under this section and to locate the information which that person seeks, and

(b) has informed him of that requirement,
the data controller is not obliged to comply with the request unless he is supplied with that further information."
Marginal Citations
M11998 c. 29.

Parliament

2. After section 35 of that Act there is inserted—

"35. A Parliamentary privilege.

Personal data are exempt from—

(a) the first data protection principle, except to the extent to which it requires compliance with the conditions in Schedules 2 and 3,

(b) the second, third, fourth and fifth data protection principles,

(c) section 7, and

(d) sections 10 and 14. (1) to (3),
if the exemption is required for the purpose of avoiding an infringement of the privileges of either House of Parliament."
Commencement Information
I1. Sch. 6 para. 2 wholly in force at 1.1.2005; Sch. 6 para. 2 not in force at Royal Assent, see s. 87. (3); Sch. 6 para. 2 in force for certain purposes at 1.1.2005 by S.I. 2004/1909, art. 2 and otherwise in force at 1.1.2005 by S.I. 2004/3122, art. 2
3. After section 63 of that Act there is inserted—

"63. A Application to Parliament.

(1) Subject to the following provisions of this section and to section 35. A, this Act applies to the processing of personal data by or on behalf of either House of Parliament as it applies to the processing of personal data by other persons.

(2) Where the purposes for which and the manner in which any personal data are, or are to be, processed are determined by or on behalf of the House of Commons, the data controller in respect of those data for the purposes of this Act shall be the Corporate Officer of that House.

(3) Where the purposes for which and the manner in which any personal data are, or are to be, processed are determined by or on behalf of the House of Lords, the data controller in respect of those data for the purposes of this Act shall be the Corporate Officer of that House.

(4) Nothing in subsection (2) or (3) is to be taken to render the Corporate Officer of the House of Commons or the Corporate Officer of the House of Lords liable to prosecution under this Act, but section 55 and paragraph 12 of Schedule 9 shall apply to a person acting on behalf of either House as they apply to any other person."

Commencement Information

I2. Sch. 6 para. 3 wholly in force at 1.1.2005; Sch. 6 para. 3 not in force at Royal Assent, see s. 87. (3); Sch. 6 para. 3 in force for certain purposes at 1.1.2005 by S.I. 2004/1909, art. 2 and otherwise in force at 1.1.2005 by S.I. 2004/3122, art. 2

4. In Schedule 2 to that Act (conditions relevant for the purposes of the first data protection principle: processing of any personal data) in paragraph 5 after paragraph (a) there is inserted—

"(aa)for the exercise of any functions of either House of Parliament,".

Commencement Information

I3. Sch. 6 para. 4 wholly in force at 1.1.2005; Sch. 6 para. 4 not in force at Royal Assent, see s. 87. (3); Sch. 6 para. 4 in force for certain purposes at 1.1.2005 by S.I. 2004/1909, art. 2 and otherwise in force at 1.1.2005 by S.I. 2004/3122, art. 2

5. In Schedule 3 to that Act (conditions relevant for the purposes of the first data protection principle: processing of sensitive personal data) in paragraph 7 after paragraph (a) there is inserted—

"(aa)for the exercise of any functions of either House of Parliament,".

Commencement Information

I4. Sch. 6 para. 5 wholly in force at 1.1.2005; Sch. 6 para. 5 not in force at Royal Assent, see s. 87. (3); Sch. 6 para. 5 in force for certain purposes at 1.1.2005 by S.I. 2004/1909, art. 2 and otherwise in force at 1.1.2005 by S.I. 2004/3122, art. 2

Honours

6. In Schedule 7 to that Act (miscellaneous exemptions) in paragraph 3. (b) (honours) after "honour" there is inserted " or dignity ".

Legal professional privilege

7. In paragraph 10 of that Schedule (legal professional privilege), for the words "or, in Scotland, to confidentiality as between client and professional legal adviser," there is substituted " or, in Scotland, to confidentiality of communications ".

Extension of transitional exemption

8. In Schedule 14 to that Act (transitional provisions), in paragraph 2. (1) (which confers transitional exemption from the prohibition on processing without registration on those registered under the Data Protection Act 1984) the words "or, if earlier, 24th October 2001" are omitted.

Schedule 6. Disclosure of information by ombudsmen

Section 76. (2).

The Parliamentary Commissioner for Administration

1. At the end of section 11 of the M1. Parliamentary Commissioner Act 1967 (provision for secrecy of information) there is inserted—
"(5)Information obtained from the Information Commissioner by virtue of section 76. (1) of the Freedom of Information Act 2000 shall be treated for the purposes of subsection (2) of this section as obtained for the purposes of an investigation under this Act and, in relation to such information, the reference in paragraph (a) of that subsection to the investigation shall have effect as a reference to any investigation."
Marginal Citations
M11967 c. 13.
2. After section 11. A of that Act there is inserted—

"11. AA Disclosure of information by Parliamentary Commissioner to Information Commissioner.

(1) The Commissioner may disclose to the Information Commissioner any information obtained by, or furnished to, the Commissioner under or for the purposes of this Act if the information appears to the Commissioner to relate to—
    (a) a matter in respect of which the Information Commissioner could exercise any power conferred by—
(i) Part V of the Data Protection Act 1998 (enforcement),
(ii) section 48 of the Freedom of Information Act 2000 (practice recommendations), or
(iii) Part IV of that Act (enforcement), or
    (b) the commission of an offence under—
(i) any provision of the Data Protection Act 1998 other than paragraph 12 of Schedule 9 (obstruction of execution of warrant), or
(ii) section 77 of the Freedom of Information Act 2000 (offence of altering etc. records with intent to prevent disclosure).
(2) Nothing in section 11. (2) of this Act shall apply in relation to the disclosure of information in accordance with this section."

The Commissions for Local Administration in England and Wales

3. In section 32 of the M2. Local Government Act 1974 (law of defamation, and disclosure of information) after subsection (6) there is inserted—
"(7)Information obtained from the Information Commissioner by virtue of section 76 of the Freedom of Information Act 2000 shall be treated for the purposes of subsection (2) above as obtained for the purposes of an investigation under this Part of this Act and, in relation to such information, the reference in paragraph (a) of that subsection to the investigation shall have effect as a reference to any investigation."

Marginal Citations
M21974 c. 7.
4. After section 33 of that Act there is inserted—

"33. A Disclosure of information by Local Commissioner to Information Commissioner.

(1) A Local Commissioner may disclose to the Information Commissioner any information obtained by, or furnished to, the Local Commissioner under or for the purposes of this Part of this Act if the information appears to the Local Commissioner to relate to—

(a) a matter in respect of which the Information Commissioner could exercise any power conferred by—
(i) Part V of the Data Protection Act 1998 (enforcement),
(ii) section 48 of the Freedom of Information Act 2000 (practice recommendations), or
(iii) Part IV of that Act (enforcement), or
(b) the commission of an offence under—
(i) any provision of the Data Protection Act 1998 other than paragraph 12 of Schedule 9 (obstruction of execution of warrant), or
(ii) section 77 of the Freedom of Information Act 2000 (offence of altering etc. records with intent to prevent disclosure).
(2) Nothing in section 32. (2) of this Act shall apply in relation to the disclosure of information in accordance with this section."

The Health Service Commissioners

5. At the end of section 15 of the M3. Health Service Commissioners Act 1993 (confidentiality of information) there is inserted—
"(4)Information obtained from the Information Commissioner by virtue of section 76 of the Freedom of Information Act 2000 shall be treated for the purposes of subsection (1) as obtained for the purposes of an investigation and, in relation to such information, the reference in paragraph (a) of that subsection to the investigation shall have effect as a reference to any investigation."
Marginal Citations
M31993 c. 46.
6. After section 18 of that Act there is inserted—

"18. A Disclosure of information to Information Commissioner.

(1) The Health Service Commissioner for England or the Health Service Commissioner for Wales may disclose to the Information Commissioner any information obtained by, or furnished to, the Health Service Commissioner under or for the purposes of this Act if the information appears to the Health Service Commissioner to relate to—

(a) a matter in respect of which the Information Commissioner could exercise any power conferred by—
(i) Part V of the Data Protection Act 1998 (enforcement),
(ii) section 48 of the Freedom of Information Act 2000 (practice recommendations), or
(iii) Part IV of that Act (enforcement), or
(b) the commission of an offence under—
(i) any provision of the Data Protection Act 1998 other than paragraph 12 of Schedule 9 (obstruction of execution of warrant), or
(ii) section 77 of the Freedom of Information Act 2000 (offence of altering etc. records with intent to prevent disclosure).

(3) Nothing in section 15 (confidentiality of information) applies in relation to the disclosure of information in accordance with this section."

The Welsh Administration Ombudsman

7. F1. . . . .
Amendments (Textual)
F1. Sch. 7 para. 7 repealed (1.4.2006 for W.) by Public Services Ombudsman (Wales) Act 2005 (c. 10), ss. 39, 40, Sch. 7; S.I. 2005/2800, art. 5
8. F2. . . . .
Amendments (Textual)
F2. Sch. 7 para. 8 repealed (1.4.2006 for W.) by Public Services Ombudsman (Wales) Act 2005 (c. 10), ss. 39, 40, Sch. 7; S.I. 2005/2800, art. 5

The Northern Ireland Commissioner for Complaints

9. At the end of Article 21 of the M4. Commissioner for Complaints (Northern Ireland) Order 1996 (disclosure of information by Commissioner) there is inserted—
"(5)Information obtained from the Information Commissioner by virtue of section 76 of the Freedom of Information Act 2000 shall be treated for the purposes of paragraph (1) as obtained for the purposes of an investigation under this Order and, in relation to such information, the reference in paragraph (1)(a) to the investigation shall have effect as a reference to any investigation."
Marginal Citations
M4. S.I. 1996/1297 (N.I. 7).
10. After that Article there is inserted—

"21. A Disclosure of information to Information Commissioner

(1) The Commissioner may disclose to the Information Commissioner any information obtained by, or furnished to, the Commissioner under or for the purposes of this Order if the information appears to the Commissioner to relate to—
    (a) a matter in respect of which the Information Commissioner could exercise any power conferred by—
(i) Part V of the Data Protection Act 1998 (enforcement),
(ii) section 48 of the Freedom of Information Act 2000 (practice recommendations), or
(iii) Part IV of that Act (enforcement), or
    (b) the commission of an offence under—
(i) any provision of the Data Protection Act 1998 other than paragraph 12 of Schedule 9 (obstruction of execution of warrant), or
(ii) section 77 of the Freedom of Information Act 2000 (offence of altering etc. records with intent to prevent disclosure).
(2) Nothing in Article 21. (1) applies in relation to the disclosure of information in accordance with this Article."

The Assembly Ombudsman for Northern Ireland

11. At the end of Article 19 of the M5. Ombudsman (Northern Ireland) Order 1996 there is inserted—
"(5)Information obtained from the Information Commissioner by virtue of section 76 of the Freedom of Information Act 2000 shall be treated for the purposes of paragraph (1) as obtained for the purposes of an investigation under this Order and, in relation to such information, the reference

in paragraph (1)(a) to the investigation shall have effect as a reference to any investigation."
Marginal Citations
M5. S.I. 1996/1298 (N.I. 8).
12. After that Article there is inserted—

"19. A Disclosure of information to Information Commissioner

(1) The Ombudsman may disclose to the Information Commissioner any information obtained by, or furnished to, the Omubudsman under or for the purposes of this Order if the information appears to the Ombudsman to relate to—

(a) a matter in respect of which the Information Commissioner could exercise any power conferred by—
(i) Part V of the Data Protection Act 1998 (enforcement),
(ii) section 48 of the Freedom of Information Act 2000 (practice recommendations), or
(iii) Part IV of that Act (enforcement), or
(b) the commission of an offence under—
(i) any provision of the Data Protection Act 1998 other than paragraph 12 of Schedule 9 (obstruction of execution of warrant), or
(ii) section 77 of the Freedom of Information Act 2000 (offence of altering etc. records with intent to prevent disclosure).
(2) Nothing in Article 19. (1) applies in relation to the disclosure of information in accordance with this Article."

The Commissioner for Local Administration in Scotland

13.
[F3. In section 30 of the M6. Local Government (Scotland) Act 1975 (limitation on disclosure of information), after subsection (5) there is inserted—
"(5. A)Information obtained from the Information Commissioner by virtue of section 76 of the Freedom of Information Act 2000 shall be treated for the purposes of subsection (2) as obtained for the purposes of an investigation under this Part of this Act and, in relation to such information, the reference in subsection (2)(a) to the investigation shall have effect as a reference to any investigation."]
Amendments (Textual)
F3. Sch. 7 para. 13 repealed (S.) (23.10.2002) by Scottish Public Services Ombudsman Act 2002 (asp 11), s. 26, Sch. 6 para. 23. (3); S.S.I. 2002/467, art. 2
Marginal Citations
M61975 c. 30.

Schedule 7. Repeals

Section 86.

Part I Repeal coming into force on passing of Act

Chapter | Short title | Extent of repeal |
1998 c. 29. | The Data Protection Act 1998. | In Schedule 14, in paragraph 2(1), the words "or, if earlier, 24th October 2001". |

Part II Repeals coming into force in accordance with section 87(2)

Chapter | Short title | Extent of repeal |
1958 c. 51. | The Public Records Act 1958. | In Schedule 1, in Part II of the Table in paragraph 3, the entry relating to the Data Protection Commissioner. |
1967 c. 13. | The Parliamentary Commissioner Act 1967. | In Schedule 2, the entry relating to the Data Protection Commissioner. |
1975 c. 24. | The House of Commons Disqualification Act 1975. | In Schedule 1, in Part III, the entry relating to the Data Protection Commissioner. |
1975 c. 25. | The Northern Ireland Assembly Disqualification Act 1975. | In Schedule 1, in Part III, the entry relating to the Data Protection Commissioner. |
In Schedule 5, Part III.
In Schedule 15, paragraphs 1. (1), 2, 4, 5. (2) and 6. (2)

Part III Repeals coming into force in accordance with section 87(3)

Chapter | Short title | Extent of repeal |
The Public Records Act 1958.
In section 5, subsections (1), (2) and (4) and, in subsection (5), the words from "and subject to" to the end.
Schedule 2.
1975 c. 24. | The House of Commons Disqualification Act 1975. | In Schedule 1, in Part II, the entry relating to the Data Protection Tribunal. |
1975 c. 25. | The Northern Ireland Assembly Disqualification Act 1975. | In Schedule 1, in Part II, the entry relating to the Data Protection Tribunal. |
In section 1. (1), in the definition of "data", the word "or" at the end of paragraph (c).
In Schedule 15, paragraphs 1. (2) and (3), 3, 5. (1) and 6. (1).

Open Government Licence v3.0

Printed in Great Britain
by Amazon

57483506R00073